Redistribution or Recognition?

Redistribution or Recognition?

A Political–Philosophical Exchange

———◆———

NANCY FRASER
and
AXEL HONNETH

Translated by Joel Golb, James Ingram,
and Christiane Wilke

VERSO
London • New York

First published by Verso 2003
© Nancy Fraser and Axel Honneth 2003
Translation © Joel Golb, James Ingram, and Christiane Wilke 2003

The moral rights of the authors and translators have been asserted

5 7 9 10 8 6 4

Verso

UK: 6 Meard Street, London W1F 0EG
USA: 20 Jay Street, Suite 1010, Brooklyn, NY 11201
www.versobooks.com

Verso is the imprint of New Left Books

ISBN 1–85984–648–3
ISBN 1–85984–492–8 (pbk)

British Library Cataloguing in Publication Data
Fraser, Nancy
    Redistribution or recognition? : a political-philosophical exchange
    1. Political science – Philosophy 2. Social justice
    I. Title II. Honneth, Axel, 1949–
    320'.011
    ISBN-13: 978-1-85984-492-2

Library of Congress Cataloging-in-Publication Data
Fraser, Nancy.
    [Umverteilung oder Anerkennung? English]
    Redistribution or recognition? : a political-philosophical exchange/Nancy Fraser and
Axel Honneth ; translated by Joel Golb, James Ingram, and Christiane Wilke.
        p. cm.
    Includes index.

    1. Social justice. 2. Capitalism–Moral and ethical aspects. 3. Identity (Philosophical
concept) 4. Recognition (Philosophy) I. Honneth, Axel, 1949– II. Title.
    HM671.F713 2003
    303.3'72–dc22
                                                                                    2003057675

Typeset in Bembo by SetSystems Ltd, Saffron Walden, Essex

From Nancy Fraser to Seyla Benhabib, another indispensable dialogue partner.

From Axel Honneth to Hans Joas, the critical companion of the last twenty-five years.

Contents

Acknowledgments ix

Introduction: Redistribution or Recognition? 1
Nancy Fraser and Axel Honneth

**1 Social Justice in the Age of Identity Politics:
Redistribution, Recognition, and Participation** 7
Nancy Fraser

    I. Redistribution or Recognition? A Critique of
        Justice Truncated 9
   II. Integrating Redistribution and Recognition:
        Problems in Moral Philosophy 26
  III. Social-Theoretical Issues: On Class and Status
        in Capitalist Society 48
  IV. Political-Theoretical Issues: Institutionalizing
        Democratic Justice 70
   V. Concluding Conjunctural Reflections: Post-
        Fordism, Postcommunism, and Globalization 88

2 **Redistribution as Recognition: A Response to**
   Nancy Fraser   110
   Axel Honneth

   I. On the Phenomenology of Experiences of
      Social Injustice   114
   II. The Capitalist Recognition Order and Conflicts
       over Distribution   135
   III. Recognition and Social Justice   160

3 **Distorted Beyond All Recognition:**
   A Rejoinder to Axel Honneth   198
   Nancy Fraser

   I. On the Place of Experience in Critical Theory:
      Against the Reduction of Political Sociology to
      Moral Psychology   201
   II. On the Cultural Turn in Social Theory: Against
       the Reduction of Capitalist Society to its
       Recognition Order   211
   III. On Liberal Equality: Against the Reduction of
        Justice to an Ethics of Intact Identity   222

4 **The Point of Recognition: A Rejoinder to the**
   Rejoinder   237
   Axel Honneth

   I. Critical Social Theory and Immanent
      Transcendence   238
   II. Capitalism and Culture: Social Integration,
       System Integration, and Perspectival Dualism   248
   III. History and Normativity: On the Limits of
        Deontology   256

   Index   269

Acknowledgments

Like all books, this one owes its existence not only to the efforts of the authors but also to the support of others. Both of us are grateful to Robin Blackburn and Jane Hindle at Verso for their sustained faith in this project, despite our long delay in bringing it to fruition. In the notes to each chapter, we thank by name individual colleagues whose comments and criticisms inspired us.

In addition, Nancy Fraser thanks her hosts at several institutions, where she found stimulation and fellowship while working on her chapters: Institut für Sozialforschung (Frankfurt), Wissenschaft-zentrum Berlin für Sozialforschung (WZB), Gender Studies Institute at the London School of Economics, and Institut für die Wissenschaften vom Menschen (Vienna). She also thanks the Graduate Faculty of the New School for a much appreciated research leave and Christiane Wilke for invaluable research assistance, including skillful and patient handling of many subtle questions of translation. Above all, she thanks Eli Zaretsky for his intense engagement and sustaining companionship at every stage of the process.

Axel Honneth thanks Monica Denz and Nora Sieverding for their great assistance during the final stages of the project, as well as Joel Golb, Christiane Wilke, and James Ingram for their excellent translations. Christine Pries's boundless patience in accompanying the seemingly never-ending discussions has been invaluable to him.

Introduction:
Redistribution or Recognition?

Nancy Fraser and Axel Honneth

"Recognition" has become a keyword of our time. A venerable category of Hegelian philosophy, recently resuscitated by political theorists, this notion is proving central to efforts to conceptualize today's struggles over identity and difference. Whether the issue is indigenous land claims or women's carework, homosexual marriage or Muslim headscarves, moral philosophers increasingly use the term "recognition" to unpack the normative bases of political claims. They find that a category that conditions subjects' autonomy on intersubjective regard well captures the moral stakes of many contemporary conflicts. And no wonder. Hegel's old figure of "the struggle for recognition" finds new purchase as a rapidly globalizing capitalism accelerates transcultural contacts, fracturing interpretative schemata, pluralizing value horizons, and politicizing identities and differences.

If recognition's salience is now indisputable, its relation to "redistribution" remains undertheorized. The latter term was central to both the moral philosophies and the social struggles of the Fordist era. Articulated in the great post-World War Two philosophies of egalitarian liberalism, the paradigm of distributive justice seemed well suited to analyzing the claims of labor and the poor in that period. In democratic welfare states whose national bases were largely taken for granted, conflicts turned chiefly on resources and were disputed in distributive terms, by appeals to universalist norms. With questions of difference usually relegated to the sidelines, claims for egalitarian redistribution appeared to typify the meaning of justice. There was no perceived need to examine their relation to claims for recognition.

Today, however, this relation cries out for interrogation. As 9/11 made painfully clear, struggles over religion, nationality, and gender are now interimbricated in ways that make the question of recognition impossible to ignore. With crosscutting axes of difference so intensely politicized, this question will continue to command center stage for the foreseeable future. At the same time, however, distributive injustice has not disappeared. On the contrary, economic inequalities are growing, as neoliberal forces promote corporate globalization and weaken the governance structures that previously enabled some redistribution within countries. Under these conditions, the question of distributive justice cannot be brushed aside. The upshot is that neither recognition nor redistribution can be overlooked in the present constellation. Forced by events to deal with both problematics, political philosophers have no choice but to examine the relations between them.

That, accordingly, is the aim of the present volume. Co-authored by two philosophers, one North American, the other European, this book stages a debate over how best to understand the relation of redistribution to recognition. The underlying premise, shared by both authors, is that an adequate understanding of justice must encompass at least two sets of concerns: those cast in the Fordist era as struggles over distribution and those often cast today as struggles for recognition. We also agree that one familiar account of the relation between them is inadequate: both of us reject the economistic view that would reduce recognition to a mere epiphenomenon of distribution.

There, however, our agreement ends. One of us, Axel Honneth, conceives recognition as the fundamental, overarching moral category, while treating distribution as derivative. Thus, he reinterprets the socialist ideal of redistribution as a subvariety of the struggle for recognition. The other one, Nancy Fraser, denies that distribution can be subsumed under recognition. Thus, she proposes a "perspectival dualist" analysis that casts the two categories as co-fundamental and mutually irreducible dimensions of justice. Expounding our respective positions in alternating chapters, we debate central issues of moral philosophy, social theory, and political analysis.

The volume opens with a chapter by Nancy Fraser that extends the analysis developed in her 1996 Tanner Lectures. To redress what she diagnoses as the current decoupling of claims for recognition from claims for redistribution, Fraser proposes a "two-dimensional" conception of justice that encompasses claims of both types without reducing either type to the other. Linking this conception to a theory of capitalism, she argues that only a framework that integrates the two analytically distinct perspectives of distribution and recognition can grasp the imbrication of class inequality and status hierarchy in contemporary society. The result is an account in which maldistribution is entwined with misrecognition but cannot be reduced to the latter.

In the second chapter, Axel Honneth develops an alternative approach. In contrast to Fraser's "perspectival dualism" of redistribution and recognition, he proposes a "normative monism" of recognition. Analyzing recognition as a differentiated concept, which encompasses both the "recognition of rights" and "cultural appreciation," as well as the claims of "love," he seeks to subsume the problematic of redistribution within it. The result is an argument that the concept of recognition, when properly understood, can accommodate, indeed even entails, a modified version of the Marxian paradigm of economic redistribution similar to that advanced in Fraser's chapter.

The remaining two chapters further focus the argument. Responding to each other's criticisms, we engage issues on three distinct levels. On the level of moral philosophy, we debate the relative merits of normative monism versus normative dualism, the priority of "the right" over "the good," and the associated implications. At the level of social theory, we dispute the relation of economy and culture, the status of the distinction between them, and the structure of capitalist society. At the level of political analysis, we examine the relation between equality and difference, between economic struggles and identity politics, between social democracy and multiculturalism. At each level, the stakes are progressively sharpened as each of us is forced to deepen our respective reflections in response to the arguments of the other.

If one result of our unfolding exchange is a sharpening of some of our differences, another is a strengthened awareness of what we share: above all, the ambition to connect the usually discrete levels of moral philosophy, social theory, and political analysis in a critical theory of capitalist society. In this respect, we part company from many of our friends and colleagues who also identify with the tradition of Critical Theory. Whereas most of them now tend to assume a disciplinary division of labor, assigning moral theory to the philosophers, social theory to the sociologists, and political analysis to the political scientists, effectively treating each of those inquiries as freestanding, both of us aspire to theorize capitalist society as a "totality." Thus, we reject the view that casts "grand theory" as epistemically unsound and politically dépassé. On the contrary, both of us believe that critique achieves both its theoretical warrant and its practical efficacy only by deploying normative concepts that are also informed by a structural understanding of contemporary society, one that can diagnose the tensions and contextualize the struggles of the present.

For both of us, moreover, the indispensable, framing category for such an understanding must be an adequate conception of capitalist society. Thus, debating the relation between redistribution and recognition has led us to another question, which is very difficult to answer but crucial for connecting moral theory, social theory, and political analysis. Should capitalism, as it exists today, be understood as a social system that differentiates an economic order that is not directly regulated by institutionalized patterns of cultural value from other social orders that are? Or should the capitalist economic order be understood rather as a consequence of a mode of cultural valuation that is bound up, from the very outset, with asymmetrical forms of recognition? At its deepest level, this book attempts to pose this question theoretically and to develop a common framework for assessing our diverging answers.

1

Social Justice in the Age of Identity Politics: Redistribution, Recognition, and Participation

Nancy Fraser

In today's world, claims for social justice seem increasingly to divide into two types. First, and most familiar, are redistributive claims, which seek a more just distribution of resources and wealth. Examples include claims for redistribution from the North to the South, from the rich to the poor, and (not so long ago) from the owners to the workers. To be sure, the recent resurgence of free-market thinking has put proponents of redistribution on the defensive. Nevertheless, egalitarian redistributive claims have supplied the paradigm case for most theorizing about social justice for the past 150 years.[1]

Today, however, we increasingly encounter a second type of social-justice claim in the "politics of recognition." Here the goal, in its most plausible form, is a difference-friendly world, where assimilation to majority or dominant cultural norms is no longer the price of equal respect. Examples include claims for the recognition of the distinctive perspectives of ethnic, "racial," and sexual minorities, as well as of gender difference. This type of claim has recently attracted the interest of political philosophers, moreover, some of whom are seeking to develop a new paradigm of justice that puts recognition at its center.

In general, then, we are confronted with a new constellation. The discourse of social justice, once centered on distribution, is now increasingly divided between claims for redistribution, on the one hand, and claims for recognition, on the other. Increasingly, too, recognition claims tend to predominate. The demise of communism, the surge of free-market ideology, the rise of "identity politics" in both its fundamentalist and progressive forms – all these developments have conspired to decenter, if not to extinguish, claims for egalitarian redistribution.

In this new constellation, the two kinds of justice claims are often dissociated from one another – both practically and intellectually. Within social movements such as feminism, for example, activist tendencies that look to redistribution as the remedy for male domination are increasingly dissociated from tendencies that look instead to recognition of gender difference. And the same is largely true in the intellectual sphere. In the academy, to continue with feminism, scholars who understand gender as a social relation maintain an uneasy arms-length coexistence with those who construe it as an identity or a cultural code. This situation exemplifies a broader phenomenon: the widespread decoupling of cultural politics from social politics, of the politics of difference from the politics of equality.[2]

In some cases, moreover, the dissociation has become a polarization. Some proponents of egalitarian redistribution reject the politics of recognition outright; citing global increases in inequality recently documented by the United Nations, they see claims for the recognition of difference as "false consciousness," a hindrance to the pursuit of social justice.[3] Conversely, some proponents of recognition disdain the politics of redistribution; citing the failure of difference-blind economic egalitarianism to assure justice for minorities and women, they see distributive politics as an outmoded materialism that can neither articulate nor challenge key experiences of injustice. In such cases, we are effectively presented with an either/or choice: redistribution or recognition? Class politics or identity politics? Multiculturalism or social democracy?

These, I maintain, are false antitheses. It is my general thesis that justice today requires *both* redistribution *and* recognition. Neither alone is sufficient. As soon as one embraces this thesis, however, the question of how to combine them becomes paramount. I shall argue that the emancipatory aspects of the two problematics should be integrated in a single comprehensive framework. Theoretically, the task is to devise a two-dimensional conception of justice that can accommodate both defensible claims for social equality and defensible claims for the recognition of difference. Practically, the task is to devise a programmatic political orientation that can integrate the best of the politics of redistribution with the best of the politics of recognition.

My discussion divides into four parts. In part I, I shall argue that neither redistribution alone nor recognition alone can suffice to overcome injustice today; thus, they need somehow to be reconciled and combined. In parts II and III, I shall examine some issues in moral philosophy and social theory that arise when we contemplate integrating redistribution and recognition in a single comprehensive account of social justice. In part IV, finally, I shall consider some political problems that arise when we seek to institutionalize such an integrated perspective in reforms aimed at remedying injustice.

I. Redistribution or Recognition?
A Critique of Justice Truncated

I begin with a terminological point. The terms "redistribution" and "recognition," as I use them here, have both a philosophical and a political reference. Philosophically, they refer to normative paradigms developed by political theorists and moral philosophers. Politically, they refer to families of claims raised by political actors and social movements in the public sphere. Each of these references merits some clarification.

As philosophical terms, "redistribution and "recognition"

have divergent provenances. "Redistribution" comes from the liberal tradition, especially its late-twentieth-century Anglo-American branch. In the 1970s and 80s this tradition was richly extended as "analytic" philosophers such as John Rawls and Ronald Dworkin developed sophisticated theories of distributive justice. Seeking to synthesize the traditional liberal emphasis on individual liberty with the egalitarianism of social democracy, they propounded new conceptions of justice that could justify socio-economic redistribution.[4]

The term "recognition," in contrast, comes from Hegelian philosophy, specifically the phenomenology of consciousness. In this tradition, recognition designates an ideal reciprocal relation between subjects in which each sees the other as its equal and also as separate from it. This relation is deemed constitutive for subjectivity; one becomes an individual subject only in virtue of recognizing, and being recognized by, another subject. Thus, "recognition" implies the Hegelian thesis, often deemed at odds with liberal individualism, that social relations are prior to individuals and intersubjectivity is prior to subjectivity. Unlike redistribution, moreover, recognition is usually seen as belonging to "ethics" as opposed to "morality," that is, as promoting substantive ends of self-realization and the good life, as opposed to the "rightness" of procedural justice. Richly elaborated by existentialist thinkers at mid-century, recognition theory is currently undergoing a renaissance, as neo-Hegelian philosophers such as Charles Taylor and Axel Honneth are making it the centerpiece of normative social philosophies aimed at vindicating "the politics of difference."[5]

Philosophically, therefore, the terms "redistribution" and "recognition" make an odd couple. Each is likely to be rejected by proponents of the other. Many liberal theorists of distributive justice contend that recognition theory carries unacceptable communitarian baggage, while some philosophers of recognition deem distributive theory individualizing and consumerist. Moreover, each of these notions elicits criticism from farther afield. Thinkers who identify with the Marxian tradition maintain that the category of distribution fails to capture the full depths of capitalist injustice because it neglects the relations of production and fails to problematize exploitation, domination, and commodification.[6] Likewise, those who embrace poststructuralist thought insist that the idea of recognition carries normalizing assumptions of centered subjectivity, which impede a more radical critique.[7]

In what follows, I shall try to show that redistribution and recognition *can* go together, despite their divergent philosophical provenances. And I shall also suggest that both notions can be conceived in ways that escape their respective critics' objections.

I propose to begin, however, by temporarily bracketing these philosophical disputes. I shall start instead by considering "redistribution" and "recognition" in their political reference. I shall consider them, that is, as ideal-typical constellations of claims that are currently contested in public spheres. From this perspective, the terms "redistribution" and "recognition" refer not to philosophical paradigms but rather to *folk paradigms of justice*, which inform present-day struggles in civil society. Tacitly presupposed by social movements and political actors, folk paradigms are sets of linked assumptions about the causes of and remedies for injustice. By reconstructing the folk paradigms of redistribution and recognition, I seek to clarify why and how these perspectives have been cast as mutually antithetical in current political debates.

1. *Anatomy of a false antithesis*

As folk paradigms, redistribution and recognition are often associated with specific social movements. Thus, the politics of redistribution is commonly equated with class politics, while the politics of recognition is assimilated to "identity politics," which is equated in turn with struggles over gender, sexuality, nationality, ethnicity, and "race." As we shall see, however, these common associations are misleading. For one thing, they treat recognition-oriented currents within feminist, anti-heter-osexist, and anti-racist movements as the whole story, rendering invisible alternative currents dedicated to righting gender-specific, "race"-specific, and sex-specific forms of economic injustice that traditional class movements ignored. For another, they obscure the recognition dimensions of class struggles, which have never aimed solely at redistributing wealth. Finally, the equation of recognition politics with identity politics reduces what we shall see is actually a plurality of different kinds of recognition claims to a single type, namely, claims for the affirmation of group specificity.

In what follows, accordingly, I shall suspend these common associations. Instead of aligning redistribution and recognition with class politics and identity politics respectively, I shall treat each folk paradigm as expressing a *distinctive perspective on social justice*, which can be applied in principle to the situation of *any* social movement.

Viewed in this way, the paradigm of redistribution can encompass not only class-centered political orientations, such as New Deal liberalism, social democracy, and socialism, but also those forms of feminism and anti-racism that look to socio-economic transformation or reform as the remedy for gender and racial-ethnic injustice. Thus, it is broader than class politics in the conventional sense. The paradigm of recognition, like-wise, can encompass not only movements aiming to revalue unjustly devalued identities – for example, cultural feminism, black cultural nationalism, and gay identity politics – but also deconstructive tendencies, such as queer politics, critical "race" politics, and deconstructive feminism, which reject the "essen-tialism" of traditional identity politics. Thus, it is broader than identity politics in the conventional sense.

Understood in this way, the folk paradigm of redistribution and the folk paradigm of recognition can be contrasted in four key respects. First, the two paradigms assume different concep-tions of injustice. The redistribution paradigm focuses on injustices it defines as socio-economic and presumes to be rooted in the economic structure of society. Examples include exploitation (having the fruits of one's labor appropriated for the benefit of others); economic marginalization (being confined to undesirable or poorly-paid work or being denied access to income-generating labor altogether), and deprivation (being denied an adequate material standard of living). The recognition paradigm, in contrast, targets injustices it understands as cultural, which it presumes to be rooted in social patterns of representation, interpretation, and communication. Examples include cultural domination (being subjected to patterns of interpretation and communication that are associated with another culture and are alien and/or hostile to one's own); nonrecognition (being rendered invisible via the authoritative representational, communicative, and interpretative practices of one's own culture); and disrespect (being routinely maligned or disparaged in stereotypic public cultural representations and/or in everyday life interactions).

Second, the two folk paradigms propose different sorts of remedies for injustice. In the redistribution paradigm, the remedy for injustice is economic restructuring of some sort. This might involve redistributing income and/or wealth, reorganizing the division of labor, changing the structure of property ownership, democratizing the procedures by which investment decisions are made, or transforming other basic economic structures. (Although these various remedies differ importantly from one another, I take this paradigm to encompass to the whole group of them under the generic term "redistribution."[8]) In the recognition paradigm, in contrast, the remedy for injustice is cultural or symbolic change. This could involve upwardly revaluing disrespected identities and the cultural products of maligned groups; recognizing and positively valorizing cultural diversity; or transforming wholesale societal patterns of representation, interpretation, and communication in ways that would change everyone's social identity. (Although these remedies, too, differ importantly from one another, I take this paradigm, too, to encompass the whole group of them under the generic term "recognition."⁹)

Third, the two folk paradigms assume different conceptions of the collectivities that suffer injustice. In the redistribution paradigm, the collective subjects of injustice are classes or class-like collectivities, which are defined economically by a distinctive relation to the market or the means of production.¹⁰ The classic case in the Marxian paradigm is the exploited working class, whose members must sell their labor power in order to receive the means of subsistence.¹¹ But the conception can cover other cases as well. Also included are racialized groups of immigrants or ethnic minorities that can be economically defined, whether as a pool of low-paid menial laborers or as an "underclass" largely excluded from regular waged work, deemed "superfluous" and not worth exploiting. When the concept of the economy is broadened to encompass unwaged labor, moreover, women are included here too – as the gender burdened with the lion's share of unwaged carework and consequently disadvantaged in employment. Also included, finally, are the complexly defined groupings that result when we theorize the political economy in terms of the intersection of class, "race," and gender.

In the folk paradigm of recognition, in contrast, the victims of injustice are more like Weberian status groups than Marxian classes. Defined not by the relations of production, but rather by the relations of recognition, they are distinguished by the lesser respect, esteem, and prestige they enjoy relative to other groups in society. The classic case in the Weberian paradigm is the low-status ethnic group, whom dominant patterns of cultural value mark as different and less worthy, to the detriment of group members' social standing and their chances of winning social esteem.¹² But the conception can cover other cases as well. In the current political conjuncture, it has been extended to gays and lesbians, who suffer pervasive effects of institutionalized stigma; to racialized groups, who are marked as different

and lesser; and to women, who are trivialized, sexually objec-
tified, and disrespected in myriad ways. It is also being
extended, finally, to encompass the complexly defined groupings that result when we theorize the relations of recognition
in terms of "race," gender, and sexuality simultaneously, as
intersecting cultural codes.

It follows, and this is the fourth point, that the two folk
paradigms assume different understandings of group differences.
The redistribution paradigm treats such differences as unjust
differentials. Far from being intrinsic properties of groups, they
are the socially constructed results of an unjust political economy. From this perspective, accordingly, we should strive to
abolish, not recognize, group differences. The recognition
paradigm, in contrast, treats differences in either of two ways.
In one version, they are benign, pre-existing cultural variations,
which an unjust interpretative schema has maliciously transformed into a value hierarchy. In another version, group
differences do not pre-exist their hierarchical transvaluation,
but are constructed contemporaneously with it. For the first
version, justice requires that we revalue devalued traits; thus,
we should celebrate, not eliminate, group differences. For the
second version, however, celebration is counterproductive;
rather, we should deconstruct the terms in which differences
are currently elaborated.

Increasingly, as I noted at the outset, redistribution and
recognition are portrayed as mutually exclusive alternatives.
Some proponents of the former, such as Richard Rorty, Brian
Barry, and Todd Gitlin, insist that identity politics is a counterproductive diversion from the real economic issues, one that
balkanizes groups and rejects universalist moral norms.[13] For
them, the sole proper object of political struggle is the economy. Conversely, some proponents of recognition, such as Iris
Marion Young, insist that a difference-blind politics of redistribution can reinforce injustice by falsely universalizing dominant
group norms, requiring subordinate groups to assimilate to
them, and misrecognizing the latter's distinctiveness.[14] For

them, the privileged political objective is cultural transformation.

With their charges and countercharges, these antagonists portray redistribution and recognition as mutually exclusive alternatives. Thus, they seem to present us with an either/or choice. Should we opt for a politics of redistribution that aims to abolish class differentials? Or should we embrace a politics of recognition that seeks to celebrate or deconstruct group differences? Apparently we cannot support both.

This, however, is a false antithesis.

2. *Exploited classes, despised sexualities, and two-dimensional categories*

To see why, let's engage in a thought experiment. Imagine a conceptual spectrum of different kinds of social divisions. At one extreme are divisions that fit the folk paradigm of redistribution. At the other extreme are divisions that fit the folk paradigm of recognition. In between are cases that prove difficult because they fit both paradigms of justice simultaneously.[15]

Consider, first, the redistribution end of the spectrum. At this end let us posit an ideal-typical social division rooted in the economic structure of society. By definition, then, any structural injustices attaching to this division will be traceable to the political economy. The core of the injustice will be socio-economic maldistribution, while any attendant cultural injustices will derive ultimately from the economic structure. At bottom, therefore, the remedy required to redress the injustice will be redistribution, as opposed to recognition.

An example that appears to approximate this ideal type is class differentiation, as understood in orthodox, economistic Marxism. (Let us leave aside the question of whether this interpretation of Marxism is adequate. And let us also bracket for the time being the question of whether this view of class fits the actual historical collectivities that have struggled for justice in the real world in the name of the working class.[16]) In this conception, class differentiation is rooted in the economic structure of capitalist society. The working class is the body of persons who must sell their labor power under arrangements that authorize the capitalist class to appropriate surplus productivity for its private benefit. The core injustice of these arrangements is exploitation, an especially deep form of maldistribution in which the proletariat's own energies are turned against it, usurped to sustain a system that benefits others. To be sure, proletarians also suffer serious cultural injustices, the "hidden injuries of class."[17] But far from being rooted directly in an autonomously unjust status order, these derive from the economic structure, as ideologies of class inferiority proliferate to justify exploitation. The remedy for the injustice, accordingly, is redistribution, not recognition. Overcoming class exploitation requires restructuring the political economy so as to alter the class distribution of benefits and burdens. In the Marxian view, such restructuring takes the radical form of abolishing the class structure as such. The task of the proletariat, therefore, is not simply to cut itself a better deal, but "to abolish itself as a class." The last thing it needs is recognition of its difference. On the contrary, the only way to remedy the injustice is to put the proletariat out of business as a distinctive group.[18]

Now consider the other end of the conceptual spectrum. At this end let us posit an ideal-typical social division that fits the folk paradigm of recognition. A division of this type is rooted in the status order of society, as opposed to in the economic structure. Thus, any structural injustices attaching to it will be traceable to the society's institutionalized patterns of cultural value. The core of the injustice will be misrecognition, while any attendant economic injustices will derive ultimately from the status order. The remedy required to redress the injustice will be recognition, as opposed to redistribution.

An example that appears to approximate this ideal type is sexual differentiation, understood through the prism of the Weberian conception of status. (As before, let us bracket for the time being the question of whether this view of sexuality fits the actually existing collectivities that have mobilized against heterosexism in the real world.[19]) According to this conception, the social division between heterosexuals and homosexuals is not grounded in the political economy, as homosexuals are distributed throughout the entire class structure of capitalist society, occupy no distinctive position in the division of labor, and do not constitute an exploited class. The division is rooted, rather, in the status order of society, as institutionalized patterns of cultural value construct heterosexuality as natural and nor-mative, homosexuality as perverse and despised. Pervasively institutionalized, such heteronormative value patterns structure broad swaths of social interaction. Expressly codified in many areas of law (including family law and criminal law), they inform legal constructions of family, intimacy, privacy, and equality. They are also entrenched in many areas of govern-ment policy (including immigration, naturalization and asylum policy) and in standard professional practices (including medi-cine and psychotherapy). Heteronormative value patterns also pervade popular culture and everyday interaction. The effect is to construct gays and lesbians as a *despised sexuality*, subject to sexually specific forms of *status subordination*. The latter include shaming and assault, exclusion from the rights and privileges of marriage and parenthood, curbs on rights of expression and association, demeaning stereotypical depictions in the media, harassment and disparagement in everyday life, and denial of the full rights and equal protections of citizenship. These harms are injustices of misrecognition.

To be sure, gays and lesbians also suffer serious economic injustices: they can be summarily dismissed from civilian employment and military service, are denied a broad range of family-based social-welfare benefits, and face major tax and inheritance liabilities. But far from being rooted directly in the economic structure of society, these derive instead from the status order, as the institutionalization of heterosexist norms produces a category of despised persons who incur economic disadvantages as a consequence of their subordinate status. The remedy for the injustice, accordingly, is recognition, not redistribution. Change the relations of recognition, that is, and the maldistribution will disappear. In general, then, overcoming homophobia and heterosexism requires changing the sexual status order, deinstitutionalizing heteronormative value patterns and replacing them with patterns that express equal respect for gays and lesbians.[20]

Matters are thus fairly straightforward at the two extremes of our conceptual spectrum. When we deal with social groups that approach the ideal type of the exploited working class, we face distributive injustices requiring redistributive remedies. What is needed is a politics of redistribution. When we deal with social groups that approach the ideal type of the despised sexuality, in contrast, we face injustices of misrecognition. What is needed *here* is a politics of recognition.

Matters become murkier, however, once we move away from these extremes. When we posit a type of social division located in the middle of the conceptual spectrum, we encounter a hybrid form that combines features of the exploited class with features of the despised sexuality. I will call such divisions "two-dimensional." Rooted at once in the economic structure and the status order of society, they involve injustices that are traceable to both. Two-dimensionally subordinated groups suffer both maldistribution and misrecognition *in forms where neither of these injustices is an indirect effect of the other, but where both are primary and co-original.* In their case, accordingly, neither a politics of redistribution alone nor a politics of recognition alone will suffice. Two-dimensionally subordinated groups need both.

Gender, I contend, is a two-dimensional social differentiation. Neither simply a class nor simply a status group, gender is a hybrid category rooted simultaneously in the economic structure and the status order of society. Understanding and redressing gender injustice, therefore, requires attending to both distribution and recognition.

From the distributive perspective, gender serves as a basic organizing principle of the economic structure of capitalist society. On the one hand, it structures the fundamental division between paid "productive" labor and unpaid "reproductive" and domestic labor, assigning women primary responsibility for the latter. On the other hand, gender also structures the division within paid labor between higher-paid, male-dominated manufacturing and professional occupations and lower-paid, female-dominated "pink collar" and domestic service occupations. The result is an economic structure that generates gender-specific forms of distributive injustice, including gender-based exploitation, economic marginalization, and deprivation.

Here, gender appears as a class-like differentiation that is rooted in the economic structure of society. When viewed under this aspect, gender injustice appears as a species of distributive injustice that cries out for redistributive redress. Much like class, gender justice requires transforming the economy so as to eliminate its gender structuring. Eliminating gender-specific maldistribution requires abolishing the gender division of labor – both the gendered division between paid and unpaid labor and the gender divisions within paid labor. The logic of the remedy is akin to the logic with respect to class: it aims to put gender out of business as such. If gender were nothing but a class-like differentiation, in sum, justice would require its abolition.

That, however, is only half the story. In fact, gender is not only a class-like division, but a status differentiation as well. As such, it also encompasses elements more reminiscent of sexuality than class, which bring it squarely within the problematic of recognition. Gender codes pervasive cultural patterns of interpretation and evaluation, which are central to the status order as a whole. As a result, not just women but all low-status groups risk feminization and thus depreciation.

Thus, a major feature of gender injustice is androcentrism: an institutionalized pattern of cultural value that privileges traits associated with masculinity, while devaluing everything coded as "feminine," paradigmatically – but not only – women. Pervasively institutionalized, androcentric value patterns structure broad swaths of social interaction. Expressly codified in many areas of law (including family law and criminal law), they inform legal constructions of privacy, autonomy, self-defense, and equality. They are also entrenched in many areas of government policy (including reproductive, immigration, and asylum policy) and in standard professional practices (including medicine and psychotherapy). Androcentric value patterns also pervade popular culture and everyday interaction. As a result, women suffer gender-specific forms of *status subordination*, including sexual assault and domestic violence; trivializing, objectifying, and demeaning stereotypical depictions in the media; harassment and disparagement in everyday life; exclusion or marginalization in public spheres and deliberative bodies; and denial of the full rights and equal protections of citizenship. These harms are injustices of recognition. They are relatively independent of political economy and are not merely "superstructural." Thus, they cannot be overcome by redistribution alone but require additional, independent remedies of recognition.

Here, gender appears as a status differentiation endowed with sexuality-like characteristics. When viewed under this aspect, gender injustice appears as a species of misrecognition that cries out for redress via recognition. Much like heterosexism, overcoming androcentrism requires changing the gender status order, deinstitutionalizing sexist value patterns and replacing them with patterns that express equal respect for women. Thus, the logic of the remedy here is akin to that concerning sexuality: it aims to dismantle androcentrism by restructuring the relations of recognition.[21]

Gender, in sum, is a two-dimensional social differentiation. It combines a class-like dimension, which brings it within the ambit of redistribution, with a status dimension, which brings it simultaneously within the ambit of recognition. It is an open question whether the two dimensions are of equal weight. But redressing gender injustice, in any case, requires changing both the economic structure and the status order of society.

The two-dimensional character of gender wreaks havoc on the idea of an either/or choice between the paradigm of redistribution and the paradigm of recognition. That construction assumes that the collective subjects of injustice are either classes or status groups, but not both; that the injustice they suffer is either maldistribution or misrecognition, but not both; that the group differences at issue are either unjust differentials or unjustly devalued variations, but not both; that the remedy for injustice is either redistribution or recognition, but not both. Gender, we can now see, explodes this whole series of false antitheses. Here we have a category that is a compound of both status and class. Here difference is constructed from both economic differentials and institutionalized patterns of cultural value. Here both maldistribution and misrecognition are fundamental. Gender injustice can only be remedied, therefore, by an approach that encompasses both a politics of redistribution and a politics of recognition.

3. Two-dimensionality: Exception or norm?

How unusual is gender in this regard? Are we dealing here with a unique or rare case of two-dimensionality in an otherwise one-dimensional world? Or is two-dimensionality, rather, the norm?

"Race," it is clear, is also a two-dimensional social division, a compound of status and class. Rooted simultaneously in the economic structure and the status order of capitalist society, racism's injustices include both maldistribution and misrecognition. In the economy, "race" organizes structural divisions between menial and non-menial paid jobs, on the one hand, and between exploitable and "superfluous" labor power, on the other. As a result, the economic structure generates racially specific forms of maldistribution. Racialized immigrants and/or ethnic minorities suffer disproportionately high rates of unem-

ployment and poverty and over-representation in low-paying
menial work. These distributive injustices can only be remedied
by a politics of redistribution.

In the status order, meanwhile, Eurocentric patterns of
cultural value privilege traits associated with "whiteness," while
stigmatizing everything coded as "black," "brown," and "yel-
low," paradigmatically – but not only – people of color. As a
result, racialized immigrants and/or ethnic minorities are constructed as deficient and inferior others who cannot be full
members of society. Pervasively institutionalized, Eurocentric
norms generate racially specific forms of status subordination,
including stigmatization and physical assault; cultural devaluation, social exclusion, and political marginalization; harassment
and disparagement in everyday life; and denial of the full rights
and equal protections of citizenship. Quintessential harms of
misrecognition, these injustices can only be remedied by a
politics of recognition.

Neither dimension of racism is wholly an indirect effect of
the other, moreover. To be sure, the distributive and recognition dimensions interact with one another. But racist maldistribution is not simply a by-product of status hierarchy; nor is
racist misrecognition wholly a by-product of economic structure. Rather, each dimension has some relative independence
from the other. Neither can be redressed indirectly, therefore,
through remedies addressed exclusively to the other. Overcoming the injustices of racism, in sum, requires both redistribution
and recognition. Neither alone will suffice.

Class, too, can be understood as two-dimensional, in spite
of the previous discussion. In fact, the economistic ideal type I
invoked for heuristic purposes occludes some significant real-
world complexities. To be sure, the ultimate cause of class
injustice is the economic structure of capitalist society.[22] But
the resulting harms include misrecognition as well as maldistribution; and status harms that originated as by-products of
economic structure may have since developed a life of their
own. Today, the misrecognition dimensions of class may be

sufficiently autonomous in their operation to require independent remedies of recognition. Left unattended, moreover, class misrecognition can impede the capacity to mobilize against maldistribution. To build broad support for economic transformation today requires challenging cultural attitudes that demean poor and working people, for example, "culture-of-poverty" ideologies that suggest they simply get what they deserve. Likewise, poor and working people may need a recognition politics to support their struggles for economic justice; they may need, that is, to build class communities and cultures in order to neutralize the hidden injuries of class and forge the confidence to stand up for themselves. Thus, a politics of class recognition may be needed both in itself and to help get a politics of redistribution off the ground.[23]

In general, then, even such an apparently one-dimensional economic category as class has a status component. To be sure, this component is subordinate, less weighty than the economic component. Nevertheless, overcoming class injustice may well require joining a politics of recognition to a politics of redistribution.[24] At the very least, it will be necessary to attend carefully to the recognition dynamics of class struggles in the process of fighting for redistribution.

What, then, of sexuality? Is it also a two-dimensional category? Here, too, the ideal type I sketched earlier for heuristic purposes may be inadequate to the real-world complexities. To be sure, the ultimate cause of heterosexist injustice is the status order, not the economic structure of capitalist society.[25] But the resulting harms include maldistribution as well as misrecognition; and economic harms that originated as by-products of the status order have an undeniable weight of their own. Left unattended, moreover, they can impede the capacity to mobilize against misrecognition. Insofar as coming out poses economic risks for gays and lesbians, their capacity to fight status subordination is diminished; so too is the capacity of their heterosexual allies, who must likewise fear the economic consequences of being (mis)identified as gay if they openly defend homosexual rights. In addition, maldistribution may be the "weak link" in the chain of heterosexist oppression. In the current climate, it may be easier to challenge the distributive inequities faced by gays and lesbians than to confront head on the deep-seated status anxieties that fuel homophobia.[26] In sum, building support for transforming the sexual status order may require fighting for economic equity. Thus, a politics of sexual redistribution may be needed both in itself and to help get a politics of recognition off the ground.

In general, then, even such an apparently one-dimensional status category as sexuality has a distributive component. To be sure, this component is subordinate, less weighty than the status component. Nevertheless, overcoming sexual injustice may well require joining a politics of redistribution to a politics of recognition. At the very least, it will be necessary to attend carefully to the distributive dynamics of sexual struggles in the process of fighting for recognition.

For practical purposes, then, virtually all real-world axes of subordination can be treated as two-dimensional. Virtually all implicate both maldistribution and misrecognition in forms where each of those injustices has some independent weight, whatever its ultimate roots. To be sure, not all axes of subordination are two-dimensional in the same way, nor to the same degree. Some, such as class, tilt more heavily toward the distribution end of the spectrum; others, such as sexuality, incline more to the recognition end; while still others, such as gender and "race," cluster closer to the center. The precise proportion of economic disadvantage and status subordination must be determined empirically in every case. Nevertheless, in virtually every case, the harms at issue comprise both maldistribution and misrecognition in forms where neither of those injustices can be redressed entirely indirectly but where each requires some independent practical attention. As a practical matter, therefore, overcoming injustice in virtually every case requires both redistribution and recognition.

The need for a two-pronged approach becomes more pressing, moreover, as soon as one ceases considering axes of subordination singly and begins considering them together. After all, gender, "race," sexuality, and class are not neatly cordoned off from one another. Rather, all these axes of subordination intersect one another in ways that affect everyone's interests and identities. No one is a member of only one such collectivity. And individuals who are subordinated along one axis of social division may well be dominant along another. Viewed in this light, the need for a two-pronged politics of redistribution and recognition does not only arise endogenously, as it were, within a single two-dimensional social division. It also arises exogenously, so to speak, across intersecting differentiations. For example, anyone who is both gay and working-class will need both redistribution and recognition, regardless of what one makes of those two categories taken singly. Seen this way, moreover, nearly every individual who suffers injustice needs to integrate those two kinds of claims. And so, furthermore, will anyone who cares about social justice, regardless of their own personal social location.

In general, then, one should roundly reject the construction of redistribution and recognition as mutually exclusive alternatives. The goal should be, rather, to develop an integrated approach that can encompass, and harmonize, both dimensions of social justice.

II.   Integrating Redistribution and Recognition: Problems in Moral Philosophy

Integrating redistribution and recognition in a single comprehensive paradigm is no simple matter, however. To contemplate such a project is to be plunged immediately into deep and difficult problems spanning several major fields of inquiry. In moral philosophy, for example, the task is to devise an overarching conception of justice that can accommodate both defensible claims for social equality and defensible claims for the recognition of difference. In social theory, as we shall see, the task is to devise an account of contemporary society that can accommodate both the differentiation of class from status and also their mutual imbrication. In political theory, meanwhile, the task is to envision a set of institutional arrangements and policy reforms that can remedy both maldistribution and misrecognition, while minimizing the mutual interferences likely to arise when the two sorts of redress are sought simultaneously. In practical politics, finally, the task is to foster democratic engagement across current divides in order to build a broad-based programmatic orientation that integrates the best of the politics of redistribution with the best of the politics of recognition.

In the present section, I shall examine some of the moral-philosophical dimensions of this project. Here, accordingly, I leave behind the political understandings of redistribution and recognition as folk paradigms of justice. In their place I now consider redistribution and recognition as *normative philosophical categories*.

1. *Justice or self-realization?*

Any attempt to integrate redistribution and recognition must address four crucial questions in moral philosophy. First, is recognition really a matter of justice, or is it a matter of self-realization? Second, do distributive justice and recognition constitute two distinct, *sui generis*, normative paradigms, or can either of them be subsumed within the other? Third, how can we distinguish justified from unjustified claims for recognition? And fourth, does justice require the recognition of what is distinctive about individuals or groups, or is recognition of our common humanity sufficient?

The first question arises given some standard distinctions in moral philosophy. In this field, questions of justice are usually understood to be matters of "the right," which belong squarely on the terrain of "morality." Questions of self-realization, in

contrast, are considered to be matters of "the good," which
belong rather to the domain of "ethics." In part this contrast is
a matter of scope. Norms of justice are universally binding; like
principles of Kantian *Moralität*, they hold independently of
actors' commitments to specific values. Claims about self-
realization, on the other hand, are usually considered to be
more restricted. Like canons of Hegelian *Sittlichkeit*, they
depend on culturally and historically specific horizons of value,
which cannot be universalized. Thus, a great deal turns on
whether claims for recognition are held to concern justice or
self-realization.

Usually, recognition is taken to be a matter of self-realization. This is the view of both Charles Taylor and Axel
Honneth, the two most prominent contemporary theorists of
recognition. For both Taylor and Honneth, being recognized
by another subject is a necessary condition for attaining full,
undistorted subjectivity. To deny someone recognition is to
deprive her or him of a basic prerequisite for human flourishing. For Taylor, for example, "nonrecognition or misrecognition . . . can be a form of oppression, imprisoning someone in
a false, distorted, reduced mode of being. Beyond simple lack
of respect, it can inflict a grievous wound, saddling people with
crippling self-hatred. Due recognition is not just a courtesy but
a vital human need."[27] For Honneth, similarly, "we owe our
integrity . . . to the receipt of approval or recognition from
other persons. [D]enial of recognition . . . is injurious because
it impairs . . . persons in their positive understanding of self –
an understanding acquired by intersubjective means."[28] Thus,
both these theorists construe misrecognition in terms of
impaired subjectivity and damaged self-identity. And both
understand the injury in ethical terms, as stunting the subject's
capacity for achieving a "good life." For Taylor and Honneth,
therefore, recognition concerns self-realization.

Unlike Taylor and Honneth, I propose to conceive recognition as a matter of justice. Thus, one should not answer the
question "what's wrong with misrecognition?" by saying that

it impedes self-realization by distorting the subject's "practical relation-to-self."[29] One should say, rather, that it is unjust that some individuals and groups are denied the status of full partners in social interaction simply as a consequence of institutionalized patterns of cultural value in whose construction they have not equally participated and which disparage their distinctive characteristics or the distinctive characteristics assigned to them.

Let me explain. To view recognition as a matter of justice is to treat it as an issue of *social status*. This means examining institutionalized patterns of cultural value for their effects on the *relative standing* of social actors. If and when such patterns constitute actors as *peers*, capable of participating on a par with one another in social life, then we can speak of *reciprocal recognition* and *status equality*. When, in contrast, institutionalized patterns of cultural value constitute some actors as inferior, excluded, wholly other, or simply invisible, hence as less than full partners in social interaction, then we should speak of *misrecognition* and *status subordination*.

I shall call this the *status model of recognition*.[30] On the status model, misrecognition is neither a psychical deformation nor an impediment to ethical self-realization. Rather, it constitutes an institutionalized relation of *subordination* and a violation of justice. To be misrecognized, accordingly, is not to suffer distorted identity or impaired subjectivity as a result of being depreciated by others. It is rather to be constituted by *institutionalized patterns of cultural value* in ways that prevent one from participating as a peer in social life. On the status model, then, misrecognition is relayed not through deprecatory attitudes or free-standing discourses, but rather through social institutions. It arises, more precisely, when institutions structure interaction according to cultural norms that impede parity of participation. Examples include marriage laws that exclude same-sex partnerships as illegitimate and perverse, social-welfare policies that stigmatize single mothers as sexually irresponsible scroungers, and policing practices such as "racial profiling" that associate racialized persons with criminality. In each of these cases, interaction is regulated by an institutionalized pattern of cultural value that constitutes some categories of social actors as normative and others as deficient or inferior: straight is normal, gay is perverse; "male-headed households" are proper, "female-headed households" are not; "whites" are law-abiding, "blacks" are dangerous. In each case, the effect is to create a class of devalued persons who are impeded from participating on a par with others in social life.

In each case, accordingly, a claim for recognition is in order. But note precisely what this means: aimed not at repairing psychical damage but rather at overcoming subordination, claims for recognition in the status model seek to establish the subordinated party as a full partner in social life, able to interact with others as a peer. They aim, that is, *to deinstitutionalize patterns of cultural value that impede parity of participation and to replace them with patterns that foster it.*

2. *Status subordination or impaired subjectivity?*

In a later section of this chapter, I shall consider the political and institutional implications of the status model. Here I want to elucidate its conceptual advantages over the self-realization model of Taylor and Honneth. Four such advantages are especially important.

First, the status model permits one to justify claims for recognition as morally binding under modern conditions of value pluralism.[31] Under these conditions, there is no single conception of self-realization or the good life that is universally shared, nor any that can be established as authoritative. Thus, any attempt to justify claims for recognition that appeals to an account of self-realization or the good life must necessarily be sectarian. No approach of this sort can establish such claims as normatively binding on those who do not share the theorist's conception of ethical value.

Unlike such approaches, the status model is deontological

and nonsectarian. Embracing the spirit of "subjective freedom" that is the hallmark of modernity, it assumes that it is up to individuals and groups to define for themselves what counts as a good life and to devise for themselves an approach to pursuing it, within limits that ensure a like liberty for others. Thus, the status model does not appeal to a conception of self-realization or the good. It appeals, rather, to a conception of justice that can – and should – be accepted by those with divergent conceptions of the good. What makes misrecognition morally wrong, in this view, is that it denies some individuals and groups the possibility of participating on a par with others in social interaction. The norm of *participatory parity* invoked here is nonsectarian in the required sense. It can justify claims for recognition as normatively binding on all who agree to abide by fair terms of interaction under conditions of value pluralism.

The status model has a second advantage as well. Conceiving misrecognition as status subordination, it locates the wrong in social relations, not in individual or interpersonal psychology. As a result, it escapes some of the self-realization model's difficulties. When misrecognition is identified with internal distortions in the structure of the self-consciousness of the oppressed, it is but a short step to blaming the victim, as imputing psychic damage to those subject to racism, for example, seems to add insult to injury. Conversely, when misrecognition is equated with prejudice in the minds of the oppressors, overcoming it seems to require policing their beliefs, an approach that is illiberal and authoritarian. For the status model, in contrast, misrecognition is a matter of externally manifest and publicly verifiable impediments to some people's standing as full members of society. To redress it, again, means to overcome subordination. This in turn means changing institutions and social practices – once again, by deinstitutionalizing patterns of cultural value that impede parity of participation and replacing them with patterns that foster it.

The status model, in other words, eschews psychologization.

What this means, however, requires some clarification. The model accepts that misrecognition can have the sort of ethical-psychological effects described by Taylor and Honneth. But it maintains that the wrongness of misrecognition does not depend on the presence of such effects. Thus, the status model decouples the normativity of recognition claims from psychology, thereby strengthening their normative force. When claims for recognition are premised on a psychological theory of "the intersubjective conditions for undistorted identity-formation," as in Honneth's model, they are made vulnerable to the vicissitudes of that theory; their moral bindingness evaporates in case the theory turns out to be false. By treating recognition as a matter of status, in contrast, the model I am proposing avoids mortgaging normative claims to matters of psychological fact. One can show that a society whose institutionalized norms impede parity of participation is morally indefensible *whether or not they distort the subjectivity of the oppressed.*

As a third advantage, the status model avoids the view that everyone has an equal right to social esteem. That view is patently untenable, of course, because it renders meaningless the notion of esteem.[32] Yet it seems to follow from at least one influential account of recognition in terms of self-realization. In Honneth's account, social esteem is among the intersubjective conditions for undistorted identity-formation, which morality is supposed to protect. It follows that everyone is morally entitled to social esteem. The account of recognition proposed here, in contrast, entails no such *reductio ad absurdum.* What it *does* entail is that everyone has an equal right to pursue social esteem under fair conditions of equal opportunity.[33] And such conditions do not obtain when institutionalized patterns of cultural value pervasively downgrade, for example, feminin-ity, "non-whiteness," homosexuality, and everything culturally associated with them. When that is the case, women and/or people of color and/or gays and lesbians face obstacles in the quest for esteem that are not encountered by others. And everyone, including straight white men, faces further obstacles when opting to pursue projects and cultivate traits that are culturally coded as feminine, homosexual, or "non-white."

Finally, the status model offers a fourth advantage, of central importance here. By construing misrecognition as a violation of justice, it facilitates the integration of claims for recognition with claims for the redistribution of resources and wealth. Here, in other words, recognition is assigned to the universally binding domain of deontological morality, as is distributive justice. With both categories thus inhabiting a single normative universe, they become commensurable — and potentially subsumable within a common framework. On the self-realization view, in contrast, the prospects for their conceptual integration are dim. That approach, as we saw, treats recognition as an ethical question, which makes it incommensurable with distributive justice. As a result, whoever wishes to endorse *both* redistribution *and* recognition seems to risk philosophical schizophrenia.

I began by noting that, as philosophical categories, redistribution and recognition have widely divergent provenances. As we saw, distribution comes from the Anglo-American liberal tradition and is often associated with Kantian *Moralität*. Recognition, in contrast, comes from the phenomenological tradition and is usually associated with Hegelian *Sittlichkeit*. It is not surprising, therefore, that the two categories are often held to be conceptually incompatible. Yet the status model overcomes this presumption of incompatibility. Treating both redistribution and recognition as matters of justice, it makes it possible to position both terms within a single normative framework. As a result, it holds out the prospect of accommodating claims of both types without succumbing to philosophical schizophrenia.

For all these reasons, recognition is better viewed as a matter of justice than as a matter of self-realization. But what follows for the theory of justice?

3. Against reductionism: A two-dimensional conception of justice

Let us suppose henceforth that recognition is a matter of justice. What exactly is its relation to distribution? Does it follow, turning now to our second question of moral philosophy, that distribution and recognition constitute two distinct, *sui generis* conceptions of justice? Or can either of them be reduced to the other?

The question of reduction must be considered from two different sides. From one side, the issue is whether standard theories of distributive justice can adequately subsume problems of recognition. In my view, the answer is no. To be sure, many distributive theorists appreciate the importance of status over and above material well-being and seek to accommodate it in their accounts.[34] But the results are not wholly satisfactory. Most such theorists assume a reductive economistic-cum-legalistic view of status, supposing that a just distribution of resources and rights is sufficient to preclude misrecognition. In fact, however, as we saw, not all misrecognition is a by-product of maldistribution, nor of maldistribution plus legal discrimination. Witness the case of the African-American Wall Street banker who cannot get a taxi to pick him up. To handle such cases, a theory of justice must reach beyond the distribution of rights and goods to examine institutionalized patterns of cultural value; it must ask whether such patterns impede parity of participation in social life.[35]

What, then, of the other side of the question? Can existing theories of recognition adequately subsume problems of distribution? Here too, I contend the answer is no. To be sure, some theorists of recognition appreciate the importance of economic equality and seek to accommodate it in their accounts. But once again the results are not wholly satisfactory. Axel Honneth, for example, assumes a reductive culturalist view of distribution. Supposing that all economic inequalities are rooted in a cultural order that privileges some kinds of labor over others, he believes that changing that cultural order is sufficient to preclude maldistribution.[36] In fact, however, as we saw, not all maldistribution is a by-product of misrecognition. Witness the case of the skilled white male industrial worker who becomes unemployed due to a factory closing resulting from a speculative corporate merger. In that case, the injustice of maldistribution has little to do with misrecognition. It is rather a consequence of imperatives intrinsic to an order of specialized economic relations whose *raison d'être* is the accumulation of profits. To handle such cases, a theory of justice must reach beyond cultural value patterns to examine the structure of capitalism. It must ask whether economic mechanisms that are relatively decoupled from structures of prestige and that operate in a relatively autonomous way impede parity of participation in social life.

In general, then, neither distribution theorists nor recognition theorists have so far succeeded in adequately subsuming the concerns of the other.[37] Absent a substantive reduction, moreover, purely verbal subsumptions are of little use. There is little to be gained by insisting as a point of semantics that, for example, recognition, too, is a good to be distributed; nor, conversely, by maintaining as a matter of definition that every distributive pattern expresses an underlying matrix of recognition. In both cases, the result is a tautology. The first makes all recognition distribution by definition, while the second merely asserts the reverse. In neither case have the substantive problems of conceptual integration been addressed.[38]

In the absence of a genuine reduction, what approach remains for those who seek to integrate distribution and recognition in a single normative framework? Instead of endorsing either one of those paradigms to the exclusion of the other, I propose to develop what I shall call a "two-dimensional" conception of justice. A two-dimensional conception treats distribution and recognition as distinct perspectives on, and dimensions of, justice. Without reducing either dimension to the other, it encompasses both of them within a broader overarching framework.

As already noted, the normative core of my conception is the notion of *parity of participation*.[39] According to this norm, justice requires social arrangements that permit all (adult) members of society to interact with one another as peers. For participatory parity to be possible, I claim, at least two conditions must be satisfied.[40] First, the distribution of material resources must be such as to ensure participants' independence and "voice." This I shall call the *objective condition* of participatory parity. It precludes forms and levels of economic dependence and inequality that impede parity of participation. Precluded, therefore, are social arrangements that institutionalize deprivation, exploitation, and gross disparities in wealth, income, and leisure time, thereby denying some people the means and opportunities to interact with others as peers.[41]

In contrast, the second condition requires that institutionalized patterns of cultural value express equal respect for all participants and ensure equal opportunity for achieving social esteem. This I shall call the *intersubjective condition* of participatory parity. It precludes institutionalized norms that systematically depreciate some categories of people and the qualities associated with them. Precluded, therefore, are institutionalized value patterns that deny some people the status of full partners in interaction – whether by burdening them with excessive ascribed "difference" or by failing to acknowledge their distinctiveness.

Both the objective condition and the intersubjective condition are necessary for participatory parity. Neither alone is sufficient. The objective condition brings into focus concerns traditionally associated with the theory of distributive justice, especially concerns pertaining to the economic structure of society and to economically defined class differentials. The intersubjective condition brings into focus concerns recently highlighted in the philosophy of recognition, especially concerns pertaining to the status order of society and to culturally defined hierarchies of status. Thus, a two-dimensional conception of justice oriented to the norm of participatory parity encompasses both redistribution and recognition, without reducing either one to the other.

This approach goes a considerable way toward achieving a conceptual integration. By construing redistribution and recognition as two mutually irreducible dimensions of justice, it broadens the usual understanding of justice to encompass intersubjective as well as objective considerations. By submitting both dimensions to the overarching norm of participatory parity, moreover, it brings both within the purview of a single integrated normative framework. The structure of that framework, including the relation between redistribution and recognition within it, will be clarified as we consider the two remaining questions of moral philosophy.

4. *Justifying claims for recognition*

Having broadened our view of justice to encompass intersubjective considerations of recognition, we arrive at our third moral-philosophical question: how can one distinguish justified from unjustified claims for recognition?

Clearly, not every claim for recognition is warranted, just as not every claim for redistribution is. In both cases, one needs an account of criteria and/or procedures for distinguishing warranted from unwarranted claims. Theorists of distributive justice have long sought to provide such accounts, whether by appealing to objectivistic criteria, such as utility maximization, or to procedural norms, such as those of discourse ethics. Theorists of recognition, in contrast, have been slower to face up to this question. They have yet to provide any principled basis for distinguishing justified from unjustified claims.

This issue poses grave difficulties for those who treat recognition as a matter of self-realization. Honneth's theory, for example, is vulnerable to serious objections on this point. According to him, everyone needs their distinctiveness recognized in order to develop self-esteem, which (along with self-confidence and self-respect) is an essential ingredient of an undistorted self-identity.[42] It seems to follow that claims for recognition that enhance the claimant's self-esteem are justified, while those that diminish it are not. On this hypothesis, however, racist identities would merit some recognition, as they enable some poor "white" Europeans and Euro-Americans to maintain their sense of self-worth by contrasting themselves with their supposed inferiors. Anti-racist claims would confront an obstacle, in contrast, as they threaten the self-esteem of poor whites. Unfortunately, cases like this one, in which prejudice conveys psychological benefits, are by no means rare. They suffice to disconfirm the view that enhanced self-esteem can supply a justificatory standard for recognition claims.

How, then, *should* recognition claims be judged? What constitutes an adequate criterion for assessing their merits? The approach proposed here appeals to participatory parity as an evaluative standard. As we saw, this norm overarches both dimensions of justice, distribution and recognition. Thus, for both dimensions the same general criterion serves to distinguish warranted from unwarranted claims. Whether the issue is distribution or recognition, claimants must show that current arrangements prevent them from participating on a par with others in social life. Redistribution claimants must show that existing economic arrangements deny them the necessary objective conditions for participatory parity. Recognition claimants must show that the institutionalized patterns of cultural value deny them the necessary intersubjective conditions. In both cases, therefore, the norm of participatory parity is the standard for warranting claims.

In both cases, too, participatory parity serves to evaluate proposed remedies for injustice. Whether they are demanding redistribution or recognition, claimants must show that the social changes they seek will in fact promote parity of participation. Redistribution claimants must show that the economic reforms they advocate will supply the objective conditions for full participation to those currently denied them – without introducing or exacerbating disparities along other dimensions in a manner that is unjustifiable. Similarly, recognition claimants must show that the socio-cultural institutional changes they seek will supply the needed intersubjective conditions – again, without unjustifiably creating or worsening other disparities. In both cases, once again, participatory parity is the standard for warranting proposals for specific reforms.

Let us consider how this standard works for some current controversies over recognition – beginning with same-sex marriage. In this case, as we saw, the institutionalization in marital law of a heterosexist cultural norm denies parity of participation to gays and lesbians. For the status model, therefore, this situation is patently unjust, and a recognition claim is in principle warranted. Such a claim seeks to remedy the injustice by deinstitutionalizing the heteronormative value pattern and replacing it with an alternative that promotes parity. This, however, can be done in more than one way. One way would be to grant the same recognition to homosexual partnerships that heterosexual partnerships currently enjoy by legalizing same-sex marriage. Another would be to deinstitutionalize heterosexual marriage, decoupling entitlements such as health insurance from marital status and assigning them on some other basis, such as citizenship and/or residency. Although there may be good reasons for preferring one of these approaches to the other, both of them would serve to foster participatory parity between gays and straights; hence both are justified in principle – assuming that neither would create or exacerbate other lines of disparity in a manner that is unjustifiable. What would not be warranted, in contrast, is an approach, like the French PACS or the "civil union" law in the US state of Vermont, that establishes a second, parallel legal status of domestic partnership that fails to confer all the symbolic or material benefits of marriage, while reserving the latter, privileged status exclusively for heterosexual couples. Although such reforms represent a

clear advance over existing laws and may command support on
tactical grounds, as transitional measures, they do not fulfill the
requirements of justice as understood via the status model.

Such tactical considerations aside, the case of same-sex
marriage presents no conceptual difficulties for the status model.
On the contrary, it illustrates a previously discussed advantage
of that model: here, the norm of participatory parity warrants
gay and lesbian claims deontologically, without recourse to
ethical evaluation – without, that is, assuming the substantive
judgment that homosexual relationships are ethically valuable. The self-realization approach, in contrast, cannot avoid
presupposing that judgment, and thus is vulnerable to counter-
judgments that deny it.[43] Thus, the status model is superior to
the self-realization model in handling this case.

Perhaps, however, this example is too easy. Let us consider some presumptively harder cases involving cultural and
religious practices. In such cases, the question arises whether
participatory parity can really pass muster as a justificatory
standard – whether, that is, it can serve to warrant claims
deontologically, without recourse to ethical evaluation of the
cultural and religious practices at issue. In fact, as we shall see,
participatory parity proves adequate here as well – provided it
is correctly applied.

What is crucial here is that participatory parity enters the
picture at two different levels. First, at the *intergroup* level, it
supplies the standard for assessing the effects of institutionalized
patterns of cultural value on the relative standing of *minorities
vis-à-vis majorities*. Thus, one invokes it when considering, for
example, whether erstwhile Canadian rules mandating uniform
headgear for Mounted Police constituted an unjust *majority
communitarianism*, which effectively closed that occupation to
Sikh men. Second, at the *intragroup* level, participatory parity
also serves to assess the *internal effects of minority practices* for
which recognition is claimed. At this level, one invokes it
when considering, for example, whether Orthodox Jewish
practices of sex segregation in education unjustly marginalize

Jewish girls and should therefore be denied public recognition in the form of tax exemptions or school subsidies.

Taken together, these two levels constitute a double requirement for claims for cultural recognition. Claimants must show, first, that the institutionalization of majority cultural norms denies them participatory parity and, second, that the practices whose recognition they seek do not themselves deny participatory parity – to some group members as well as to nonmembers. For the status model, both requirements are necessary; neither alone is sufficient. Only claims that meet both of them are deserving of public recognition.

To apply this double requirement, consider the French controversy over the *foulard*. Here the issue is whether policies forbidding Muslim girls to wear headscarves in state schools constitute unjust treatment of a religious minority. In this case, those claiming recognition for the *foulard* must establish two points: they must show, first, that the ban on the scarf constitutes an unjust majority communitarianism, which denies educational parity to Muslim girls; and second, that an alternative policy permitting the *foulard* would not exacerbate female subordination – in Muslim communities or in society at large. Only by establishing both points can they justify their claim. The first point, concerning French majority communitarianism, can be established without difficulty, it seems, as no analogous prohibition bars the wearing of Christian crosses in state schools; thus, the policy denies equal standing to Muslim citizens. The second point, concerning the non-exacerbation of female subordination, has proved controversial, in contrast, as some French republicans have argued that the *foulard* is itself a marker of such subordination and must therefore be denied recognition. Disputing this interpretation, however, some multiculturalists have rejoined that the scarf's meaning is highly contested in French Muslim communities today, as are gender relations more generally; thus, instead of construing it as univocally patriarchal, which effectively accords to male supremacists the sole authority to interpret Islam, the state should treat the *foulard* as a symbol of Muslim identity in transition, one whose meaning is contested, as is French identity itself, as a result of transcultural interactions in a multicultural society. From this perspective, permitting the *foulard* in state schools could be a step toward, not away from, gender parity.

In my view, the multiculturalists have the stronger argument here. (This is *not* the case, incidentally, for those who would recognize what they call "female circumcision" – actually genital mutilation – which clearly denies parity in sexual pleasure and in health to women and girls.) But that is not the point I wish to stress here. The point, rather, is that the argument is rightly cast in terms of parity of participation. For the status model, this is precisely where the controversy should be joined. As in the case of same-sex marriage, so in the case of cultural and religious claims, too: participatory parity is the proper standard for warranting claims. Differences in its interpretation notwithstanding, the norm of participatory parity serves to evaluate such recognition claims deontologically, without any need for ethical evaluation of the cultural or religious practices in question.

In general, then, the status model sets a stringent standard for warranting claims. Yet it remains wholly deontological. Unlike the self-realization model, it can justify claims for recognition under modern conditions of value pluralism.

5. *Decision theory or democratic deliberation?*

Participatory parity, I have been arguing, supplies a powerful justificatory standard. Yet the previous example shows that it cannot be applied monologically, in the manner of a decision procedure. There, as we saw, the issue ultimately turns on the effects of the *foulard* on the status of girls. But those effects cannot be calculated by an algorithmic metric or method. On the contrary, they can only be determined dialogically, by the give-and-take of arguments in which conflicting judgments are sifted and rival interpretations are weighed. More generally, there is no wholly transparent perspicuous sign that accompanies participatory parity, announcing its arrival for all to see. Anything purporting to be such a sign would itself remain subject to interpretation and contestation.

Thus, the norm of participatory parity must be applied dialogically and discursively, through democratic processes of public debate. In such debates, participants argue about whether existing institutionalized patterns of cultural value impede parity of participation and about whether proposed alternatives would foster it – without unjustifiably introducing or exacerbating other disparities.[44] For the status model, then, participatory parity serves as an idiom of public contestation and deliberation about questions of justice. More strongly, it represents *the principal idiom of public reason*, the preferred language for conducting democratic political argumentation on issues of both distribution and recognition.

This dialogical approach contrasts favorably, once again, with alternative models of recognition. It precludes the populist view, held by some proponents of identity politics, that misrecognized subjects alone should determine whether and how they are adequately recognized, hence that those whose self-esteem is at risk should have the final say as to what is required to secure it. At the same time, it also precludes the authoritarian view, assumed by some theorists of self-realization, that a philosophical expert can and should decide what is needed for human flourishing. Both those approaches are monological, vesting in a single subject the authority to interpret the requirements of justice. In contrast to such approaches, the status model treats participatory parity as a standard to be applied dialogically, in democratic processes of public deliberation. No given view – neither that of the claimants nor that of the "experts" – is indefeasible. Rather, precisely because interpretation and judgment are ineliminable, only the full, free participation of all the implicated parties can suffice to warrant claims for recognition. By the same token, however, every consensus or majority decision is fallible. In principle revisable, each provisional determination remains open to later challenges.

This last point brings us full circle, to be sure. Fair democratic deliberation concerning the merits of recognition claims requires parity of participation for all actual and possible deliberators. That in turn requires just distribution and reciprocal recognition. Thus, there is an unavoidable circularity in this account: claims for recognition can only be justified under conditions of participatory parity, which conditions include reciprocal recognition. The circularity is not vicious, however. Far from reflecting any defect of conceptualization, it faithfully expresses the reflexive character of justice as understood from the democratic perspective. In the democratic perspective, justice is not an externally imposed requirement, determined over the heads of those whom it obligates. Rather, it binds only insofar as its addressees can also rightly regard themselves as its authors.[45]

The solution, accordingly, is not to abolish the circularity in theory. It is rather to work to abolish it in practice by changing social reality. This requires raising (first-order) claims for redistribution and recognition, to be sure. But it also requires raising second-order or meta-level claims about the conditions in which first-order claims are adjudicated. By arguing publicly that the conditions for genuinely democratic public argument are currently lacking, one expresses the reflexivity of democratic justice in the process of struggling to realize it practically.

Thus, the approach proposed here incorporates a meta-level of deliberation about processes of deliberation. As a result, it offers the further advantage of preserving the possibility of radical critique. Much discourse about justice has an in-built conservative bias; focused on securing fair access to existing social goods, it tends not to question whether those are "the right goods." In contrast, the approach proposed here can counteract this conservative tendency. As we have seen, this approach enjoins equal participation in democratic debates over claims aimed at ensuring parity in actually existing forms of social interaction. But that is not the whole extent of its reach. In addition, it also enjoins parity in the social practices of critique, including deliberation about what forms of interaction *should* exist. Moreover, by applying the norm of participatory parity reflexively, to debates about debates, it tends to invite explicit discussion of the built-in biases of such debates, including biases favoring preservation of *status-quo* social practices over creation of new ones. Thus, unlike other approaches, the dialogical approach allows for historical dynamism.

6. *Recognizing distinctiveness? A pragmatic approach*

The preceding account of justification shares in the spirit of discourse ethics and of democratic pragmatism more generally. Its pragmatic spirit is appropriate as well for approaching our fourth and final normative-philosophical question: does justice require the recognition of what is distinctive about individuals or groups, over and above the recognition of our common humanity?

Here it is important to note that participatory parity is a universalist norm in two senses. First, it encompasses all (adult) partners to interaction. And second, it presupposes the equal moral worth of human beings. But moral universalism in these senses still leaves open the question of whether recognition of individual or group distinctiveness could be required by justice as one element among others of the intersubjective condition for participatory parity.

This question cannot be answered, I contend, by an *a priori* account of the kinds of recognition that everyone always needs. It needs rather to be approached in the spirit of a pragmatism informed by the insights of social theory. From this perspective, recognition is a remedy for social injustice, not the satisfaction of a generic human need. Thus, the form(s) of recognition justice requires in any given case depend(s) on the form(s) of *mis*recognition to be redressed. In cases where misrecognition involves denying the common humanity of some participants, the remedy is universalist recognition; thus, the first and most fundamental redress for South African apartheid was universal "non-racial" citizenship. Where, in contrast, misrecognition involves denying some participants' distinctiveness, the remedy could be recognition of specificity; thus, many feminists claim that overcoming women's subordination requires recognizing their unique and distinctive capacity to give birth.[46] In every case, the remedy should be tailored to the harm.

This pragmatist approach overcomes the liabilities of two other, mirror-opposite views. First, it rejects the claim, espoused by some distributive theorists, that justice requires limiting public recognition to those capacities all humans share. Favored by opponents of affirmative action, that approach dogmatically forecloses recognition of what distinguishes people from one another, without considering whether such recognition might be necessary in some cases to overcome obstacles to participatory parity. Second, the pragmatist approach rejects the opposite claim, equally decontextualized, that everyone always needs their distinctiveness recognized.[47] Favored by most recognition theorists, including Honneth, this second approach cannot explain why it is that not all, but only some, social differences generate claims for recognition, nor why only some of those claims, but not others, are morally justified. For example, it cannot explain why those occupying advantaged positions in the status order, such as men and heterosexuals, usually shun recognition of their (gender and sexual) distinctiveness, claiming not specificity but universality;[48] nor why, on those occasions when they do seek such recognition, their claims are usually spurious. By contrast, the approach proposed here sees claims for the recognition of difference pragmatically and contextually − as remedial responses to specific, pre-existing injustices. Thus, it appreciates that the recognition needs of subordinated social actors differ from those of dominant actors and that only those claims that promote participatory parity are morally justified.

For the pragmatist, accordingly, everything depends on precisely what currently misrecognized people need in order to be able to participate as peers in social life. And there is no reason to assume that all of them need the same thing in every context. In some cases, they may need to be unburdened of excessive ascribed or constructed distinctiveness. In other cases, they may need to have hitherto underacknowledged distinctiveness taken into account. In still other cases, they may need to shift the focus onto dominant or advantaged groups, outing the latter's distinctiveness, which has been falsely parading as universal. Alternatively, they may need to deconstruct the very terms in which attributed differences are currently elaborated. Finally, they may need all of the above, or several of the above, in combination with one another and in combination with redistribution. Which people need which kind(s) of recognition in which contexts depends on the nature of the obstacles they face with regard to participatory parity. That, however, cannot be determined by an abstract philosophical argument. It can only be determined with the aid of a critical social theory, a theory that is normatively oriented, empirically informed, and guided by the practical intent of overcoming injustice.

In the following section, accordingly, I shall examine some relevant aspects of social theory. First, however, let me conclude this discussion of normative philosophical issues by recapping the main claims argued here. First, recognition should be treated as a matter of justice, not one of self-realization. Second, theorists of justice should reject the idea of an either/or choice between the distributive paradigm and the recognition paradigm; instead, they should adopt a two-dimensional conception of justice premised on the norm of participatory parity. Third, to justify their claims, recognition claimants must show in public processes of democratic deliberation that institutionalized patterns of cultural value unjustly deny them the intersubjective conditions of participatory parity and that replacing those patterns with alternative ones would represent a step in the direction of parity. Fourth and finally, justice could in principle require recognizing distinctiveness, over and above our common humanity; but whether it does so in any given case can only be determined pragmatically in light of the obstacles to participatory parity specific to the case.

III. Social-Theoretical Issues: On Class and Status in Capitalist Society

This brings us to the social-theoretical issues that arise when we try to encompass redistribution and recognition in a single framework. Here the principal task is to understand the relations between maldistribution and misrecognition in contemporary society. This, we shall see, entails theorizing the relations between the class structure and the status order in late-modern globalizing capitalism. An adequate approach must allow for the full complexity of these relations. It must account *both for the differentiation of class from status and for the causal interactions between them*. It must accommodate, as well, *both the mutual irreducibility of maldistribution and misrecognition and their practical entwinement with each other*.

Such an account must, moreover, be historical. Sensitive to recent shifts in social structure and political culture, it must identify the distinctive dynamics and conflict tendencies of the present conjuncture. Attentive both to national specificities and to transnational forces and frames, it must explain why today's grammar of social conflict takes the form that it does: why, that is, struggles for recognition have recently become so salient; why egalitarian redistribution struggles, hitherto central to social life, have lately receded to the margins; and why, finally, the two kinds of claims for social justice have become decoupled and antagonistically counterposed.

First, however, some conceptual clarifications. The terms class and status, as I use them here, denote socially entrenched orders of subordination. To say that a society has a class structure is to say that it institutionalizes economic mechanisms that systematically deny some of its members the means and opportunities they need in order to participate on a par with others in social life. To say, likewise, that a society has a status hierarchy is to say that it institutionalizes patterns of cultural value that pervasively deny some members the recognition they need in order to be full, participating partners in social interaction. The existence of either a class structure or a status hierarchy constitutes an obstacle to parity of participation and thus an injustice.

These understandings differ from some more familiar definitions of status and class. Unlike stratification theory in postwar US sociology, for example, I do not conceive status as a prestige quotient that is ascribable to an individual and compounded of quantitatively measurable factors, including economic indices such as income. In my conception, in contrast, status represents an order of intersubjective subordination derived from institutionalized patterns of cultural value that constitute some members of society as less than full partners in interaction. Unlike Marxist theory, likewise, I do not conceive class as a relation to the means of production. In my conception, rather, class is an order of objective subordination derived from economic arrangements that deny some actors the means and resources they need for participatory parity.[49]

According to my conceptions, moreover, status and class do not map neatly onto current folk distinctions among social movements. Struggles against sexism and racism, for example, do not aim solely at transforming the status order, as gender and "race" implicate class structure as well. Nor, likewise, should labor struggles be reduced exclusively to matters of economic class, as they properly concern status hierarchies, too. More generally, as I noted earlier, virtually all axes of subordination partake simultaneously of the status order and the class structure, albeit in different proportions. Thus, far from corresponding to folk distinctions, status and class represent analytically distinct orders of subordination, which typically cut across social movements.

What status and class *do* correspond to, however, are misrecognition and maldistribution respectively. Each of them is associated with an analytically distinct type of impediment to participatory parity – hence with an analytically distinct dimension of justice. Status corresponds to the recognition dimension, which concerns the effects of institutionalized meanings and norms on the relative standing of social actors. Class, in contrast, corresponds to the distributive dimension, which concerns the allocation of economic resources and wealth. In general, then, the paradigmatic status injustice is misrecognition, which *may*, however, be accompanied by maldistribution, whereas the quintessential class injustice is maldistribution, which *may* in turn be accompanied by misrecognition.

1. *Beyond culturalism and economism*

Given these clarifications, we can now supply the counterpart in social theory to the moral theory of the previous section. The key point is that each of the two dimensions of justice is associated with an analytically distinct aspect of social order. The recognition dimension corresponds to the *status order* of society, hence to the constitution, by socially entrenched patterns of cultural value, of culturally defined categories of social actors – statuses – each distinguished by the relative respect, prestige, and esteem it enjoys vis-à-vis the others. The distributive dimension, in contrast, corresponds to the *economic structure* of society, hence to the constitution, by property regimes and labor markets, of economically defined categories of actors, or classes, distinguished by their differential endowments of resources. Each dimension, too, corresponds to an analytically distinct form of subordination: the recognition dimension corresponds to *status subordination*, rooted in institutionalized patterns of cultural value; the distributive dimension, in contrast, corresponds to *economic class subordination*, rooted in structural features of the economic system.

These correspondences enable us to situate the problem of

integrating redistribution and recognition within a broad social-theoretical frame. From this perspective, societies appear as complex fields that encompass at least two analytically distinct modes of social ordering: an economic mode, in which inter-action is regulated by the functional interlacing of strategic imperatives, and a cultural mode, in which interaction is regulated by institutionalized patterns of cultural value. As we shall see, economic ordering is typically institutionalized in markets; cultural ordering may work through a variety of different institutions, including kinship, religion, and law. In all societies economic ordering and cultural ordering are mutually imbricated. The question arises, however, as to how precisely they relate to each other in a given social formation. Is the economic structure institutionally differentiated from the cul-tural order, or are they effectively fused? Do the class structure and the status hierarchy diverge from one another, or do they coincide? Do maldistribution and misrecognition convert into each other, or are such conversions effectively blocked?

The answers to these questions depend on the nature of the society under consideration. Consider, for example, an ideal-typical pre-state society of the sort described in the classical anthropological literature, while bracketing the question of ethnographic accuracy. In such a society, the master idiom of social relations is kinship. Kinship organizes not only marriage and sexual relations, but also the labor process and the distri-bution of goods; relations of authority, reciprocity, and obliga-tion; and symbolic hierarchies of status and prestige. Of course, it could well be the case that such a society has never existed in pure form. Still, we can imagine a world in which neither distinctively economic institutions nor distinctively cultural institutions exist. A single order of social relations secures (what *we* would call) both the economic integration and the cultural integration of the society. Class structure and status order are accordingly fused. Because kinship constitutes the overarching principle of distribution, kinship status dictates class position. In the absence of any quasi-autonomous economic institutions, status subordination translates immediately into (what *we* would consider to be) distributive injustice. Misrecognition directly entails maldistribution.

Now consider the opposite extreme of a fully marketized society, in which economic structure dictates cultural value. In such a society, the master determining instance is the market. Markets organize not only the labor process and the distribution of goods, but also marriage and sexual relations; political relations of authority, reciprocity, and obligation; and symbolic hierarchies of status and prestige. Granted, such a society has never existed, and it may be that one never could.[50] For heuristic purposes, however, we can imagine a world in which a single order of social relations secures not only the economic integration but also the cultural integration of society. Here too, as in the previous case, class structure and status order are effectively fused. But the determinations run in the opposite direction. Because the market constitutes the sole and all-pervasive mechanism of valuation, market position dictates social status. In the absence of any quasi-autonomous cultural value patterns, distributive injustice translates immediately into status subordination. Maldistribution directly entails misrecognition.

These two societies are effectively mirror images of each other that share one major characteristic: neither of them differentiates economic ordering from cultural ordering, institutions that prioritize strategic action from those that prioritize value-regulated interaction. In both societies, accordingly, (what *we* would call) class and status map perfectly onto each other. So, as well, do (what *we* would call) maldistribution and misrecognition, which convert fully and without remainder into one another. As a result, one can understand both these societies reasonably well by attending exclusively to a single dimension of social life. For the fully kin-governed society, one can read off the economic dimension of subordination directly from the cultural; one can infer class directly from status and maldistribution directly from misrecognition. For the fully marketized society, conversely, one can read off the cultural dimension of subordination directly from the economic; one can infer status directly from class and misrecognition directly from maldistribution. For understanding the forms of subordination proper to the fully kin-governed society, therefore, culturalism is a perfectly appropriate social theory.[51] If, in contrast, one is seeking to understand the fully marketized society, one could hardly improve on economism.[52]

When we turn to other types of societies, however, such simple and elegant approaches no longer suffice. They are patently inappropriate for our own society, which contains both marketized arenas, in which strategic action predominates, and non-marketized arenas, in which value-oriented interaction predominates. Here, accordingly, zones of economic ordering are differentiated from zones of cultural ordering, the economic structure from the cultural order. The result is a partial uncoupling of the economic mechanisms of distribution from the structures of prestige – thus a gap between status and class. In our society, then, the class structure ceases perfectly to mirror the status order, even though each of them influences the other. Because the market does not constitute the sole and all-pervasive mechanism of valuation, market position does not dictate social status. Partially market-resistant cultural value patterns prevent distributive injustices from converting fully and without remainder into status injuries. Maldistribution does not directly entail misrecognition, although it certainly contributes to the latter. Conversely, because no single status principle such as kinship constitutes the sole and all-pervasive principle of distribution, status does not dictate class position. Relatively autonomous economic institutions prevent status injuries from converting fully and without remainder into distributive injustices. Misrecognition does not directly entail maldistribution, although it, too, surely contributes to the latter. As a result, one cannot understand this society by attending exclusively to a single dimension of social life. One cannot read off the economic dimension of subordination directly from the cultural, nor the cultural directly from the economic. Likewise, one cannot infer class directly from status, nor status directly from class. Finally, one cannot deduce maldistribution directly from misrecognition, nor misrecognition directly from maldistribution.

It follows that neither culturalism nor economism suffices for understanding contemporary society. Instead, one needs an approach that can accommodate differentiation, divergence, and interaction at every level. Before attempting to sketch such an approach, however, it is worth pausing to explicate a tacit presupposition of the preceding discussion.

2. *Cultural modernity and status inequality: Hybridization, differentiation, contestation*

Throughout this chapter I have assumed that the category of status remains relevant to contemporary society. I have assumed, that is, that it is not the case that status hierarchy is an exclusively premodern phenomenon, which disappeared with the rise of "contract." I have likewise assumed that the forms of status subordination that are extant today are not simply archaic precapitalist vestiges. On the contrary, it is a presupposition of my approach that injustices of status are intrinsic to the social structure of modern capitalism, including in its contemporary globalizing phase. Let me explain, and justify, these assumptions.

The need for an explanation arises because contemporary society differs sharply from those "traditional" societies for which the concept of status was originally developed. To appreciate the difference, let us return for a moment to our hypothetical fully kin-governed society. In that society, as we saw, cultural ordering was the primary mode of social integration, and status hierarchy was the root form of subordination. We can see retrospectively, moreover, that the anthropologists who envisioned the society tacitly assumed that its cultural order possessed five major characteristics. First, it was sharply bounded; because intercultural contacts were restricted to the margins, there was no significant cultural hybridization, nor any great difficulty in establishing where one culture ended and another began. Second, the cultural order was institutionally undifferentiated; because a single overarching institution, kinship, regulated all forms of social interaction, a single pattern of cultural value supplied the template for the status order. Third, the society was ethically monistic; all of its members operated within the terms of a single, shared horizon of evaluation, which was all-pervasive and uniformly diffused; there existed no encapsulated subcultures subscribing to alternative ethical horizons. Fourth, the cultural order was exempt from contestation; in the absence of any alternative evaluative horizon, there was no perspective from which to criticize the institutionalized pattern of cultural value, nor any perspective that supported contestation. Fifth and finally, the resulting hierarchy was socially legitimate; however much individuals may have chafed under it, they lacked any principled basis for challenging its authority. In our hypothetical fully kin-governed society, in sum, the cultural order was sharply bounded, institutionally undifferentiated, ethically monistic, uncontested, and socially legitimate. As a result, the status order took the form of *a single fixed, all-encompassing status hierarchy*.

None of these conditions holds for contemporary society. First, the cultural order of this society is not sharply bounded. No longer restricted to the margins, transcultural flows pervade the central "interior" spaces of social interaction. Thanks to mass migrations, diasporas, globalized mass culture, and transnational public spheres, it is impossible to say with certainty exactly where one culture ends and another begins; all, rather, are internally hybridized. Second, the cultural order of contemporary society is institutionally differentiated. No single master institution, such as kinship, supplies a template of cultural value that effectively governs all social interaction. Rather, a multiplicity of institutions regulates a multiplicity of action arenas according to different patterns of cultural value, at least some of which are mutually incompatible; the schema for interpreting and evaluating sexuality that organizes mass culture, for example, diverges from that institutionalized in the laws governing marriage.[53] Third, the cultural order of contemporary society is ethically pluralistic. Not all members share a common, uniformly diffused evaluative horizon. On the contrary, different subcultures or "communities of value" subscribe to different, and at times incompatible, horizons of value. Although neither internally homogeneous nor sharply bounded, these subcultures constitute a third source of cultural complexity, over and above hybridization and institutional differentiation. Fourth, value patterns and evaluative horizons are intensely contested. The combination of transcultural hybridization, institutional differentiation, and ethical pluralism ensures the availability of alternative perspectives that can be used to criticize the dominant values. Nowhere exempt from cultural contestation, contemporary societies are veritable cauldrons of cultural struggle. Virtually none of their narratives, discourses, and interpretative schemata goes unchallenged; all are contested, rather, as social actors struggle to institutionalize their own horizons of value as authoritative. Finally, status hierarchy is illegitimate in modern society. The most basic principle of legitimacy in this society is liberal equality, as expressed both in market ideals, such as equal exchange, the career open to talents, and meritocratic competition, and in democratic ideals, such as equal citizenship and status equality. Status hierarchy violates all these ideals. Far from being socially legitimate, it contravenes fundamental norms of market and democratic legitimacy.[54]

In general, then, contemporary society is light years away from our hypothetical fully kin-governed society. Unlike the cultural order of that society, with its stable, monolithic, pervasively institutionalized pattern of value, culture today bears all the marks of modernity. Hybridized, differentiated, pluralistic, and contested, it is suffused with anti-hierarchical norms. Today's status order, accordingly, does not resemble that of the fully kin-governed society. Where that society instantiated a fixed, uncontested, all-encompassing status hierarchy, ours gives rise to a shifting field of cross-cutting status distinctions. In this field, social actors do not occupy any preordained "place." Rather, they participate actively in *a dynamic regime of ongoing struggles for recognition.*

Yet it is not the case that everyone enters these struggles on equal terms. On the contrary, some contestants lack the resources to participate on a par with others, thanks to unjust economic arrangements. And what is more to the point here, some lack the social standing, thanks to institutionalized patterns of cultural value that are inequitable. Cultural contradiction and complexity notwithstanding, parity-impeding value patterns continue to regulate interaction in most important social institutions – witness religion, education, and law. To be sure, such value patterns do not comprise a seamless, coherent, all-encompassing, and unbreachable web, as in the fully kin-governed society; and they no longer go without saying. Nevertheless, norms favoring whites, Europeans, heterosexuals, men, and Christians are institutionalized at many sites throughout the world. They continue to impede parity of participation – and thus to define axes of status subordination.

In general, then, status subordination persists in contemporary society – albeit in another guise. Far from having been eliminated, it has undergone a qualitative transformation. In the modern regime, there is no stable pyramid of corporations or social estates. Nor is every social actor assigned to a single, exclusive "status group," which defines his or her standing across the board. Rather, individuals are nodes of convergence for multiple, cross-cutting axes of subordination. Frequently disadvantaged along some axes and simultaneously advantaged along others, they wage struggles for recognition in a modern regime.

Two broad historical processes have contributed to modernizing status subordination. The first is marketization, which is a process of societal differentiation. Markets have always existed, of course, but their scope, autonomy, and influence attained a qualitatively new level with the development of modern capitalism. In a capitalist society, markets constitute the core institutions of a specialized zone of economic relations, legally differentiated from other zones. In this marketized zone, interaction is not directly regulated by patterns of cultural value. It is governed, rather, by the functional interlacing of strategic imperatives, as individuals act to maximize self-interest. Marketization, accordingly, introduces breaks in the cultural order, fracturing pre-existing normative patterns and rendering traditional values potentially open to challenge. But capitalist markets do not cause status distinctions simply to "melt into air," as Marx and Engels predicted.[55] For one thing, markets neither occupy the totality of social space nor govern the entirety of social interaction; rather, they coexist with, indeed *rely on*, institutions that regulate interaction according to values that encode status distinctions – above all, the family and the state.[56] Even on their own turf, moreover, markets do not simply dissolve status distinctions; rather, they instrumentalize them, bending pre-existing patterns of cultural value to capitalist purposes. For example, racial hierarchies that long predated capitalism were not abolished with the dismantling of New World slavery or even of Jim Crow, but reconfigured to suit a market society. No longer explicitly codified in law, and no longer socially legitimate, racist norms have been wired into the infrastructure of capitalist labor markets.[57] Thus, the net result of marketization is the modernization, not supersession, of status subordination.

The second status-modernizing historical process is the rise of a complex, pluralistic civil society. This, too, involves differentiation, but of another sort. With civil society comes the differentiation of a broad range of nonmarketized institutions – legal, political, cultural, educational, associational, religious, familial, aesthetic, administrative, professional, intellectual. As these institutions acquire some autonomy, each develops its own relatively customized pattern of cultural value for regulating interaction. These patterns overlap, to be sure, but they do not fully coincide. In civil society, therefore, different loci of interaction are governed by different patterns cultural value; and social actors are differently positioned at different sites – denied parity here or there, according to which distinctions trump which in a given setting. In addition, the rise of civil society is often linked to the advent of toleration, which permits the coexistence of different subcultures and further pluralizes value horizons. Finally, a modern civil society tends to encourage transcultural contacts; accommodating trade, travel, and transnational networks of communication, it sets in motion, or accelerates, processes of cultural hybridization. In general then, civil society pluralizes and hybridizes value horizons, thereby serving, like marketization, to modernize status subordination.

The moral is that a critical theory of contemporary society cannot neglect status subordination. Rather, it must reconstruct classical sociological concepts for a modern dynamic regime. Thus, a critical theory must eschew the Durkheimian assumption of a single, overarching pattern of cultural value.[58] In addition, it must eschew the traditional pluralist assumption of a series of discrete, internally homogeneous cultures coexisting alongside, but not constitutively affecting, one another.[59] Finally, it must eschew the "stable pyramid" picture of subordination, which assigns every individual to a single "status group." In their place, it must develop conceptions – like those proposed here – that can grasp modern forms of status subordination.[60]

Lastly, a critical theory of contemporary society must include an account of the relation of status subordination to class subordination, misrecognition to maldistribution. Above all, it must clarify the prospects for emancipatory change for a time in which struggles for recognition are increasingly decoupled from struggles for egalitarian redistribution – even as justice requires that the two be joined.

3. *An argument for perspectival dualism*

What sort of social theory can handle this task? What approach can theorize the dynamic forms of status subordination characteristic of late-modern globalizing capitalism? What approach can theorize, too, the complex relations between status and class, misrecognition and maldistribution, in this society? What sort of theory can grasp at once their conceptual irreducibility, empirical divergence, and practical entwinement? And what sort of theory can do all this *without reinforcing the current dissociation of the politics of recognition from the politics of redistribution?*

Earlier we saw that neither economism nor culturalism is up to the task: contemporary society cannot be understood by approaches that reduce status to class or class to status. The same is true of a third approach that I shall call "poststructuralist anti-dualism." Proponents of this approach, who include Judith Butler and Iris Marion Young, reject distinctions between economic ordering and cultural ordering as "dichotomizing." They claim that culture and economy are so deeply interconnected, so mutually constitutive, that they cannot meaningfully be distinguished at all. They also claim that contemporary society is so monolithically systematic that a struggle against any one aspect of it necessarily threatens the whole; hence, it is divisive and counterproductive to distinguish claims for recognition from claims for redistribution. Instead of theorizing the relations between status and class, therefore, poststructuralist anti-dualists advocate deconstructing the distinction altogether.[61]

Although more fashionable than economism and culturalism, poststructuralist anti-dualism is no more adequate for theorizing contemporary society. Simply to stipulate that all injustices, and all claims to remedy them, are simultaneously economic and cultural is to paint a night in which all cows are grey: obscuring actually existing divergences of status from class, this approach surrenders the conceptual tools that are needed to understand social reality. Likewise, to treat contemporary capitalism as a monolithic system of perfectly interlocking oppressions is to cover over its actual complexity; far from advancing efforts to join struggles for recognition to struggles for redistribution, this approach makes it impossible to entertain pressing political questions about how the two types of struggles might be synergized and harmonized, when at present they diverge and conflict.[62]

In general, then, none of the three approaches considered here so far can provide an acceptable theory of contemporary society. None can conceptualize today's complex relations between cultural ordering and economic ordering, status subordination and class subordination, misrecognition and maldistribution. If neither economism nor culturalism nor poststructuralist anti-dualism is up to the task, then what alternative approaches are possible?

Two possibilities present themselves, both of them species of dualism. The first approach I shall call "substantive dualism." It treats redistribution and recognition as two different "spheres of justice," pertaining to two different societal domains. The former pertains to the economic domain of society, the relations of production. The latter pertains to the cultural domain, the relations of recognition. When we consider economic matters, such as the structure of labor markets, we should assume the standpoint of distributive justice, attending to the impact of economic structures and institutions on the relative economic position of social actors. When, in contrast, we consider cultural matters, such as the representation of female sexuality on MTV, we should assume the standpoint of recognition, attending to the impact of institutionalized patterns of cultural value on the relative standing of social actors.

Substantive dualism may be preferable to economism, culturalism, and poststructuralist anti-dualism, but it is nevertheless inadequate. Treating economy and culture as two separate spheres, it overlooks their interpenetration. In fact, as we have just seen, the economy is not a culture-free zone, but a culture-instrumentalizing and culture-resignifying one. Thus, what presents itself as "the economy" is always already permeated with interpretations and norms – witness the distinctions between "working" and "caregiving," "men's jobs" and "women's jobs," which are so fundamental to historical capitalism. In these cases, gender meanings and norms have been appropriated from the cultural order and bent to capitalist purposes, with major consequences for both distribution and recognition. Likewise, what presents itself as "the cultural sphere" is deeply permeated by "the bottom line" – witness global mass entertainment, the art market, and transnational advertising, all fundamental to contemporary culture. *Contra* substantive dualism, then, nominally economic matters usually affect not only the economic position but also the status and identities of social actors. Likewise, nominally cultural matters affect not only status but also economic position. In neither case, therefore, are we dealing with separate spheres.[63]

Practically, moreover, substantive dualism fails to challenge the current dissociation of cultural politics from social politics. On the contrary, it reinforces that dissociation. Casting the economy and the culture as impermeable, sharply bounded separate spheres, it assigns the politics of redistribution to the former and the politics of recognition to the latter. The result is effectively to constitute two separate political tasks requiring two separate political struggles. Decoupling cultural injustices from economic injustices, cultural struggles from social struggles, it reproduces the very dissociation we are seeking to overcome. Substantive dualism is not a solution to, but a symptom of, our problem. It reflects, but does not critically interrogate, the institutional differentiations of modern capitalism.

A genuinely critical perspective, in contrast, cannot take the appearance of separate spheres at face value. Rather, it must probe beneath appearances to reveal the hidden connections between distribution and recognition. It must make visible, and *criticizable*, both the cultural subtexts of nominally economic processes and the economic subtexts of nominally cultural practices. Treating *every* practice as simultaneously economic and cultural, albeit not necessarily in equal proportions, it must assess each of them from two different perspectives. It must assume both the standpoint of distribution and the standpoint of recognition, without reducing either one of these perspectives to the other.

Such an approach I call "perspectival dualism." Here redistribution and recognition do not correspond to two substantive societal domains, economy and culture. Rather, they constitute two analytical perspectives that can be assumed with respect to any domain. These perspectives can be deployed critically, moreover, against the ideological grain. One can use the recognition perspective to identify the cultural dimensions of what are usually viewed as redistributive economic policies. By focusing on the institutionalization of interpretations and norms in income-support programs, for example, one can assess their effects on the social status of women and immigrants.[64] Conversely, one can use the redistribution perspective to bring into focus the economic dimensions of what are usually viewed as issues of recognition. By focusing on the high "transaction costs" of living in the closet, for example, one can assess the effects of heterosexist misrecognition on the economic position of gays and lesbians.[65] With perspectival dualism, then, one can assess the justice of any social practice, regardless of where it is institutionally located, from two analytically distinct normative vantage points, asking: does the practice in question work to ensure both the objective and intersubjective conditions of participatory parity? Or does it, rather, undermine them?

The advantages of this approach should be clear. Unlike poststructuralist anti-dualism, perspectival dualism permits us to distinguish distribution from recognition – and thus to analyze the relations between them. Unlike economism and culturalism, however, it avoids reducing either one of those categories to the other and short-circuiting the complexity of the links. Unlike substantive dualism, finally, it avoids dichotomizing economy and culture and obscuring their mutual imbrication. In contrast to these approaches, perspectival dualism allows us to theorize the complex connections between two orders of subordination, grasping at once their conceptual irreducibility, empirical divergence, and practical entwinement. Understood perspectivally, then, the distinction between distribution and recognition does not simply reproduce the ideological dissociations of our time. Rather, it provides an indispensable conceptual tool for interrogating, working through, and eventually overcoming those dissociations.

4. *Countering unintended effects*

Perspectival dualism offers another advantage as well. Alone among all the approaches considered here, it allows us to conceptualize some practical difficulties that can arise in the course of political struggles. Conceiving the economic and the cultural as differentiated but interpenetrating modes of social ordering, perspectival dualism appreciates that neither claims for redistribution nor claims for recognition can be contained within a separate sphere. On the contrary, they impinge on one another in ways that can give rise to unintended effects.

Consider, first, that redistribution impinges on recognition. Virtually any claim for redistribution will have some recognition effects, whether intended or unintended. Proposals to redistribute income through social welfare, for example, have an irreducible expressive dimension;[66] they convey interpretations of the meaning and value of different activities, for example, "childrearing" versus "wage-earning," while also constituting and ranking different subject positions, for example "welfare mothers" versus "taxpayers."[67] Thus, redistributive claims affect the standing and identities of social actors, as well as their economic position. These status effects must be thematized and scrutinized, lest one end up fueling misrecognition in the course of trying to remedy maldistribution.

The classic example, once again, is "welfare." Means-tested

benefits aimed specifically at the poor are the most directly redistributive form of social welfare. Yet such benefits tend to stigmatize recipients, casting them as deviants and scroungers and invidiously distinguishing them from "wage-earners" and "taxpayers" who "pay their own way." Welfare programs of this type "target" the poor – not only for material aid but also for public hostility. The end result is often to add the insult of misrecognition to the injury of deprivation. Redistributive policies have misrecognition effects when background patterns of cultural value skew the meaning of economic reforms, when, for example, a pervasive cultural devaluation of female caregiving inflects support for single-mother families as "getting something for nothing."[68] In this context, welfare reform cannot succeed unless it is joined with struggles for cultural change aimed at revaluing caregiving and the feminine associations that code it. In short, *no redistribution without recognition.*

Consider, next, the converse dynamic, whereby recognition impinges on distribution. Virtually any claim for recognition will have some distributive effects, whether intended or unintended. Proposals to redress androcentric evaluative patterns, for example, have economic implications, which can work to the detriment of the intended beneficiaries. For example, campaigns to suppress prostitution and pornography for the sake of enhancing women's status may have negative effects on the economic position of sex workers, while no-fault divorce reforms, which appeared to dovetail with feminist efforts to enhance women's status, have had negative effects on the economic position of some divorced women, although their extent is currently in dispute.[69] Thus, recognition claims can affect economic position, above and beyond their effects on status. These effects, too, must be scrutinized, lest one end up fueling maldistribution in the course of trying to remedy misrecognition. Recognition claims, moreover, are liable to the charge of being "merely symbolic."[70] When pursued in contexts marked by gross disparities in economic position, reforms aimed at affirming distinctiveness tend to devolve into empty gestures; like the sort of recognition that would put women on a pedestal, they mock, rather than redress, serious harms. In such contexts, recognition reforms cannot succeed unless they are joined with struggles for redistribution. In short, *no recognition without redistribution.*

The need, in all cases, is to think integratively, as in recent campaigns for "comparable worth." Here a claim to redistribute income between men and women was expressly integrated with a claim to change gender-coded patterns of cultural value. The underlying premise was that gender injustices of distribution and recognition are so complexly intertwined that neither can be redressed entirely independently of the other. Thus, efforts to reduce the gender wage gap cannot fully succeed if, remaining wholly "economic," they fail to challenge the gender meanings that code low-paying service occupations as "women's work," largely devoid of intelligence and skill. Likewise, efforts to revalue female-coded traits such as interpersonal sensitivity and nurturance cannot succeed if, remaining wholly "cultural," they fail to challenge the structural economic conditions that connect those traits with dependency and powerlessness. Only an approach that redresses the cultural devaluation of the "feminine" precisely *within* the economy (and elsewhere) can deliver serious redistribution and genuine recognition.

Comparable worth epitomizes the advantages of perspectival dualism. That approach, we have seen, aligns distribution and recognition with two modes of social ordering – the economic and the cultural, which are conceived not as separate spheres but as differentiated and interpenetrating. As a result, it enables us to grasp the full complexity of the relations between class subordination and status subordination, maldistribution and misrecognition, in contemporary society. In addition, perspectival dualism provides us with practical insight into possible pitfalls of political struggles for redistribution and recognition. Enjoining us to assess claims of each type from both normative perspectives, it can help us anticipate, and hopefully avoid, the perverse effects of faulty political strategies.

5. *Concluding conceptual reflections*

In the following section, I shall turn in earnest to the political-theoretical implications of this approach. First, however, I want to explicate some conceptual implications of the preceding argument. Three points in particular deserve attention.

The first concerns the distinctions between class and status, economy and culture, maldistribution and misrecognition. In the argument made here, these were not treated as ontological distinctions. *Contra* some poststructuralist critics, I did not align distribution with the material and recognition with the "merely symbolic."[71] Rather, I assumed that status injustices can be just as material as class injustices – witness gay-bashing, gang rape, and genocide. Far from ontologizing the distinction, I *historicized* it, tracing it to historical developments in social organization. Thus, I traced the distinction between cultural ordering and economic ordering to the historical differentiation of markets from value-regulated social institutions. Likewise, I traced the distinction between status and class to the historical decoupling of specialized mechanisms of economic distribution from culturally defined structures of prestige. Finally, I traced the distinction between maldistribution and misrecognition to the historical differentiation of economic from cultural obstacles to participatory parity. In short, I traced all three distinctions to the rise of capitalism, arguably the first social formation in history that systematically elaborates two distinct orders of subordination, premised on two distinct dimensions of injustice.[72]

The second point concerns the conceptual openness of this account. In the preceding argument, I considered two modes of social ordering, the economic and the cultural, corresponding to two types of subordination and two types of obstacles to participatory parity. But I did not rule out the possibility of additional modes. On the contrary, I left open the question of whether there might exist other modes of social ordering corresponding to other types of subordination and other dimensions of justice. The most plausible candidate for a third dimension is "the political." "Political" obstacles to participatory parity would include decision-making procedures that systematically marginalize some people even in the absence of maldistribution and misrecognition – for example, single-member district winner-take-all electoral rules that deny voice to quasi-permanent minorities.[73] The corresponding injustice would be "political marginalization" or "exclusion," the corresponding remedy, "democratization."[74]

In the following sections, I shall incorporate some considerations pertaining to this third dimension. Here I note only that it holds out the prospect of answering an objection mentioned earlier. I refer to the Marxian objection that the approach proposed here does not adequately address the problem of class oppression, which encompasses not only maldistribution and misrecognition but also exploitation and lack of control over work; as these are due to the capitalist property form, so the objection runs, they cannot be redressed by redistribution and recognition, but only by abolishing that property form. One can respond to this objection by disaggregating several injustices that are bundled together in the notion of the capitalist property form: first, the right of the capitalist to appropriate a disproportionate portion of surplus value and to exclude the workers from their rightful share; second, the right of the capitalist to command labor at the workplace and to exclude the workers from decision-making concerning the conditions and organization of their work; and third, the right of the capitalist class to determine unilaterally how the social surplus shall be invested and to exclude the citizenry from such decision-making. Thus disaggregated, these injustices can be fitted into the framework presented here, now expanded to included the "political" dimension: whereas the first injustice is an instance of maldistribution, the second and third are "political" – the one representing a deficit of workplace democracy, the other a deficit of economic democracy in the broader sense of citizen control over the overall direction of economic life. Thus, the remedies required to redress the injustice include redistribution and democratization – as well as, presumably, recognition. What, if anything, would remain of the capitalist property form in the event of such redress is a matter for further examination elsewhere.

A third and final point concerns the interpretation of the present political conjuncture. It is an implication of the argument developed here that the current decoupling of the politics of recognition from the politics of redistribution is not the result of a simple mistake. Rather, the possibility of such a decoupling is built into the structure of modern capitalist society. In this society, as we have seen, the cultural order is hybridized, differentiated, pluralistic, and contested, while status hierarchy is considered illegitimate. At the same time, economic ordering is institutionally differentiated from cultural ordering, as is class from status and maldistribution from misrecognition. Taken together, these structural features of our society encode the possibility of today's political dissociations. They encourage the proliferation of struggles for recognition, while also enabling the latter's decoupling from struggles for redistribution.

At the same time, however, the argument presented here implies that the structure of modern society is such that neither class subordination nor status subordination can be adequately understood in isolation from the other. On the contrary, misrecognition and maldistribution are so complexly intertwined today that each must be grasped from a larger, integrated perspective that also encompasses the other. Only when status and class are considered in tandem, in sum, can our current political dissociations be overcome.

IV. Political-Theoretical Issues: Institutionalizing Democratic Justice

Let us turn now to the political-theoretical issues that arise when we try to encompass redistribution and recognition in a single framework. Here the principal questions are: what institutional arrangements can ensure both the objective and inter-subjective conditions for participatory parity? What policies and reforms can ameliorate injustices of status and class simultaneously? What programmatic political orientation can satisfy both defensible claims for redistribution and defensible claims for recognition, while minimizing the mutual interferences that can arise when the two types of claims are pursued in tandem?

In preparing to take up these questions, we should consider what kind of answers we are looking for – and hence what sort of stance should govern the inquiry. One possibility is to adopt the mindset of latter-day philosopher kings, charged with operationalizing the requirements of justice. In that case, the answers to our questions will resemble blueprints, whether in the utopian guise of overarching institutional designs or in the realist guise of policy proposals for piecemeal reforms. A second possibility is to assume the standpoint of democratic justice, seeking to foster citizen deliberation about how best to implement the requirements of justice. In that case, the answers will resemble dialogical guideposts, heuristics for organizing democratic debate. Ever since Plato and Aristotle, political theorists have wavered uneasily between these two stances, with some inclining more to the first and others leaning more to the second. Which approach is preferable here?

The Platonic stance has its virtues, to be sure. Far from taking refuge in empty proceduralism, it yields substantive political conclusions. These are backed, moreover, by argumentation whose validity can (supposedly) be assessed by any rational inquirer. Yet this approach is largely insensitive to issues of context. Naively assuming that normative principles can determine their own application, it fails to appreciate that implementation requires political judgment. In addition, the Platonic approach overlooks "the fact of pluralism"; neglecting the plurality of reasonable perspectives on how best to interpret the requirements of justice, it substitutes an inadequate mono-logical decision-procedure for dialogical deliberation.[75] Finally, the Platonic stance neglects the importance of democratic legitimacy; effectively usurping the role of the citizenry, it authorizes a theoretical expert to circumvent the deliberative process by which those subject to the requirements of justice can come to regard themselves as the latter's authors.

For all these reasons, the Aristotelian stance is *prima facie* preferable. It is especially well suited to the current globalizing moment, in which issues of "difference" are intensely politi-cized, the boundaries of political membership are increasingly contested, and the quest for democratic legitimacy is acquiring new urgency. In this context, monological approaches are counterproductive, while proceduralist alternatives gain plausi-bility. The latter, however, are vulnerable to a serious objec-tion: precisely because of their democratic commitments, such approaches devolve easily into empty formalisms. At times overly fearful of supplanting the citizenry, they rush to jettison substantive content. The result can be an abstract insistence on democratic procedure that has little to say about justice.

Thus, neither monologism nor proceduralism will suffice. What is needed, rather, is an approach that strikes a proper balance between those extremes. Avoiding both authoritarian usurpation and self-effacing vacuity, such an approach must allow for an appropriate division of labor between theorist and citizenry. Delimiting the philosopher's province from that of the *demos*, it must discern the point at which theoretical argumentation rightly ends and dialogical judgment should begin. Where that point lies, however, is not immediately self-evident.[76] After all, theoretical arguments are often introduced into citizen debates; and contextual considerations can and should inform theorizing. Thus, there are no clearly marked borders separating political theory from the collective reflection of democratic citizens. Yet it is possible to state a rule of thumb: when we consider institutional questions, theory can help to clarify the range of policies and programs that are compatible with the requirements of justice; weighing the choices within that range, in contrast, is a matter for citizen deliberation. This division of labor is by no means absolute, but its rationale runs as follows: delimiting the range of permissible options entails measuring institutional proposals by a normative yardstick, which is largely an exercise in conceptual analysis. Choosing among the set of acceptable options, in contrast, entails situated hermeneutical reflection on matters that are context-specific, including what citizens value in addition to justice, given their histories, traditions, and collective identities. Political theorists *qua* theorists may be able to help clarify the former; the citizens themselves should do the latter.

In what follows, I shall be guided by this rule of thumb. Seeking to avoid both the Scylla of monologism and the Charybdis of proceduralism, I shall adopt a modified version of the standpoint of democratic justice. Thus, in considering programmatic scenarios for integrating redistribution and recognition, I shall not aim to devise institutional blueprints. Rather, I shall make it my primary objective to clarify the parameters of public debate. At the same time, however, I shall not forgo substantive conclusions. Rather, I shall identify a range of programmatic options that can serve to foster parity of participation along both dimensions of justice simultaneously; and I shall propose some heuristics for a democratic discussion by which their relative merits can be weighed.

1. *Affirmation or transformation?*

With this orientation, let us turn now to the issues before us: what institutional reforms can remedy injustices of status and class simultaneously? What political strategy can successfully integrate redistribution and recognition, while also mitigating the mutual interferences that can arise when those two aims are pursued in tandem?

Consider, again, the remedy for injustice, restated now in its most general form: removal of impediments to participatory parity. At first sight, what this means is clear. To remedy maldistribution one must remove economic impediments via redistribution; what is needed, accordingly, is economic restructuring aimed at ensuring the objective conditions for participatory parity. To remedy misrecognition, likewise, one must remove cultural impediments via recognition; what is required here are policies that can supply the intersubjective prerequisites – by deinstitutionalizing patterns of cultural value that impede parity of participation and replacing them with patterns that foster it. Finally, applying this schema to "the third dimension," we could say that to remedy political exclusion or marginalization one must remove political obstacles via democratization, an idea I shall return to later.

The initial appearance of clarity is misleading, however, even for redistribution and recognition. In both those cases, the general formula of removing obstacles to participatory parity is subject to more than one institutional application. As noted earlier, economic restructuring could mean redistributing income and/or wealth; reorganizing the division of labor; changing the rules and entitlements of property ownership; or democratizing the procedures by which decisions are made about how to invest social surpluses. Likewise, as also noted, misrecognition can be redressed in more than one way: by universalizing privileges now reserved for advantaged groups or by eliminating those privileges altogether; by deinstitutionalizing preferences for traits associated with dominant actors or by entrenching norms favoring subordinates alongside them; by privatizing differences or by valorizing them or by deconstructing the oppositions that underlie them. Given this plethora of possible interpretations, the institutional implications are no longer so clear. Which remedies for maldistribution and misrecognition should proponents of justice seek to effect?

To answer this question, we need a way of organizing, and evaluating, the alternatives. I propose to proceed by distinguishing two broad strategies for remedying injustice that cut across the redistribution–recognition divide: *affirmation* and *transformation*.[77] After sketching these strategies generically, I shall show how they can be used to categorize approaches to redistribution and recognition. On this basis, finally, I shall reformulate the problem of integrating those two dimensions of justice in a single political strategy.

I begin, accordingly, by distinguishing affirmation and transformation. The distinction turns on the contrast between underlying social structures, on the one hand, and the social outcomes they generate, on the other. Affirmative strategies for redressing for injustice aim to correct inequitable outcomes of social arrangements without disturbing the underlying social structures that generate them. Transformative strategies, in contrast, aim to correct unjust outcomes precisely by restructuring the underlying generative framework. This distinction is *not* equivalent to reform versus revolution, nor to gradual versus apocalyptic change. Rather, the nub of the contrast is the level at which injustice is addressed: whereas affirmation targets end-state outcomes, transformation addresses root causes.

The distinction between affirmation and transformation can be applied, first of all, to the perspective of distributive justice. In this perspective, the paradigmatic example of an affirmative strategy is the liberal welfare state, which aims to redress maldistribution through income transfers.[78] Relying heavily on public assistance, this approach seeks to increase the consumption share of the disadvantaged, while leaving intact the underlying economic structure. In contrast, the classic example of a transformative strategy is socialism. Here the aim is to redress unjust distribution at the root – by transforming the framework that generates it. Far from simply altering the end-state distribution of consumption shares, this approach would change the division of labor, the forms of ownership, and other deep structures of the economic system.

Today, of course, economic transformation is out of fashion, as much of the traditional institutional content of socialism has proven problematic.[79] But it is a mistake to conclude that we should drop the idea of deep economic restructuring *tout court*. That idea is still meaningfully contrasted with affirmative redistribution, which leaves the root causes of maldistribution in place. In today's neoliberal climate especially, it is important to retain the general idea of economic transformation, even if we are currently uncertain of its precise institutional content.

The contrast between affirmation and transformation is intuitively familiar in the perspective of distribution. What may be more surprising, however, is that it can also be applied to remedies for misrecognition. An example of an affirmative strategy in the latter perspective is what I shall call "mainstream multiculturalism."[80] This approach proposes to redress disrespect by revaluing unjustly devalued group identities, while leaving intact both the contents of those identities and the group differentiations that underlie them. It can be contrasted with a transformative strategy that I shall call "deconstruction."[81] This second approach would redress status subordination by deconstructing the symbolic oppositions that underlie currently institutionalized patterns of cultural value. Far from simply raising the self-esteem of the misrecognized, it would destabilize existing status differentiations and change *everyone's* self-identity.

The idea of deconstructive recognition may sound to some like an oxymoron, as it mixes Hegelian and Derridean motifs. Nevertheless, it has a precise and useful sense in contemporary politics. To illustrate that sense, consider two alternative strategies for remedying heterosexism: gay identity politics, which aims to revalue gay and lesbian sexuality, and "queer politics," which proposes to deconstruct the binary opposition between homosexuality and heterosexuality.[82] Whereas the first – affirmative – approach seeks to enhance the standing of an existing sexual orientation, the second – transformative – one would destabilize the current grid of mutually exclusive sexual statuses.

Deconstructive strategies can also be found in feminist and anti-racist movements, where they aim to substitute a shifting field of multiple differences for rigid male/female and black/ white oppositions. Of course, such strategies assume that the status distinction in question is oppressive *per se*. Where a status distinction is only contingently oppressive, however, alternative forms of transformation may be preferable, as we shall see.[83]

In general, then, the distinction between affirmation and transformation applies equally to distribution and recognition. It can be used in both perspectives to sort the plethora of possible remedies for injustice. Of course, the ultimate aim of the sorting is to draw some conclusions concerning what is to be done. To do that, however, one needs to assess the relative merits of affirmation and transformation. Which of those approaches is better able to redress maldistribution and misrecognition simultaneously?

Considered abstractly, independent of context, affirmative strategies have at least two major drawbacks. First, when applied to misrecognition, affirmative remedies tend to reify collective identities. Valorizing group identity along a single axis, they drastically simplify people's self-understandings – denying the complexity of their lives, the multiplicity of their identifications, and the cross-pulls of their various affiliations. At their worst, moreover, such approaches tend to pressure individuals to conform to a group type, discouraging dissidence and experimentation, which are effectively equated with disloyalty. Suppressing exploration of intragroup divisions, they mask the power of dominant fractions and reinforce cross-cutting axes of subordination. Far from promoting interaction across differences, then, affirmative strategies for redressing misrecognition lend themselves all too easily to separatism and repressive communitarianism.[84]

Meanwhile, affirmative remedies also prove problematic for a second reason: when applied to maldistribution, they often provoke a backlash of misrecognition. In the liberal welfare state, for example, public assistance programs channel aid to the poor, while leaving intact the deep structures that generate poverty; thus, they must make surface reallocations again and again. The result is to mark the disadvantaged as inherently deficient and insatiable, as always needing more and more. In such cases, affirmative approaches not only fail to redress maldistribution; they also intensify misrecognition. Their net effect is to add the insult of disrespect to the injury of deprivation.

In contrast, transformative strategies largely escape these difficulties. Applied to misrecognition, deconstructive remedies are in principle dereifying, as they aim to destabilize invidious status distinctions. Acknowledging the complexity and multiplicity of identifications, they seek to replace overweening master dichotomies, such as black/white or gay/straight, with a decentered congeries of lower-case differences. When successful, such reforms discourage the *en bloc* conformism that often accompanies mainstream multiculturalism. And far from promoting separatism or repressive communitarianism, they foster interaction across differences.

Applied to maldistribution, meanwhile, transformative approaches are solidaristic. Focused on expanding the pie and restructuring the general conditions of labor, they tend to cast entitlements in universalist terms; thus, they reduce inequality without creating stigmatized classes of vulnerable people perceived as beneficiaries of special largesse. Far from generating backlash misrecognition, then, they tend to promote solidarity. Thus, an approach aimed at redressing maldistribution can help to redress misrecognition as well – or, rather, those forms of misrecognition that derive directly from the economic structure of society.[85]

All other things being equal, then, transformative strategies are preferable. But they are not altogether without difficulties. Calls for deconstructing binary oppositions are far removed from the immediate concerns of most subjects of misrecognition, who are more disposed to seek self-respect by affirming a depreciated identity than by espousing the blurring of status distinctions. Similarly, calls for economic transformation are experientially remote for most subjects of maldistribution, who stand to gain more immediate benefit from income transfers than from democratic socialist planning. More generally, transformative strategies are highly vulnerable to collective action problems. In their pure form, at least, they become feasible only under unusual circumstances, when events conspire to wean many people simultaneously from current constructions of their interests and identities.

If transformative strategies are preferable in principle, but more difficult to effect in practice, then something, apparently, must give. Should one sacrifice principle on the altar of realism?

2. *The* via media *of nonreformist reform*

Fortunately, the dilemma is less intractable than it first appears. In fact, the distinction between affirmation and transformation is not absolute, but contextual.[86] Reforms that appear to be affirmative in the abstract can have transformative effects in some contexts, provided they are radically and consistently pursued. For example, Unconditional Basic Income grants would guarantee a minimum standard of living to every citizen, regardless of labor force participation, while leaving intact the deep structure of capitalist property rights.[87] Thus, in the abstract they appear to be affirmative. That appearance would jibe with reality, moreover, in a neoliberal regime, where the grants would effectively subsidize employers of low-wage, temporary labor and possibly depress wages overall. In a social democracy, however, the effects could be dramatically different. According to proponents, if the level of the grants were set high enough, Basic Income would alter the balance of power between capital and labor, creating a more favorable terrain on which to pursue further change. The long-term result could be to undermine the commodification of labor power.[88] In that case, an apparently affirmative remedy for maldistribution would have deeply transformative effects with respect to economic class subordination.

By the same token, Unconditional Basic Income grants would not, in the abstract, be transformative with respect to gender. To be sure, they would enable primary caregivers, along with others, to withdraw periodically from the labor market. But in and of themselves they would do little to alter a gender division of labor that assigns unpaid caregiving overwhelmingly to women, while leaving male recipients free to surf.[89] In some contexts, in fact, Basic Income would serve to consolidate a "Mommy Track," a market in flexible, noncontinuous, largely female labor, thereby reinforcing, instead of transforming, the deep structures of gender maldistribution.[90] On the other hand, instituted as one element among others of a social-democratic-cum-feminist regime, Basic Income could be deeply transformative. Combined, for example, with comparable worth and high-quality, abundant public childcare, it could alter the balance of power within heterosexual households, helping to spark changes in the gender division of labor.

Such examples suggest a way of finessing our Hobson's choice. They point to the possibility of a *via media* between an affirmative strategy that is politically feasible but substantively flawed and a transformative one that is programmatically sound but politically impracticable. What defines this alternative strategy is its reliance on "nonreformist reforms."[91] These would be policies with a double face: on the one hand, they engage people's identities and satisfy some of their needs as interpreted within existing frameworks of recognition and distribution; on the other hand, they set in motion a trajectory of change in which more radical reforms become practicable over time. When successful, nonreformist reforms change more than the specific institutional features they explicitly target. In addition, they alter the terrain upon which later struggles will be waged. By changing incentive structures and political opportunity structures, they expand the set of feasible options for future

reform. Over time their cumulative effect could be to transform
the underlying structures that generate injustice.

At its best, the strategy of nonreformist reform combines the
practicability of affirmation with the radical thrust of transformation, which attacks injustice at the root. In the Fordist
period, it informed some left-wing understandings of social
democracy. From this perspective, social democracy was not
seen as a simple compromise between an affirmative liberal
welfare state, on the one hand, and a transformative socialist
one, on the other. Rather, it was viewed as a dynamic regime
whose trajectory would be transformative over time. The idea
was to institute an initial set of apparently affirmative redistributive reforms, including universalist social-welfare entitlements,
steeply progressive taxation, macroeconomic policies aimed at
creating full employment, a large non-market public sector,
and significant public and/or collective ownership. Although
none of these policies altered the structure of the capitalist
economy *per se*, the expectation was that together they would
shift the balance of power from capital to labor and encourage
transformation in the long term.[92] That expectation is arguable,
to be sure. In the event, it was never fully tested, as neoliberalism effectively put an end to the experiment. The question
may now be moot, moreover, as nonreformist economic
reform may no longer be possible within a single country,
given current conditions of economic globalization. Nevertheless, the general idea of a progressively self-transformative
regime is by no means discredited. On the contrary, the strategy
of nonreformist economic reform is well worth pursuing today
– on a transnational scale.

Is such an approach also conceivable for the politics of
recognition? Certainly, some proponents of identity politics
support affirmative strategies in anticipation of transformative
effects further down the road. Cultural feminists, for example,
pursue a recognition politics aimed at revaluing traits associated
with femininity. Yet not all of them view the affirmation of
"women's difference" as an end in itself. Some consider it a

transitional strategy that will lead eventually to the destabilization of the male/female dichotomy. One such strategy would celebrate femininity as a way of empowering women to struggle against the gratuitous gendering of social roles; another would valorize women's traditional activities as a way of encouraging men to take them up too. In both cases, proponents of "strategic essentialism" expect an affirmative strategy to have long-term transformative effects.[93] Whether this expectation is plausible, however, depends on contextual factors – on whether, for example, there exist sufficiently powerful forces to counter the reifying tendencies inherent in such a politics. In the context of a neotraditional culture, where gender difference is considered natural, strategic cultural feminism is likely to succumb to reification. In a postmodernist culture, in contrast, where there exists a lively sense of the constructedess and contingency of all classifications and identifications, it is more likely to promote transformation. In contexts, finally, where neotraditionalism and postmodernism coexist as competing cultural currents, strategic essentialism's probable effects are more difficult to gauge. This last case, of course, is the one we are facing today – which is why many feminists are skeptical of this strategy.[94]

In any case, there is another way of conceiving nonreformist reform in relation to recognition. The preceding strategy assumed that gender differentiation is inherently oppressive and should eventually be deconstructed. Where differentiations are not inherently oppressive, however, the preferred *telos* of social change may not be their deconstruction. In such cases, where distinctions are only contingently tied to institutionalized disparities in participation, the goal could be rather to eliminate the disparities and leave the distinctions to flourish or die, according to the choices of later generations.

Consider, again, *l'affaire foulard*. Here the remedy for misrecognition is not to deconstruct the distinction between Christian and Muslim. As we saw, it is rather to eliminate institutionalized preferences for majority practices by taking

affirmative steps to include minorities – without requiring
assimilation or exacerbating the subordination of women. In
the short term, this approach counts as affirmative, to be sure,
as it affirms the right of an existing group to full participation
in public education. In the longer term, however, it could have
transformative consequences – such as reconstructing French
national identity to suit a multicultural society, refashioning
Islam for a liberal-pluralist and gender-egalitarian regime, and/
or generally decreasing the political salience of religion by
rendering such differences routine and mundane. As before,
whether or not such transformations occur depends on contextual factors.

The key point, in any case, is this: where status distinctions
can be detached from subordination, the strategy of nonreformist reform need not predetermine their ultimate fate.
Rather, one can leave it to future generations to decide
whether a given distinction is worth preserving. One need only
strive now to ensure that that decision can be made freely,
unconstrained by institutionalized subordination. This, however, requires a measure of institutional restraint: strategies of
nonreformist reform should avoid constitutionalizing group
rights or otherwise entrenching status distinctions in forms that
are difficult to change.[95]

Doubtless there are other ways of conceiving nonreformist
reform with respect to recognition. My aim here is not to
defend a specific variant, however, but to suggest the general
interest of such an approach. Whatever their orientation, nonreformist reforms seek to spark transformations in the status
order – not only directly, by immediate institutional interven-
tion, but also politically, by changing the terrain on which
future struggles for recognition are waged. Thus, for recognition as for distribution, this approach represents a *via media*
between affirmation and transformation that combines the best
features of both.

3. Postures of integration: Cross-redressing and boundary awareness

In general, then, the strategy of nonreformist reform holds some promise for both dimensions of justice. But it cannot be applied in an additive way. Thus, it will not suffice to develop one such strategy for distribution and another for recognition.[96] As we saw, remedies for maldistribution that are perfectly plausible when considered alone can exacerbate misrecognition – and vice-versa. And individual reforms that could successfully counter injustice in a given dimension can undermine one another when pursued together. What is needed, therefore, is an integrated approach that can redress maldistribution and misrecognition simultaneously.

How might one proceed to develop such an approach? We have already noted the uses of perspectival dualism, which facilitates integration by enabling one to monitor both the distributive implications of recognition reforms and the recognition implications of distributive reforms. Two further postures of thought can be similarly helpful.

The first I call *cross-redressing*. This means using measures associated with one dimension of justice to remedy inequities associated with the other – hence, using distributive measures to redress misrecognition and recognition measures to redress maldistribution.[97] Cross-redressing exploits the imbrication of status and class in order to mitigate both forms of subordination simultaneously. To be sure, it cannot be used wholesale, across the board. Thus, I argued earlier against the reductive economistic view that one can redress all misrecognition by redistribution, while likewise opposing the vulgar culturalist view that one can remedy all maldistribution by recognition. But cross-redressing is perfectly viable on a more limited scale.

Consider, first, some cases in which redistribution can mitigate misrecognition. Theorists of rational choice contend that increased earnings enhance women's exit options from marriage and improve their bargaining position in households; thus, higher wages strengthen women's capacity to avoid the status harms associated with marriage, such as domestic violence and marital rape.[98] Based on this sort of reasoning, some policy analysts claim that the surest way to raise poor women's status in developing countries is to provide them access to paid work.[99] To be sure, such arguments are sometimes over-extended to the point of dismissing the need for recognition reforms altogether; and in such forms they are clearly fallacious. But the point is persuasive when stated more modestly: in some cases, redistribution can mitigate status subordination.

That conclusion is also supported by my previous discussion of transformative redistribution. As we saw, that approach favors universal entitlements to social welfare over targeted aid for the poor; thus, instead of stigmatizing the needy, it fosters social solidarity. In fact, transformative remedies for maldistribution have the potential to reduce misrecognition in ways that are especially useful for combating racism. By enlarging the pie, such policies soften the economic insecurity and zero-sum conflicts that typically exacerbate ethnic antagonisms. And by reducing economic differentials, they create a common material form of life, thereby lessening incentives for maintaining racial boundaries.[100] In such cases, redistributive policies can diminish misrecognition – or, rather, those forms of misrecognition that are closely tied to economic conditions.

Consider, too, some cases in which cross-redressing works in the opposite direction. As we saw, gays and lesbians suffer serious economic disadvantages as a consequence of status subordination. For them, accordingly, measures associated with recognition can mitigate maldistribution. Legalizing gay marriage or domestic partnerships would effectively remove economic penalties currently entrenched in welfare entitlements and in tax and inheritance law; and outlawing heterosexist discrimination in employment and military service would mean higher income and better fringe benefits. The point holds more broadly for despised groups: enhanced respect translates into reduced discrimination – not only in employment, but also in housing and access to credit, hence into improved economic position. In such cases, where maldistribution is tied to status subordination, recognition can help to correct it.

In general, then, cross-redressing represents a useful tactic for integrating redistribution and recognition. Deployed judiciously, as part of a larger coordinated strategy of nonreformist reform, it can help circumvent unpalatable trade-offs.

A second posture that facilitates integration I call *boundary awareness*. By this I mean awareness of the impact of various reforms on group boundaries. As we saw, some efforts to redress injustice serve to differentiate social groups, whereas others serve to de-differentiate them. For example, efforts to redress maldistribution have as their stated aim the abolition or reduction of economic differentials; whether the preferred strategy is affirmative or transformative, the goal is to lessen or abolish class divisions – thus to soften or eliminate boundaries. In contrast, affirmative approaches to recognition aim to valorize group specificity; effectively validating group differentiation, they would affirm existing boundaries. Finally, transformative recognition strategies propose to deconstruct dichotomous classifications; effectively blurring sharp status distinctions, they would destabilize the boundaries between groups.

Efforts to integrate redistribution and recognition must reckon with these varying aims. Absent awareness of boundary dynamics, one can end up pursuing reforms that work at cross-purposes with one another. For example, affirmative efforts to redress racist misrecognition by revaluing "blackness" tend to consolidate racial differentiation; in contrast, transformative efforts to redress racist maldistribution by abolishing the racial division of labor would undermine racial boundaries. Thus, the two sorts of reforms pull in opposite directions; pursued together, they could interfere with, or work against, each other. Boundary awareness can anticipate such contradictions; exposing the self-defeating character of certain combinations of reforms, it can identify more productive alternatives.[101]

The need for boundary-awareness increases, moreover, given the possibility of unintended effects. After all, reforms of every type may fail to achieve their stated aims. We have seen, for example, that affirmative remedies for maldistribution often generate backlash misrecognition, thereby sharpening the very divisions they sought to reduce; thus, while ostensibly seeking to soften group boundaries, they may actually serve to consolidate them. In such cases, too, boundary awareness can anticipate, and help to forestall, perverse effects. Combined with perspectival dualism and cross-redressing, it facilitates efforts to devise an approach that integrates redistribution and recognition.

By themselves, however, these ideas do not add up to a substantive programmatic strategy for integrating redistribution and recognition. Rather, they represent postures of reflection conducive to devising such a strategy. The question remains as to who precisely should use them to that end.

4. Guidelines for deliberation

The task of developing an integrated strategy is not a job for an individual theorist. It is, rather, a project for an emerging counterhegemonic bloc of social movements.[102] Instead of proposing a programmatic blueprint, therefore, I shall conclude this section by suggesting some general guidelines for public deliberations aimed at advancing this political project. Three points in particular follow from the preceding discussion.

The first concerns the role of redistribution in deliberations about how to institutionalize justice. *Contra* fashionable culturalist ideologies, distribution is a fundamental dimension of justice; it cannot be reduced to an epiphenomenon of recognition. *Contra* substantive dualism, moreover, this dimension is not restricted to the official economy, although it is crucially important there; rather, it runs through the entirety of social relations, including those usually considered as cultural. *Contra* reductive economism, finally, maldistribution is not exclusively an injustice of class in the conventional sense; rather, subordinated genders, "races," sexualities, and nationalities are also subject to systematic economic disadvantage. It follows that distributive questions must be central to *all* deliberations about institutionalizing justice. Granted, redistribution alone is not sufficient to redress all modes of subordination; but it remains an indispensable aspect of every defensible program for social change. Movements that ignore or truncate the distributive dimension are likely to exacerbate economic injustice, however otherwise progressive their aims.

A second point concerns the role of recognition in deliberations about institutionalizing justice. Like distribution, recognition is a fundamental and irreducible dimension of justice, which runs throughout the entire social field. Thus, it too must be central to *all* programmatic discussions. Usually, however, misrecognition is interpreted as depreciated identity, and the politics of recognition means identity politics, aimed at affirming a given group identity. But that interpretation is problematic, as it reifies identities, encourages separatism, and masks intra-group domination. Thus, it should not inform policy deliberations. Instead, misrecognition should be treated as status subordination, in which institutionalized patterns of cultural value impede parity of participation for some. Thus, only reforms that replace those patterns with parity-fostering alternatives should be counted as viable remedies. Today, moreover, policy discussions should not assume a stable status pyramid that assigns every individual to a fixed place. Rather, they should assume a dynamic regime of ongoing struggles for recognition. In this regime, where individuals are multiply positioned by cross-cutting axes of status subordination, reforms must allow for complexity and historical change. Tailored to multiple sites and modes of misrecognition, they should avoid entrenching thick group identities, constitutionalizing group rights, or otherwise foreclosing future emancipatory transformations.

A third and final point concerns "the political dimension." Deliberations about institutionalizing justice should explicitly consider the problem of "the frame." For every issue, they should ask: who precisely are the relevant subjects of justice?

Who are the social actors among whom parity of participation is required? Earlier, before the current acceleration of globalization, the answers to such questions were largely taken for granted. It was assumed, usually without explicit discussion, that spheres of justice were coextensive with the reach of states, hence that those entitled to consideration were fellow citizens. Today, however, that answer can no longer go without saying. Given the increased salience of both transnational and subnational processes, the Westphalian sovereign state can no longer serve as the sole unit or container of justice. Rather, notwithstanding its continuing importance, that state is one frame among others in an emerging new multi-leveled structure. In this situation, deliberations about institutionalizing justice must take care to pose questions at the right level, determining which matters are genuinely national, which local, which regional, and which global. They must delimit various arenas of participation so as to mark out the set of participants rightfully entitled to parity within each. Certainly, this problem has not received an adequate discussion here.[103] But it remains crucial to implementing the requirements of justice. Thus, discussion of the frame should play a central role in deliberations about institutional arrangements.

Each of these three points runs counter to prevailing trends. Today, unfortunately, recognition policies are often debated as identity issues, while the distributive dimension and the problem of the frame are largely ignored. Together, accordingly, these three guidelines invite some concluding reflections on the current conjuncture.

V. Concluding Conjunctural Reflections: Post-Fordism, Postcommunism, and Globalization

At the outset, I noted that the present inquiry was rooted in a specific political conjuncture: the new salience of struggles for recognition, their decoupling from struggles for redistribution, and the relative decline of the latter, at least in their class-centered egalitarian form. Now, as I prepare to summarize the argument of this chapter, I want to examine this conjuncture in greater detail.

Consider, first, the remarkable proliferation of struggles for recognition in the current period. Today, claims for recognition drive many of the world's social conflicts – from battles around multiculturalism to struggles over gender and sexuality, from campaigns for national sovereignty and subnational autonomy to newly energized movements for international human rights. These struggles are heterogeneous, to be sure; they run the gamut from the patently emancipatory to the downright reprehensible, which is why I have insisted on normative criteria. Nevertheless, such widespread recourse to a common grammar is striking, suggesting an epochal shift in the political winds: a massive resurgence of the politics of status.

Consider, too, the corresponding decline in the politics of class. Once the hegemonic grammar of political contestation, the language of economic equality is less salient today than in the recent past. Political parties once identified with projects of egalitarian redistribution now embrace an elusive "third way"; when the latter has genuine emancipatory substance, it has more to do with recognition than redistribution. Meanwhile, social movements that not long ago boldly demanded an equitable share of resources and wealth no longer typify the spirit of the times. They have not wholly disappeared, to be sure; but their impact has been greatly reduced. Even in the best cases, moreover, when struggles for redistribution are not cast as antithetical to struggles for recognition, they tend to be dissociated from the latter.

In general, then, we are facing a new constellation of political culture. In this constellation, the center of gravity has shifted from redistribution to recognition. How can we account for this shift? What explains the recent resurgence of struggles over status and the corresponding decline of struggles over class? And what accounts for their mutual decoupling?

As we saw in a previous section, the potential for such a development is built into the structure of contemporary society: taken together, capitalism's partial uncoupling of class from status plus modernity's dynamic cultural matrix effectively encode the current constellation as a possible scenario. Yet structurally rooted possibilities are only realized under specific historical conditions. To understand why this one has materialized now, we need to turn to recent history.

The recent shift from redistribution to recognition reflects the convergence of several developments. For the sake of brevity, we can summarize these via the portmanteau terms, post-Fordism, postcommunism, and globalization. To be sure, each of these developments is immensely complex, far too complex to be recapitulated here. But their combined effect on political culture is clear: together, they have shattered the postwar paradigm that had consigned recognition concerns to a secondary place within a predominantly distributive political grammar. In the OECD countries the Fordist paradigm had shunted political claims into the redistributionist channels of the national-Keynesian welfare state, where recognition issues were submerged as subtexts of distributive problems. Post-Fordism ruptured that paradigm, releasing contestation over status – first over "race" (in the United States), then over gender and sexuality, and finally over ethnicity and religion. Meanwhile, in a parallel universe, communism had effected an analogous containment of recognition in "the second world." Postcommunism likewise burst open that container, fueling the broad delegitimation of economic egalitarianism and unleashing new struggles for recognition – especially around nationality and religion. In "the third world," finally, under the joint auspices of Bretton Woods and the Cold War, some countries had established "developmental states" in which distributive concerns assumed pride of place. Post-Fordism and postcommunism put an end to that project, thereby intensifying struggles for recognition – especially around religion and ethnicity. Thus, these developments have effectively upended the postwar distributive paradigm. The result has been to open up space for a worldwide resurgence of the politics of status.

That result has been amplified, moreover, by the accompanying acceleration of globalization. A long-term, open-ended process, globalization is multidimensional – as much cultural and political as economic.[104] Its current cultural effects include a newly felt proximity of "the other" and heightened concerns about "difference," which have intensified struggles for recognition. Equally important, globalization is destabilizing the modern Westphalian state system. The cumulative weight of transnational processes is calling into question an underlying premise of that system, the premise of exclusive, indivisible citizenship, determined by nationality and/or territorial residence. The result is to reproblematize a matter that had previously seemed settled, at least in principle: the sources and boundaries of political membership.[105] More generally, globalization is currently decentering the national frame that previously delimited most struggles for justice, whether focused on status or class.

To be sure, the foregoing sketch is far too schematic to do justice to the developments in question. But situating the shift from redistribution to recognition in relation to post-Fordism, postcommunism, and globalization sheds light on the current constellation. Specifically, it highlights three political tendencies that, if left unchecked, could threaten the project of integrating redistribution and recognition.

First, struggles for recognition are proliferating today despite (or because of) increased transcultural interaction and communication. They occur, that is, just as accelerated migration and global media flows are fracturing and hybridizing all cultural forms, including those experienced as previously "intact." Appropriately, some recognition struggles seek to adapt institutions to this condition of increased complexity. Yet many others take the form of a communitarianism that drastically simplifies and reifies group identities. In such forms, struggles for recognition do not promote respectful interaction across differences in increasingly multicultural contexts. They tend, rather, to encourage separatism and group enclaves, chauvinism and intolerance, patriarchalism and authoritarianism. I shall call this *the problem of reification*.

Second, the shift from redistribution to recognition is occurring despite (or because of) an acceleration of economic globalization. Thus, status conflicts have achieved paradigmatic status at precisely the moment when an aggressively expanding neoliberal capitalism is radically exacerbating economic inequality. In this context, they are serving less to supplement, complicate, and enrich redistribution struggles than to marginalize, eclipse, and displace them. I shall call this *the problem of displacement*.

Third, the current configuration is emerging despite (or because of) the decentering of the national frame. It is occurring, that is, just as it is becoming increasingly implausible to posit the Westphalian state as the sole container, arena, and regulator of social justice. Under these conditions, it is imperative to pose questions at the right level: as we saw, one must determine which matters are genuinely national, which local, which regional, and which global. Yet current conflicts often assume an inappropriate frame. For example, numerous movements are seeking to secure ethnic enclaves at precisely the moment when increased mixing of populations is rendering such projects utopian. And some defenders of redistribution are turning protectionist at precisely the moment when economic globalization is making Keynesianism in one country an impossibility. In such cases, the effect is not to promote parity of participation. It is rather to exacerbate disparities by forcibly imposing a national frame on processes that are inherently transnational. I shall call this *the problem of misframing*.

All three problems – reification, displacement, and misframing – are extremely serious. Insofar as the politics of recognition is reifying collective identities, it risks sanctioning violations of human rights and freezing the very antagonisms it purports to mediate. Insofar as it is displacing the politics of redistribution, it may actually promote economic inequality. Insofar, finally, as struggles of either type are misframing transnational processes, they risk truncating the scope of justice and excluding relevant social actors. Taken together, these three tendencies threaten to derail the project of integrating redistribution and recognition in a comprehensive political framework.

In this chapter, I have proposed an approach that offers some help in defusing these threats. I have argued that to pose an either/or choice between the politics of redistribution and the politics of recognition is to posit a false antithesis. On the contrary, justice today requires both. Thus, I have proposed a comprehensive framework that encompasses both redistribution and recognition so as to challenge injustice on both fronts. On the plane of moral theory, first, I proposed a *status model of recognition* and a two-dimensional conception of justice centered on the normative principle of *parity of participation*. This approach, I argued, can encompass both redistribution and recognition, without reducing either one of them to the other. On the plane of social theory, meanwhile, I proposed a *perspectival dualist* understanding of redistribution and recognition. That approach, I sought to show, can accommodate both the differentiation of class from status in contemporary society and also their causal interaction, while also comprehending specifically modern forms of status subordination. On the plane of political theory, finally, I proposed a strategy of *nonreformist reform* as a way of thinking about institutional change; and I identified some postures of reflection for envisioning concrete reforms that can redress maldistribution and misrecognition simultaneously.

Together, these conceptions can help to defuse the threats of reification, displacement, and misframing. First, by substituting a status model of recognition for the more familiar but defective identity model, the approach proposed here helps to avoid reifying group identities. Second, by theorizing the interimbrication of status and class, it discourages the displacement of redistribution. Finally, by positing parity of participation as a normative standard, it puts the problem of the frame on the political agenda; that standard cannot be applied, after all, without delimiting arenas of participation so as to mark out the set of participants rightfully entitled to parity within each; in that respect, it constitutes a potentially powerful resource against misframing.

In general, then, the approach proposed here provides some conceptual resources for answering what I take to be the key political question of our day: how can we develop a coherent programmatic perspective that integrates redistribution and recognition? How can we develop a framework that integrates what remains cogent and unsurpassable in the socialist vision with what is defensible and compelling in the apparently "postsocialist" vision of multiculturalism? If we fail to ask this question, if we cling instead to false antitheses and misleading either/or dichotomies, we will miss the chance to envision social arrangements that can redress both economic and status subordination. Only by looking to integrative approaches that unite redistribution and recognition can we meet the requirements of justice for all.

Notes

1 This chapter is a revised and expanded version of my Tanner Lectures on Human Values, delivered at Stanford University, April–May 1996 and published in *The Tanner Lectures on Human Values*, vol. 19, ed. Grethe B. Peterson (Salt Lake City 1998), 1–67. Portions of the original version are reprinted with permission. I am grateful to the Tanner Foundation and Stanford University, especially the Program in Ethics and Society, the Philosophy Department, and Professor Susan Moller Okin, for their support of this work. I benefited greatly from the responses presented at Stanford by Professors Elizabeth Anderson and Axel Honneth, although I have not always been able to respond to them adequately. Conversations with Richard J. Bernstein, Rainer Forst, Axel Honneth, Theodore Koditschek, Steven Lukes, Jane Mansbridge, Linda Nicholson, and Eli Zaretsky influenced my thinking greatly at key points during the preparation of the original lectures. Subsequent com-

ments from Seyla Benhabib, Judith Butler, Rainer Forst, Anne Phillips, Erik Olin Wright, and Eli Zaretsky were invaluable in the process of revision.

2 It may be that the political dissociation of redistribution from recognition is more advanced in the United States than elsewhere. But it is not a uniquely American problem. On the contrary, similar tendencies can be observed in varying degrees throughout much of the world, even in countries where social-democratic parties remain strong. The rise of neoliberal currents within such parties portends a willingness to jettison longstanding redistributive commitments while pursuing some relatively limited emancipatory reforms in the relations of recognition.

3 United Nations Development Program, *Human Development Report 1996* (Oxford 1996). Highlights of the findings are reported by Barbara Crossette, "UN Survey Finds World Rich–Poor Gap Widening," *New York Times*, July 15, 1996, A4. Data from the latest HDR (2003) are less dramatic but nevertheless alarming. See "HDR 2003 Charts Decade-Long Income Drop in 54 Countries," July 8, 2003, which reports findings of Human Development Report 2003, available at http//www.undp.org/hdr2003/.

4 See especially John Rawls, *A Theory of Justice* (Cambridge, MA 1971) and Ronald Dworkin, "What is Equality? Part 2: Equality of Resources," *Philosophy and Public Affairs* 10, no. 4 (Fall 1981): 283–345.

5 For Hegel on recognition, see "Independence and Dependence of Self-Consciousness: Lordship and Bondage," *The Phenomenology of Spirit*. Important secondary treatments include Alexandre Kojève, *Introduction to the Reading of Hegel*, especially "In Place of an Introduction," 3–30 and Axel Honneth, *The Struggle for Recognition: The Moral Grammar of Social Conflicts*, trans. Joel Anderson (Cambridge 1995), especially Part I, 3–63. For existentialist elaborations, see Jean-Paul Sartre, *Being and Nothingness*, especially "The Look," and *Anti-Semite and Jew* (New York 1948); Frantz Fanon, *Black Skin, White Masks*, especially "The Fact of Blackness"; and Simone de Beauvoir, *The Second Sex*. For current work on recognition, see Axel Honneth, *The Struggle for Recognition*, and Charles Taylor, "The Politics of Recognition," in Amy Gutmann, ed., *Multiculturalism: Examining the Politics of Recognition* (Princeton 1994). Reconstructing the demands of Québec nationalists as claims for recognition, Taylor has defended them as promoting the collective end of "cultural survival."

6 I am grateful to Eli Zaretsky and Moishe Postone for insisting on this point in conversation.

7 I am grateful to Simon Hollis and Simon Critchley for insisting on this point in conversation.

8 In this usage, "redistribution" is not limited to the sort of end-state

reallocations that are associated with the liberal welfare state. Rather, it also encompasses the sort of deep-structural economic changes that have historically been associated with socialism. Thus, it encompasses both "affirmative" approaches, which seek to alter economic outcomes without changing the underlying mechanisms that generate them, and "transformative" approaches, which seek to alter the underlying mechanisms. For the distinction between affirmative redistribution and transformative redistribution, see Nancy Fraser, "From Redistribution to Recognition? Dilemmas of Justice in a 'Postsocialist' Age," *New Left Review* 212 (July/August 1995): 68–93; reprinted in Nancy Fraser, *Justice Interruptus: Critical Reflections on the "Postsocialist" Condition* (London & New York 1997). Later in this chapter I shall discuss this contrast in some detail. For now, I note only that because this usage of "redistribution" accommodates radical economic restructuring, it should help to allay Marxist worries that the term fails to address the nub of capitalist injustice.

9 Once again, in this usage, "recognition" is not limited to the sort of valorization of group differences that is associated with mainstream multiculturalism. Rather, it also encompasses the sort of deep restructuring of the symbolic order that is associated with deconstruction. Thus, it, too, encompasses both "affirmative" approaches, which seek to alter recognition outcomes without changing the framework that underlies them, and "transformative" approaches, which seek to alter the underlying framework. Later in this chapter I shall discuss this contrast, too, in some detail. For now, I note only that because this usage of "recognition" accommodates deconstruction, it should help to allay poststructuralist worries about the term.

10 This initial formulation skirts the issue of the proper theoretical definition of class. It leaves open whether class is to be understood in the traditional Marxian sense of relation to the means of production or in the Weberian sense of relation to the market. In this section, I shall assume the Marxian definition for the purpose of simplifying the argument. In later sections, however, I shall use the Weberian definition for reasons to be explained then.

11 For a succinct and elegant formulation of the Marxian definition of class, see Karl Marx, "Wage Labor and Capital," in *The Marx–Engels Reader*, ed. Robert C. Tucker (New York 1978).

12 For the Weberian definition of status, see Max Weber, "Class, Status, Party," in *From Max Weber: Essays in Sociology*, ed. Hans H. Gerth and C. Wright Mills (Oxford 1958).

13 Brian Barry, *Culture and Equality: An Egalitarian Critique of Multiculturalism* (Cambridge, MA 2001); Todd Gitlin, *The Twilight of Common*

SOCIAL JUSTICE IN THE AGE OF IDENTITY POLITICS 97

Dreams: Why America is Wracked by Culture Wars (New York 1995);
Richard Rorty, *Achieving Our Country: Leftist Thought in Twentieth-Century America* (Cambridge, MA 1998) and "Is 'Cultural Recognition' a Useful Notion for Left Politics?" in Nancy Fraser, *Adding Insult to Injury: Social Justice and the Politics of Recognition*, ed. Kevin Olson (London & New York forthcoming).

14 Iris Marion Young, *Justice and the Politics of Difference* (Princeton 1990). Young, to be sure, does not use the term "recognition"; nor does she acknowledge privileging cultural transformation. Nevertheless, I believe that the deep logic of her thought supports this characterization and interpretation. For an extended argument to this effect, see Nancy Fraser, "Culture, Political Economy, and Difference: On Iris Young's *Justice and the Politics of Difference*," in Fraser, *Justice Interruptus*.

15 The following discussion revises a section of my 1995 essay, "From Redistribution to Recognition?"

16 For the sake of argument, I begin by conceiving class in an orthodox, economistic way in order to sharpen the contrast to the other ideal-typical kinds of collectivity discussed below. Thus, I treat class as rooted wholly in the economic structure of society, as opposed to in the status order. This, of course, is hardly the only interpretation of the Marxian conception of class. At a later step in the argument, I shall introduce a less economistic interpretation, one that gives more weight to the cultural, historical and discursive dimensions of class emphasized by such writers as E.P. Thompson and Joan Wallach Scott. See Thompson, *The Making of the English Working Class* (New York 1963); and Scott, *Gender and the Politics of History* (New York 1988).

17 Richard Sennett and Jonathan Cobb, *The Hidden Injuries of Class* (Cambridge, MA 1972).

18 One might object that the result would not be the proletariat's abolition but only its universalization. Even in that case, however, the proletariat's group distinctiveness would disappear.

19 Here, too, I begin, for the sake of argument, by conceiving sexuality in a highly stylized, culturalist way in order to sharpen the contrast to class. Thus, I treat sexual differentiation as rooted wholly in the status order, as opposed to in the political economy. Of course, this is not the only interpretation of sexuality. At a later step in the argument, I shall introduce an alternative interpretation, which gives more weight to political economy.

20 In principle, this could be done in more than one way – for example, by recognizing homosexual specificity or by deconstructing the straight/gay binary opposition. In the first case, the logic of the remedy is to valorize the group's "groupness" by recognizing its distinctiveness.

In the second case, in contrast, it is to put the group out of business as a group. I shall return to this point later in this chapter.

21 Once again recognition can be accorded in more than one way – for example, by according positive recognition to women's specificity or by deconstructing the binary opposition between masculinity and femininity. In the first case, once again, the logic of the remedy is to valorize the group's "groupness" by recognizing its distinctiveness. In the second case, as before, it is to put the group out of business as a group. I will return to this point too in a subsequent section.

22 It is true that pre-existing status distinctions, for example, between lords and commoners, shaped the emergence of the capitalist system. Nevertheless, it was only the creation of a differentiated economic order with a relatively autonomous life of its own that gave rise to the class division between capitalists and workers.

23 I am grateful to Erik Olin Wright (personal communication 1997) for several of the formulations in this paragraph.

24 In fact, as historians such as E.P. Thompson have famously shown, actual historical class struggles have always encompassed a recognition dimension, as working people fought not only to mitigate or abolish exploitation, but also to defend their class cultures and to establish the dignity of labor. In the process, they elaborated class identities, often in forms that privileged cultural constructions of masculinity, heterosexuality, "whiteness," and/or majority nationality, thus in forms problematic for women and/or members of sexual, "racial" and national minorities. In such cases, the recognition dimension of class struggle was not an unalloyed force for social justice. On the contrary, it incorporated and exacerbated, if it did not itself performatively create, gender, sexual, "racial" and/or national misrecognition. But of course the same is true for struggles focused on gender, "race," and sexuality, which have typically proceeded in forms that privileged elites and middle-class people, as well as other advantaged strata, including "whites," men, and/or heterosexuals, within the group. For the recognition dimension of class struggle, see Thompson, *The Making of the English Working Class*. For the *mis*recognition dimension, see David R. Roediger, *The Wages of Whiteness: Race and the Making of the American Working Class* (London & New York 1991) and Scott, *Gender and the Politics of History*. For the misrecognition dimension of feminist and anti-racist struggles, see, for example, Evelyn Brooks Higginbotham, "African American Women's History and the Metalanguage of Race," *Signs* 17, no. 2 (1992): 251–74; and Elizabeth Spelman, *Inessential Woman* (Boston 1988).

25 In capitalist society, the regulation of sexuality is relatively decoupled from the economic structure, which comprises an order of economic

relations that is differentiated from kinship and oriented to the expansion of surplus value. In the current "postfordist" phase of capitalism, moreover, sexuality increasingly finds its locus in the relatively new, latemodern sphere of "personal life," where intimate relations that can no longer be identified with the family are lived as disconnected from the imperatives of production and reproduction. Today, accordingly, the heteronormative regulation of sexuality is increasingly removed from, and not necessarily functional for, the capitalist economic order. As a result, the economic harms of heterosexism do not derive in any straightforward way from the economic structure. They are rooted, rather, in the heterosexist status order, which is increasingly out of phase with the economy. For a fuller argument, see Nancy Fraser, "Heterosexism, Misrecognition, and Capitalism: A Response to Judith Butler," and Judith Butler, "Merely Cultural," *Social Text*, nos. 53/54 (Winter/Spring 1998). Both these essays are reprinted in Fraser, *Adding Insult to Injury*.

26 Here again I owe several of these formulations to Erik Olin Wright (personal communication 1997).

27 Taylor, "The Politics of Recognition," 25.

28 Axel Honneth, "Integrity and Disrespect: Principles of a Conception of Morality Based on the Theory of Recognition," *Political Theory* 20, no. 2 (May 1992): 188–89.

29 See Axel Honneth, *The Struggle for Recognition* and "Integrity and Disrespect."

30 For a fuller discussion of the status model, see Nancy Fraser, "Rethinking Recognition: Overcoming Displacement and Reification in Cultural Politics," *New Left Review* 3 (May/June 2000): 107–20.

31 I am grateful to Rainer Forst for help in formulating the following argument.

32 Here I am assuming the distinction, now fairly standard in moral philosophy, between respect and esteem. According to this distinction, respect is owed universally to every person in virtue of shared humanity; esteem, in contrast, is accorded differentially on the basis of persons' specific traits, accomplishments, or contributions. Thus, while the injunction to respect everyone equally is perfectly sensible, the injunction to esteem everyone equally is an oxymoron.

33 This point can be restated as follows: although no one has a right to equal social esteem in the positive sense, everyone has a right not to be *dis*esteemed on the basis of institutionalized group classifications that undermine her or his standing as a full partner in social interaction. I owe this formulation to Rainer Forst (personal conversation).

34 John Rawls, for example, at times conceives "primary goods" such as income and jobs as "social bases of self-respect," while also speaking of

self-respect itself as an especially important primary good whose distribution is a matter of justice. Ronald Dworkin, likewise, defends the idea of "equality of resources" as the distributive expression of the "equal moral worth of persons." Amartya Sen, finally, considers both a "sense of self" and the capacity "to appear in public without shame" as relevant to the "capability to function," hence as falling within the scope of an account of justice that enjoins the equal distribution of basic capabilities. See Rawls, *A Theory of Justice*, §67 and §82; and *Political Liberalism* (New York 1993), 82, 181, and 318ff; Dworkin, "What is Equality? Part 2"; and Amartya Sen, *Commodities and Capabilities* (Amsterdam, New York & North-Holland 1985).

35 The outstanding exception of a theorist who has sought to encompass issues of culture within a distributive framework is Will Kymlicka. Kymlicka proposes to treat access to an "intact cultural structure" as a primary good to be fairly distributed. This approach was tailored for multinational polities, such as Canada, as opposed to polyethnic polities, such as the United States. Thus, it is not applicable to cases where mobilized claimants for recognition do not divide neatly into groups with distinct and relatively bounded cultures. Nor for cases where claims for recognition do not take the form of demands for (some level of) sovereignty but aim rather at parity of participation within a polity that is crosscut by multiple, intersecting lines of difference and inequality. For the argument that an intact cultural structure is a primary good, see Will Kymlicka, *Liberalism, Community and Culture* (Oxford 1989). For the distinction between multinational and polyethnic politics, see Will Kymlicka, "Three Forms of Group-Differentiated Citizenship in Canada," in *Democracy and Difference*, ed. Seyla Benhabib (Princeton 1996).

36 Honneth, *The Struggle for Recognition*.

37 To be sure, this could conceivably change. Nothing I have said rules out *a priori* that someone could successfully extend the distributive paradigm to encompass issues of culture. Nor that someone could successfully extend the recognition paradigm to encompass the structure of capitalism, although that seems more unlikely to me. In either case, it will be necessary to meet several essential requirements simultaneously: first, one must avoid hypostatizing culture and cultural differences; second, one must respect the need for nonsectarian, deontological moral justification under modern conditions of value pluralism; third, one must allow for the differentiated character of capitalist society, in which status and class can diverge; and fourth, one must avoid overly unitarian or Durkheimian views of cultural integration that posit a single pattern of cultural values that is shared by all and that pervades all institutions and social practices. I discuss each of these requirements below.

38 In fact, such purely definitional "reductions" could actually serve to impede progress in solving these problems. By creating the misleading appearance of reduction, such approaches could make it difficult to see, let alone address, possible tensions and conflicts between claims for redistribution and claims for recognition. I shall examine such tensions and conflicts later in this chapter.

39 Since I coined this phrase in 1990, the term "parity" has come to play a central role in feminist politics in France. There, it signifies the demand that women occupy a full 50 percent of seats in parliament and other representative political bodies. "Parity" in France, accordingly, means strict numerical gender equality in political representation. For me, in contrast, "parity" means the condition of being a *peer*, of being on a *par* with others, of standing on an equal footing. I leave the question open exactly what degree or level of equality is necessary to ensure such parity. In my formulation, moreover, the moral requirement is that members of society be ensured the *possibility* of parity, if and when they choose to participate in a given activity or interaction. There is no requirement that everyone actually participate in any such activity. For my earliest discussion of participatory parity, see Nancy Fraser, "Rethinking the Public Sphere: A Contribution to the Critique of Actually Existing Democracy," *Social Text* 25/26 (Fall 1990): 56–80; reprinted in Fraser, *Justice Interruptus*. For the differences between my usage and the French usage of parity, see Nancy Fraser, "Pour une politique féministe à la de la reconnaissance," *Actuel Marx* 30 (September 2001).

40 I say *"at least* two conditions must be satisfied" in order to allow for the possibility of more than two. I have in mind a possible third condition for the possibility of participatory parity that could be called "political," as opposed to economic or cultural. I discuss this third condition in a later section of the present chapter.

41 It is an open question how much economic inequality is consistent with parity of participation. Some such inequality is inevitable and unobjectionable. But there is a threshold at which resource disparities become so gross as to impede participatory parity. Where exactly that threshold lies is a matter for further investigation.

42 Honneth, *The Struggle for Recognition.*

43 Let me forestall any possible misunderstanding: I myself accept the view that attributes ethical value to homosexual relationships. But I still insist that it cannot adequately ground claims for recognition in societies where citizens hold divergent views of the good life and disagree among themselves as to the ethical value of same-sex unions.

44 Actually, there are several different issues here that are potentially in need of deliberative resolution: 1) determining whether a claim for the

existence of an injustice of misrecognition is justified; i.e. whether institutionalized patterns of cultural value really do entrench status subordination;
2) if so, determining whether a proposed reform would really remedy the
injustice by mitigating the disparity in question; 3) if so, determining
whether a proposed reform would create or exacerbate other disparities in
participation in a way and to a degree that is unjustifiable. This last
formulation is intended to acknowledge the possibility that "clean solu-
tions" may be unavailable. It could be the case, in other words, that under
existing arrangements there is no way to remedy a given disparity without
creating or exacerbating another one. To say in such cases that any
proposed reform is unwarranted would be too restrictive, however, as it
holds claimants to a higher standard than everyone else. Rather, one should
allow that in such cases tradeoffs may be justifiable in principle. Whether
any given proposed tradeoff is justifiable, then, is a further matter for
deliberative resolution. I am grateful to Erik Olin Wright (personal
communication) for this clarification.

45 This celebrated formula is associated historically with Rousseau
and Kant. For a recent elaboration and defense of this sort of democratic
approach to justice, see Ian Shapiro, *Democratic Justice* (New Haven 1999).

46 I say the remedy *could* be recognition of difference, not that it
must be. As I shall explain later in this chapter, there are other possible
remedies for the denial of distinctiveness – including deconstruction of
the very terms in which differences are currently elaborated.

47 Both Taylor and Honneth hold this view. See Taylor, "The
Politics of Recognition," and Honneth, *The Struggle for Recognition*.

48 Linda Nicholson, "To Be or Not to Be: Charles Taylor and the
Politics of Recognition," *Constellations: An International Journal of Critical
and Democratic Theory* 3, no. 1 (1996): 1–16.

49 To be sure, these economic arrangements can be theorized in
Marxian terms; but my emphasis is less on the mechanisms of exploitation
than on their normative consequences, which I conceive in terms of the
impact of distributive outcomes on social participation.

50 For an argument against the possibility of a fully marketized
society, see Karl Polanyi, *The Great Transformation* (Boston 1957).

51 By culturalism, I mean a monistic social theory that holds that
political economy is reducible to culture and that class is reducible to
status. As I read him, Axel Honneth subscribes to such a theory. See
Honneth, *The Struggle for Recognition*.

52 By economism, I mean a monistic social theory that holds that
culture is reducible to political economy and that status is reducible to
class. Karl Marx is often (mis)read as subscribing to such a theory.

53 Intracultural differentiation is not the same thing as the differenti-

ation discussed in the previous section. There the issue was the differentiation of market-regulated from value-regulated social arenas. Here the issue is differentiation among a plurality of value-regulated arenas, which institutionalize a plurality of different evaluative horizons.

54 Both sets of norms are counterfactual, to be sure. Nevertheless, they profoundly affect the status order in modern capitalist society. Even as fixed status hierarchy is presumed illegitimate, that presumption can serve to mask newer forms of status subordination. For more on this point, see note 57 below.

55 Karl Marx and Friedrich Engels, "The Communist Manifesto," in *The Marx–Engels Reader*.

56 On this one point, at least, Hegel's argument was better than Marx's. In his *Elements of the Philosophy of Right*, ed. Allen W. Wood, trans. H.B. Nisbet (Cambridge 1991), Hegel argued that "contract" cannot be the sole principle of social integration, as the functioning of a contractually-based zone of interaction ("the system of needs") presupposes, and requires, the existence of the noncontractually-based institutions of family and state.

57 This is not to say that status distinctions cease altogether to function in more traditional ways – witness the US criminal justice system, where, in a scenario eerily reminiscent of lynching, blacks are disproportionately subject to police brutality, incarceration, and capital punishment. Ironically, moreover, modern norms of liberal equality can serve to mask new forms of status subordination. In recent US debates, for example, some conservatives have argued that racial discrimination was ended with the dismantling of Jim Crow, hence that affirmative action is unnecessary, unjustified, and a violation of minority dignity; they thus appeal to the absence of a fixed, legally codified racial status hierarchy in order to mask newer forms of racism and to discredit policies aimed at remedying them, while insinuating that any remaining racial inequalities reflect bonafide disparities in competence and ability. In cases like this, liberal-egalitarian ideals become grist for the process by which distinctively modern forms of status subordination are elaborated and reproduced in capitalist society. For an account of the modernization of racial and gender status subordination in the United States, see Reva Siegel, "Why Equal Protection No Longer Protects: The Evolving Forms of Status-Enforcing State Action," *Stanford Law Review* 49, no. 5 (May 1977): 1111–48. See also Nancy Fraser and Linda Gordon, "A Genealogy of 'Dependency': Tracing A Keyword of the U.S. Welfare State," *Signs* 19, no. 2 (Winter 1994): 309–36, reprinted in Fraser, *Justice Interruptus*.

58 It is yet another weakness of Axel Honneth's theory that it maintains this Durkheimian assumption. See his *Struggle for Recognition*.

59 This assumption is presupposed in the theories of recognition of Charles Taylor and Will Kymlicka, both of whom subscribe to outmoded notions of cultural boundedness. Defending political policies aimed at ensuring the "survival" or "autonomy" of minority cultures, they assume that it is still possible to sharply demarcate "distinctive societies" or "societal cultures" from one another. They also assume that one can uncontroversially distinguish the practices and beliefs that are intrinsic to a culture from those that are inauthentic or extrinsic. Effectively treating national cultures as internally homogeneous, moreover, they fail to give adequate weight to other modes of cultural difference, including those, such as gender and sexuality, that are internal to, and/or cut across, nationality. Thus, neither Taylor nor Kymlicka fully appreciates the capacity of cross-national and subnational pluralisms to destabilize the national "cultures" whose "survival" or "autonomy" they seek to ensure. In general, both theorists reify culture, neglecting the multiplicity of evaluative horizons and the inescapability of hybridization in contemporary society. See Charles Taylor, "The Politics of Recognition"; Will Kymlicka, *Multicultural Citizenship: A Liberal Theory of Minority Rights* (Oxford 1995). For a critique of the reification of culture in the writings of Charles Taylor, see Amelie Rorty, "The Hidden Politics of Cultural Identification," *Political Theory* 22, no. 1 (1994): 152–66. For a critique of the reification of culture in the writings of Will Kymlicka, see Seyla Benhabib, "*Nous et 'les autres'*: The Politics of Complex Cultural Dialogue in a Global Civilization," in *Multicultural Questions*, ed. Christian Joppke and Steven Lukes (Oxford 1999). For a general critique of conceptions of recognition that reify culture, see Fraser, "Rethinking Recognition."

60 For an extended argument that the standard, "identity model" of recognition is inadequate to this task, see Fraser, "Rethinking Recognition."

61 Iris Marion Young, "Unruly Categories: A Critique of Nancy Fraser's Dual Systems Theory," *New Left Review* 222 (March/April 1997): 147–60; and Judith Butler, "Merely Cultural."

62 For a more detailed rebuttal of poststructuralist anti-dualism, see Fraser, "A Rejoinder to Iris Young," *New Left Review* 223 (May/June 1997): 126–29; and Fraser, "Heterosexism, Misrecognition, and Capitalism."

63 For more detailed criticism of an influential example of substantive dualism, see Nancy Fraser, "What's Critical About Critical Theory? The Case of Habermas and Gender," in *Unruly Practices: Power, Discourse, and Gender in Contemporary Social Theory* (Minneapolis 1989).

64 I have discussed this issue in "Women, Welfare, and the Politics of Need Interpretation" and "Struggle Over Needs," both in *Unruly Practices*. See also Fraser and Gordon, "A Genealogy of 'Dependency'."

65 Jeffrey Escoffier has discussed these issues insightfully in "The Political Economy of the Closet: Toward an Economic History of Gay and Lesbian Life before Stonewall," in Escoffier, *American Homo: Community and Perversity* (Berkeley 1998), 65–78.

66 I owe this expression to Elizabeth Anderson (response to my Tanner Lecture, presented at Stanford University, April 30–May 2, 1996).

67 See Nancy Fraser, "Clintonism, Welfare, and the Antisocial Wage: The Emergence of a Neoliberal Political Imaginary," *Rethinking Marxism* 6, no. 1 (1993): 9–23.

68 This was the case with Aid to Families with Dependent Children (AFDC), the major means-tested welfare program in the United States. Claimed overwhelmingly by solo-mother families living below the poverty line, AFDC became a lightening rod for racist and sexist anti-welfare sentiments in the 1990s. In 1997, it was "reformed" in such a way as to eliminate the federal entitlement that had guaranteed (some, inadequate) income support to the poor.

69 See Lenore Weitzman, *The Divorce Revolution: The Unexpected Social Consequences for Women and Children in America* (New York 1985).

70 I am grateful to Steven Lukes for insisting on this point in conversation.

71 For the poststructuralist anti-dualist misreading, see Judith Butler, "Merely Cultural." For a rebuttal, see Fraser, "Heterosexism, Misrecognition, and Capitalism."

72 This is not to say, however, that these distinctions cannot be used to discuss precapitalist social formations. On the contrary, one can say, as I did earlier, that in such societies a single order of social relations handles both economic integration and cultural integration, matters that are relatively decoupled in capitalist society. For a fuller discussion of the implications, and advantages, of historicizing social-theoretical categories, see Fraser, "Heterosexism, Misrecognition, and Capitalism."

73 For an insightful account of this example, see Lani Guinier, *The Tyranny of the Majority* (New York 1994).

74 The possibility of a third, "political" class of obstacles to participatory parity adds a further Weberian twist to my use of the class/status distinction, as Weber's own distinction was tripartite not bipartite. See his "Class, Status, Party." I develop an account of the political dimension in "Postnational Democratic Justice: Redistribution, Recognition, and Representation" (unpublished manuscript).

75 I borrow the expression "fact of pluralism" from John Rawls's *Political Liberalism*. But my use of it differs from his. Whereas Rawls's pluralism pertains to (reasonable) "comprehensive doctrines" that can be bracketed in debates about justice, mine assumes that such bracketing is

not always possible. Thus, I assume that there is likely to be a plurality of reasonable perspectives on how best to interpret not only the good life but also the requirements of justice.

76 Its precise location is one of the principal bones of contention in the celebrated Rawls–Habermas debate. See Jürgen Habermas, "Reconciliation through the Public Use of Reason: Remarks on John Rawls's *Political Liberalism*," trans. Ciaran Cronin, *The Journal of Philosophy* 92, no. 3 (March 1995): 109–31, reprinted in Habermas, *The Inclusion of the Other: Studies in Political Theory*, ed. Ciaran Cronin and Pablo De Greiff (Cambridge, MA 1998), 49–73; and John Rawls, "Reply to Habermas," *The Journal of Philosophy* 92, no. 3 (March 1995): 132–80, reprinted "with some minor editorial but not substantive changes" in Rawls, *Political Liberalism*, second edition (New York 1996), 372–434.

77 Portions of the following discussion are drawn from Fraser, "From Redistribution to Recognition?" But some key aspects of the argument have been revised.

78 By "liberal welfare state," I mean the sort of regime established in the US in the aftermath of the New Deal. It has been usefully distinguished from the social-democratic welfare state and the conservative-corporatist welfare state by Gøsta Esping-Andersen in *The Three Worlds of Welfare Capitalism* (Princeton 1990).

79 Virtually no one, even among radical egalitarians, continues to defend a command economy in which there is little or no place for markets. Moreover, egalitarians do not agree on the place and extent of public ownership in a democratic egalitarian society.

80 Not all versions of multiculturalism fit the model described here. The latter is an ideal-typical reconstruction of what I take to be the majority understanding of multiculturalism. It is also mainstream in the sense of being the version that is usually debated in mainstream public spheres. Other versions are discussed in Linda Nicholson, "To Be or Not To Be"; and in Michael Warner et al., "Critical Multiculturalism," *Critical Inquiry* 18, no. 3 (Spring 1992): 530–56.

81 To be sure, my use of the term "deconstruction" is unorthodox, as it denotes a specific type of institutional remedy for misrecognition. Thus, Jacques Derrida might not approve this usage, especially given his recent identification of deconstruction with justice *tout court*. Nevertheless, my usage retains something of the flavor of Derrida's earlier work, as it suggests a utopian cultural ideal of fluid, shifting differences. For Derrida's earlier utopian vision of a deconstructive culture, see Jacques Derrida and Christie V. McDonald, "Choreographies," *Diacritics* 12 (1982): 66–76. For Derrida's later account of deconstruction's relation to justice, see Jacques Derrida, "Force of Law: The 'Mystical Foundation of Authority',"

in *Deconstruction and the Possibility of Justice*, ed. Drucilla Cornell, Michel Rosenfeld, and David Gray Carlson (New York 1992), 3–67.

82 Still another approach is gay-rights humanism, which would privatize existing sexualities.

83 Erik Olin Wright has suggested several additional approaches, including: *destruction* (of one identity, but not the other, within a binary pair – e.g. destroying whiteness, but not blackness, as a source of identity; or, alternatively, of only specific oppressive elements of an identity – e.g. the misogynist and homophobic elements of a religious identity); *separation* (radical disengagement of the parties to decrease social interaction among them and minimize the occasion for oppressive practices); and *depoliticization* (transforming publicly salient antagonisms into private matters of taste or belief). I shall consider some of these alternatives later in this section. Wright has also proposed to correlate specific remedies with specific axes of misrecognition: thus, he contends that ethnic misrecognition is best redressed by affirmative approaches that valorize diversity; that sexual misrecognition is best redressed by deconstruction followed by depoliticization; that gender misrecognition is best redressed by deconstruction; that religious misrecognition is best redressed by depoliticization; that racial misrecognition is best redressed by destruction; and that national misrecognition is best redressed by separation. Most of these correlations are intuitively plausible. Nevertheless, I believe that the political questions are too complex to be resolved by this level of categorial argument. Thus, I propose to refrain from such conclusions, while leaving it to democratic publics to decide such matters through deliberation. See Erik Olin Wright, "Comments on a General Typology of Emancipatory Projects" (unpublished manuscript, February 1997), hereafter cited as "Comments."

84 See Fraser, "Rethinking Recognition," for an extended discussion of such difficulties.

85 Redressing forms of misrecognition that are rooted in the status order, in contrast, requires additional independent recognition remedies.

86 I owe this point to Erik Olin Wright. I have borrowed several of the formulations in this paragraph from his "Comments."

87 Philippe Van Parijs, "Why Surfers Should Be Fed: The Liberal Case for an Unconditional Basic Income," *Philosophy and Public Affairs* 20, no. 2 (Spring 1991): 101–31; and *Real Freedom for All: What (If Anything) Can Justify Capitalism?* (Oxford 1995).

88 Ibid.

89 In "Why Surfers Should Be Fed," Philippe Van Parijs posited the surfer as the litmus test recipient for Basic Income – without remarking its gender subtext.

90 Nancy Fraser, "After the Family Wage: A Postindustrial Thought Experiment," in Fraser, *Justice Interruptus.*

91 For the idea of nonreformist reform, see André Gorz, *Strategy for Labor: A Radical Proposal*, trans. Martin A. Nicolaus and Victoria Ortiz (Boston 1967). Thanks to Erik Olin Wright, "Comments," for suggesting that I incorporate Gorz's idea here.

92 A version of this argument appears in Esping-Andersen, *The Three Worlds of Welfare Capitalism.*

93 The term "strategic essentialism" was originated by Gayatri Spivak. See Gayatri Spivak with Ellen Rooney, "In a Word: Interview," *differences* 1–2 (Summer 1989): 124–56. The view that an affirmative politics of identity can lead to cultural transformation has been defended by Iris Marion Young in "Unruly Categories."

94 I count myself among the skeptics. To date, unfortunately, the feminist debate on this question has remained largely abstract. Cultural feminists have yet to specify a plausible concrete scenario by which the valorization of feminine identity could lead to the deconstruction of gender difference; and the discussion has not been pursued in an institutionally grounded way. A notable exception is Anne Phillips's judicious weighing of the transformative prospects and reificatory perils attending gender quotas in political representation. See Anne Phillips, *The Politics of Presence* (Oxford 1995).

95 For a persuasive argument against constitutionalizing group rights, see Benhabib, "*Nous et 'les autres'.*"

96 Some readers of my essay, "From Redistribution to Recognition?" inferred that I was proposing such an additive strategy – doubtless because I advocated "socialism in the economy and deconstruction in the culture." Nevertheless, my intention was not to simply to piggyback a politics of recognition on top of a politics of redistribution. Rather, I sought an integrated approach that could obviate mutual interferences and the need for tradeoffs. Here, I hope to forestall this sort of misunderstanding by avoiding formulations that sound additive.

97 The term "cross-redressing" is my own. However, I owe the point to Erik Olin Wright. See his "Comments."

98 Susan Moller Okin, *Justice, Gender and the Family* (New York 1989); Nancy Fraser, "After the Family Wage"; and Barbara Hobson, "No Exit, No Voice: Women's Economic Dependency and the Welfare State," *Acta Sociologica* 33, no. 3 (Fall 1990): 235–50. See also the general argument about exit and voice in Albert O. Hirschman, *Exit, Voice, and Loyalty: Responses to Decline in Firms, Organizations, and States* (Cambridge, MA 1970).

99 Amartya Sen, "Gender and Cooperative Conflicts," in *Persistent*

Inequalities: Women and World Development, ed. Irene Tinker (New York 1990).

100 Wright, "Comments."

101 For a detailed comparative assessment of the compatibility of various reform packages with respect to boundary dynamics, see Fraser, "From Redistribution to Recognition?"

102 There are two ways of conceiving such a counterhegemonic bloc. In the first ("united front") scenario, the component movements join together to devise a single, integrated programmatic strategy for redressing both maldistribution and misrecognition – along all major axes of subordination. In the second (more decentralized) scenario, they remain relatively separate, and coordination is an ongoing process of attunement within a loose congeries of social movements, each aware of the others, and each thinking two-dimensionally – about both distribution and recognition.

103 For a discussion of the frame problem, see Nancy Fraser, "Postnational Democratic Justice."

104 The case for viewing globalization as an ongoing, open-ended, multidimensional process, not limited to economics, is persuasively argued in David Held, Anthony McGrew, David Goldblatt, and Jonathan Perraton, *Global Transformations: Politics, Economics, and Culture* (Stanford 1999).

105 Seyla Benhabib, "Citizens, Residents, and Aliens in a Changing World: Political Membership in the Global Era," *Social Research* 66, no. 3 (Fall 1999): 709–44.

2

Redistribution as Recognition:
A Response to Nancy Fraser*

Axel Honneth

In a series of articles and responses over recent years, Nancy Fraser has tried to outline a thesis that deserves our attention not only on account of its orienting power for a diagnosis of the times. Rather, if I understand her correctly, with her reflections she seeks to establish the conceptual underpinnings of an attempt to reconnect to critical social theory's old claim: both reflexively to conceptualize the emancipatory movements of the age and prospectively to work towards realizing their objectives.[1] As the texts that emerged from the Institute of Social Research in its founding phase already indicate, the two tasks taken together not only call for a sociologically rich interpretation of the normative claims implicit in the social conflicts of the present. Beyond this, they also require a justification, however indirect, of the moral objectives that social-theoretical analysis has shown to determine or character-ize the state of contemporary conflict. Now, in contrast to her earlier essays, the particular challenge of Nancy Fraser's contri-bution to this volume is that both tasks are to be accomplished in a single line of argument. In the course of an attempt to conceptually clarify the normative objectives now pursued in a rather diffuse and mostly implicit way by various social movements, a moral standard is to be formulated that can demonstrate the goals' public justifiability, while moreover improving their political prospects.

The theoretical originality and sociological circumspection with which Nancy Fraser tries to renew the far-reaching claims of Critical Theory are surely reason enough for deep engagement with the present essay. As well, in the course of her argument she also manages to clarify the importance of a series of contemporary political-theoretical approaches in the framework of the social conflicts that mark at least the highly developed countries of the West. But another and, for me, more essential reason for considering her reflections with great care arises from the specific thesis that establishes the guiding thread of her attempt to renew Critical Theory: her conviction – indeed fear – that the shift away from key concepts of critical social theory toward a theory of recognition will lead to neglect of the demands for economic redistribution that once constituted the normative heart of the theoretical tradition that goes back to Marx. And, alongside the relevant essay by Charles Taylor,[2] she views my own theoretical efforts since I started investigating the "struggle for recognition" as typical of this recognition-theoretical turn.[3]

The starting point of Fraser's argument is the now hardly disputable observation that a great many contemporary social movements can only be properly understood from a normative point of view if their motivating demands are interpreted along the lines of a "politics of identity" – a demand for the cultural recognition of their collective identity. The more recent emancipatory movements – as represented by feminism, ethnic minorities, gay and lesbian subcultures – no longer struggle mainly for economic equality or material redistribution, but for respect for the characteristics by which they see themselves culturally bound together. But if the rise of a specific type of social movement prompts a complete shift of critical social theory's key normative concepts toward demands for recognition, then, according to Fraser, something necessarily falls out of view that has lost none of its moral urgency in view of growing immiseration and economic inequality: the persistence, beyond "postmodern" forms of identity politics, and especially under conditions of unrestrained neoliberal capitalism, of those social struggles and conflicts connected to the experience of economic injustice.[4] If Critical Theory is still to be able to understand itself as a theoretical reflection of the emancipatory movements of the age, it must not hastily give itself over to the conceptual framework of recognition that has arisen over recent years. Rather, it should develop a normative frame of reference in which the two competing objectives of recognition and redistribution both receive their due. For Fraser, in the end this means that the standpoint of the just distribution of material resources continues to deserve priority on account of its moral urgency, while demands for cultural recognition must be adjusted to the resulting limits. Through this reassessment of contemporary goals, she moreover hopes, finally, to contribute to a harmonization of two wings of the emancipatory movement which threaten to fall apart absent the introduction of a reflective mediating instance.

Now, in view of the social situation even in the highly developed capitalist countries, there can hardly be disagreement between Fraser and myself when it comes to this general conclusion. The trend toward growing impoverishment of large parts of the population; the emergence of a new "underclass" lacking access to economic as well as sociocultural resources; the steady increase of the wealth of a small minority – all these scandalous manifestations of an almost totally unrestrained capitalism today make it appear self-evident that the normative standpoint of the just distribution of essential goods be given the highest priority. The debate signaled by the juxtaposition of the key terms "recognition" and "redistribution" can therefore not reside at this level of weighing political-moral tasks. Rather, in my view the argument is located on, so to speak, a lower level, where what is at issue is the "philosophical" question: which of the theoretical languages linked to the respective terms is better suited to consistently reconstructing and normatively justifying present-day political demands within the framework of a critical theory of society? Not the superficial ranking of normative goals, but rather their placement in a categorial framework shaped by the far-reaching claims of Critical Theory thus constitutes the core of our discussion. And it is in fact at precisely this point that I depart from Fraser in a decisive and far-reaching respect. *Contra* her proposal that the normative objectives of critical social theory now be conceived as the product of a synthesis of "material" and "cultural" considerations of justice, I am convinced that the terms of recognition must represent the unified framework for such a project. My thesis is that an attempt to renew the comprehensive claims of Critical Theory under present conditions does better to orient itself by the categorial framework of a sufficiently differentiated theory of recognition, since this establishes a link between the social causes of widespread feelings of injustice and the normative objectives of emancipatory movements. Moreover, such an approach does not run the risk Fraser's does of introducing a theoretically unbridgeable chasm between "symbolic" and "material" aspects of social reality, since, on the assumptions of a theory of recognition, the relation between the two can be seen as the historically mutable result of cultural processes of institutionalization.

However, fundamental questions of social theory, like those raised by this last problem, play only a subordinate role in the debate between Fraser and myself. In the foreground is the general question of which categorial tools are most promising for reviving Critical Theory's claim to at once appropriately articulate and morally justify the normative claims of social movements. To be sure, the first step of my argument already problematizes a theoretical premise that this question seems to assume as self-evident: that in the interest of renewing Critical Theory, it is advisable to be oriented by normative claims that have already gained public notice as social movements. We need only recall the original intentions of the Frankfurt Institute for Social Research, however, to realize that an abstractive fallacy is involved in such an attachment to goals that have already been publicly articulated insofar as it neglects the everyday, still unthematized, but no less pressing embryonic form of social misery and moral injustice. Simply recalling this everyday dimension of moral feelings of injustice makes it clear that – in agreement with much recent research – what is called "injustice" in theoretical language is experienced by those affected as social injury to well-founded claims to recognition (I). Following these preliminary reflections – which might be somewhat pretentiously termed a "phenomenology" of social experiences of injustice – in a second step the category of recognition will be differentiated in order to clarify different aspects of socially caused injuries to recognition claims. In this way, I hope to be able to offer evidence for the strong thesis that even distributional injustices must be understood as the institutional expression of social disrespect – or, better said, of unjustified relations of recognition (II). If this can be shown – and Fraser's dichotomy of "recognition" and "redistribution" thus turns out to be questionable – then the question of the normative justification of demands for recognition remains as a final and decisive problem. And here, too, I will formulate a counter-thesis to Fraser's: I would like to demonstrate that without anticipating a conception of the good life, it is impossible to adequately criticize any of the contemporary injustices she tries to conceive in Marxist fashion, and I in terms of a theory of recognition (III).

I.   On the Phenomenology of Experiences of Social Injustice

In the last twenty-five years or so, it has become almost self-evident that when critical social theory reconsiders the normative goals of the present, it should be oriented toward a social phenomenon whose name already signals a break with the past. Empirical indicators of the spark-point of moral discontent in developed societies are no longer expected from the labor movement or similar protest currents, but rather from the diffuse complex of newer activist groups and protest movements brought under the umbrella concept of the "new social movements." It is true that from the start there was a certain lack of clarity about what the commonality in the "new" of these movements consisted in. Thus, with the initial selective orientation toward the peace and ecology movements, the idea predominated that we were facing the result of a cultural turn away from "material" values and a growing interest in questions about the quality of our way of life;[5] while today, with the focus on the phenomenon of multiculturalism, the idea of a "politics of identity" is dominant, according to which cultural minorities increasingly struggle for recognition of their collective value convictions.[6] But in any case, the theoretical motive hidden behind these different versions of an orientation to the "new social movements" remains the same insofar as the traditional problems of capitalist societies are no longer held to be the key to present moral discontent. Rather, it is suggested that only such newly emerging movements can inform us of the moral objectives toward which a critical social theory should be oriented in the long term.

It is with this indirect demand for a link between critical social theory and present-day social movements that I am interested in this first round of our debate. The danger I see in such an affiliation is an unintended reduction of social suffering and moral discontent to just that part of it that has already been made visible in the political public sphere by publicity-savvy organizations. A critical social theory that supports only normative goals that are already publicly articulated by social movements risks precipitously affirming the prevailing level of political-moral conflict in a given society: only experiences of suffering that have already crossed the threshold of mass media attention are confirmed as morally relevant, and we are unable to advocatorially thematize and make claims about socially unjust states of affairs that have so far been deprived of public attention. Of course, it has long since become clear in the Marxist tradition that endowing the working class with a privileged status in the articulation of moral discontent in capitalist society, prior to any empirical scrutiny, is merely an unaddressed residue of metaphysical historical speculation. And a great merit of the thinkers brought together in the early Institute for Social Research was to have opened the way for shaking off this philosophical-historical dogma by programmatically subjecting the task of scouting out system-transcending conflict potentials to the check of empirical social research.[7] But the now widespread acceptance of a merely opposed perspective, whereby only moral discontent articulated by the "new" social movements is valid as a theory-guiding objective, holds no less danger for the project of a critical social theory. It is all too easy to abstract from social suffering and injustice that, owing to the filtering effects of the bourgeois public sphere, has not yet reached the level of political thematization and organization.

Now, Nancy Fraser seems to be completely clear about this risk, as her contributions over recent years show. Indeed, the whole drift of the present essay pursues precisely this aim by warning against hastily adjusting our normative terminology to political objectives that owe their prominence to selective attention to only one type of social movement. Nevertheless, I would like to suggest that in the dramaturgy of Fraser's line of thinking, her choice of examples and positioning of arguments, a conviction comes to dominate that is not so far from today's widespread idealization of the "new social movements." For in her case, too, the legitimacy of a critical social theory's normative framework is primarily to be measured by whether it is in a position to express the political objectives of social movements. This is why she is so concerned to point out again and again the extent to which, even today, demands for "material redistribution" are among the objectives of organized political movements. The point at which I depart from the conceptual model underlying this argumentative strategy is best anticipated by a rhetorical question: what would be the implications for the categorial framework of a critical social theory if, at a particular time and for contingent reasons, problems of distribution no longer played a role in the political public sphere? Would the consequence of the doctrine that basic normative concepts must essentially mirror the objectives of social movements then be that demands for redistribution would completely disappear from the theory's moral vocabulary? The obvious answer makes it clear that the introduction of central normative concepts into a critical social theory should not follow directly from an orientation toward "social movements." Rather, an "independent" terminology is required, since the forms of institutionally caused suffering and misery to be identified also include those that exist prior to and independently of political articulation by social movements. Before trying to show how carrying out this task raises a certain type of moral-psychological question that has long been neglected within the tradition of Critical Theory (2), I would first like to briefly explain why Nancy Fraser is not altogether free from unreflective ties to the contingent successes of social movements (1).

1. On the demystification of "identity struggles"

The picture that Nancy Fraser develops of the "post-socialist" conditions of contemporary politics at the beginning of her reflections is wholly determined by the central place of a certain type of social movement. What we face first and foremost in the framework of a critical social theory is a multitude of politically organized efforts by cultural groups to find social recognition for their own value convictions and lifestyles. It is obvious which empirical phenomena Fraser has in mind with this diagnosis: in the highly developed countries of the West, the women's movement and ethnic and sexual minorities increasingly resist disrespect and marginalization rooted in an institutionalized value structure constitutively tailored to the idealized characteristics of the white, male, heterosexual citizen. The struggle thus aims to change a country's majority culture by overcoming stereotypes and ascriptions in a way that can also in the end win social recognition for one's own traditions and way of life. It is true that in view of the tendency to elevate precisely this type of social movement into the embodiment of a post-socialist conflict scenario, certain doubts may arise about whether Fraser's initial diagnosis already involves an overgeneralization of American experience. For in countries like France, Great Britain, and Germany, social struggles of the "identity politics" type have so far played only a subordinate role, whereas the "traditional" problems of labor policies, social welfare, and ecology more strongly shape debate in the political public sphere. But what interests me in this suggestive picture of a new, post-socialist era is a different question altogether, which has less to do with tendencies to empirical overgeneralization than with a certain reductionism: which morally relevant forms of social deprivation and suffering do we have to abstract away from in order to arrive at the diagnosis that today we are essentially facing struggles for "cultural" recognition? I see three such reductive abstractions at work, which had to be carried out sequentially for the "identity politics" of certain social movements to emerge as the central conflict of our time.

a) Anyone seeking a rough overview of typical forms of socially caused suffering in the highly developed capitalist countries would not be ill advised to consult the impressive study *The Weight of the World*, by Pierre Bourdieu and his associates. Here we find a multitude of reports and interviews that make it clear that the overwhelming share of cases of everyday misery are still to be found beyond the perceptual threshold of the political public sphere.[8] A few remarks suffice to sketch in broad outline the characteristics of these phenomena of social deprivation: they include the consequences of the "feminization" of poverty, which primarily affects single mothers with limited job qualifications; long-term unemployment, which goes along with social isolation and private disorganization; the depressing experience of the rapid disqualification of job skills that had enjoyed high esteem at the start of a career and now have been made useless by accelerated technological development; the immiseration of the rural economy, where, despite deprivation and back-breaking work, yields on small farms never seem to be sufficient; and finally, the everyday privations of large families, where low pay renders even the efforts of both parents insufficient to support the children. Each of these social crisis situations – and the list could easily be expanded – goes along with a series of exhausting, embittered activities for which the concept of "social struggle" would be entirely appropriate. Such tendencies toward immiseration are constantly fought by the afflicted with forms of opposition extending from confrontations with the authorities, to desperate efforts to maintain the integrity of both family and psyche, to the mobilization of aid by relatives or friends. But, as Bourdieu insists in his Postscript, none of these social efforts is recognized by the political public sphere as a relevant form of social conflict. Instead, a sort of perceptual filter ensures that only those problems that have already attained the organizational level of a political movement are taken seriously in moral terms:

> With only the old-fashioned category of "social" at their disposal to think about these unexpressed and often inexpressible malaises, political organizations cannot perceive them and, still less, take them on. They could do so only by expanding the narrow vision of "politics" they have inherited from the past and by encompassing not only all the claims brought into the public arena by ecological, antiracist or feminist movements (among others), but also all the diffuse expectations and hopes which, because they often touch on the ideas that people have about their own identity and self-respect, seem to be a private affair and therefore legitimately excluded from political debate.[9]

Referring Bourdieu's vehement objections back to Fraser's initial image of a post-socialist conflict scenario, the full extent of the retouching this construction required becomes visible: in unintended agreement with the exclusionary mechanisms that direct the attention of the political public sphere, out of the multitude of everyday struggles only the relatively insignificant number that have already found official recognition as "new" social movements are picked out, as if by artificial light. This gives rise, first of all, to the misleading notion that developed capitalist societies are marked primarily by social conflicts driven by demands for cultural recognition. And to counteract the normative consequences of considering only these object- ives within the framework of a critical social theory, the marginalized social movements (still) demanding distributive justice must then be remembered in a second step. The error here lies in the tacit initial premise that "social movements" can serve critical social theory as a kind of empirically visible guiding thread for diagnosing normatively relevant problem areas. What such a procedure completely overlooks is the fact that official designation as a "social movement" is itself the result of an underground struggle for recognition conducted by groups or individuals afflicted by social suffering to make the public perceive and register their problems. But this co-enact- ment of an exclusion already contained in the designation "social movement" is not the only retouching Nancy Fraser had to carry out to arrive at her initial diagnosis.

b) For all its one-sidedness, it is of course not entirely wrong to locate a new focus of conflict within the highly developed societies in the growing tendency of cultural groups to demand recognition of their collective identities. Albert Hirschman also basically assumes that we are facing a shift from "divisible" to "indivisible" conflicts, whose peculiarity consists in the fact that the contested good – precisely this "collective identity" – cannot be parceled out from the standpoint of distributive justice. On his premises, the danger is therefore growing of social conflicts whose resolution can no longer rely on the normative agreement of the members of a political community.[10] But those who believe they can in fact discern in this tendency the central conflict scenario of the highly developed societies must also take the next step and consider in their empirical diagnosis that many such cultural groups try to assert their collective identity by aggressively excluding all "outsiders." The social movements today demanding recognition of their value convictions include not only peaceful groups like feminists or marginalized minorities, but also racist and nationalist groups such as Farrakhan's Nation of Islam and German skinheads. In this respect, the second retouch Fraser had to carry out to her initial picture of a new post-socialist conflict scenario consists in leaving out a not inconsiderable portion of the "identity politics" enterprise. The different movements, that is, can only be tied to the common aim of non-exclusive, democratically-oriented demands for cultural recognition when we abstract away from those that militantly try to assert their "particularity" with the threat of violence by tacitly applying a normative criterion. In an essay that grapples with contemporary theoretical approaches to the "new social movements," Craig Calhoun leaves no doubt about such a tendency toward normative idealism in the conception of "identity politics":

> The new social movements idea is, however, problematic and obscures the greater significance of identity politics. Without much theoretical rationale, it groups together what seem to the researchers relatively "attractive" movements, vaguely on the left, but leaves out such other contemporary movements as the new religious right and fundamentalism, the resistance of white ethnic communities against people of color, various versions of nationalism, and so forth. Yet these are equally manifestations of "identity politics" and there is no principle that clearly explains their exclusion from the lists drawn up by NSM theorists.[11]

To this extent, the current privileging of the social movements with which Fraser opens her analysis not only results from leaving out many of the social struggles that occur in the shadows of the political public sphere. Moreover, it must abstract away from those "identity politics" projects that pursue their goals by means of social exclusion in order to arrive at the idea that today feminism, antiracist movements, and sexual minorities are at the center of social conflict. However, these two bits of retouching do not yet complete the initial picture. Before it can take its final form, in a third step all historical precursors that might reveal similarities with the movements in question are excised. For only thus can the suggestive impression emerge that with today's struggles for "cultural" recognition we face an entirely novel historical phenomenon.

c) In the famous essay that revealed the "politics of recognition" to a broad public as a contemporary problem, Charles Taylor in a way already supposes a highly misleading chronology. According to his central historical thesis, while the history of liberal-capitalist societies has hitherto been marked by struggles for legal equality, today their place has largely been taken by the struggles of social groups demanding recognition of their culturally defined difference.[12] What interests me at this point is not that, by assuming a much too narrow notion of legal recognition, Taylor schematically shrinks it into a kind of homogenizing equal treatment; I will have to return to this later in the context of conceptual clarification, since the same tendency seems to be at work with Fraser as well. For the moment, however, what is of interest are the historical stylizations and one-sidedness that give Taylor's thesis its linear chronology. Just as all legal components of contemporary struggles for recognition must be suppressed in advance, so, conversely, must all the cultural, "identity-political" elements be removed from the legal conflicts of the past in order to arrive at the idea of a historical sequence of two distinguishable types of social movement. The thesis that today we face above all struggles for the recognition of cultural difference thus tacitly assumes a specific picture of traditional social movements – as if, despite all the focus on legal equality, an objective like demanding social recognition for one's values and ways of life had been completely alien to these movements. It does not require much detailed historical knowledge to see how misleading – indeed false – this characterization is.

The notion that identity politics is a new phenomenon is, in sum, clearly false. The women's movement has roots at least two hundred years old. The founding of communes was as important in the early 1800s as in the 1960s. Weren't the European nationalisms of the nineteenth century instances of identity politics? What of the struggles of African-Americans in the wake of slavery? What of anticolonial resistance? Neither is identity politics limited to the relatively affluent (the "postmaterialists" as Inglehart calls them), as though there were some clear hierarchy of needs in which clearly defined material interests precede culture and struggles over the constitution of the nature of interests – both material and spiritual.[13]

Today's "identity-political" movements can no more be reduced to their cultural objectives than the traditional resistance movements of the late nineteenth and early twentieth centuries can be pinned down to material and legal goals. In the end, even the efforts of the labor movement – to name another important example Calhoun leaves off his list – aimed in essential part at finding recognition for its traditions and forms of life within a capitalist value horizon.[14] The whole sequential schema on which Taylor bases his historical diagnosis is therefore misleading: it suggests two phases in the history of modern social movements, where it is to a large extent merely a matter of differences of nuance and emphasis. And insofar as Fraser lets her initial picture be influenced by this suggestive periodization, she necessarily takes on the false premises of a historical opposition of interest-based or legal politics on the one side, and "identity politics" on the other. As a result, she too, in a third and final retouch, must leave out all the cultural elements of the traditional social movements in order to arrive at the idea that the struggle for cultural recognition is a historically new phenomenon.

Bringing together these three abstractions, it becomes clear that Fraser's initial diagnosis is a sociological artifact: first, from the multitude of current social conflicts, only those are picked out that have attracted the attention of the political public sphere as social movements (in the USA) under the official title of "identity politics"; then, tacitly applying a normative criterion, from these identity-political movements precisely those are excluded that pursue aims by the illegitimate means of social exclusion and oppression; and finally, by leaving out historical forerunners, the small group of social movements that remain are stylized into the new key phenomenon of the post-socialist era, to which the normative conceptualization of critical social theory must feel partially bound. What chiefly concerns me about such an approach in this first round of the debate is what happens in the first of the sequential exclusions. On the dubious premise that a critical social theory should be normatively oriented toward social movements, the whole spectrum of social discontent and suffering is reduced to that small part of it that wins official recognition in the political public sphere. The justification for this thematic one-sidedness is for the most part implicitly supplied by the fatal mistake Marxist theory made over and over again, from its beginnings up to the recent past. While Marx and his successors had a historical-philosophical tendency to see the proletariat alone as the stand-in for all social discontent, in a countermove, all dogmatic definitions are now to be avoided by interpreting social movements as the empirical indicators of such discontent.[15] This gives rise to the questionable tendency of merely taking on board all the prior thematic decisions by which, on the basis of selection processes, certain forms of social suffering move to the center of the political public sphere. Today, such a – surely unintended – complicity with political domination can only be undone by introducing a normative terminology for identifying social discontent independently of public recognition. Of course, this requires precisely the kind of moral-psychological considerations Fraser seeks to avoid.

2. *Injustice as humiliation and disrespect*

So far, I have demonstrated nothing more against Fraser than that normatively orienting a critical social theory toward the publicly perceptible demands of social movements has the unintended consequence of reproducing political exclusions. This does not, however, seem to show all that much in view of her further arguments, since in a second step she proceeds to insist on the normative relevance of questions of distribution against the hegemony of "identity-political" goals. However, if we recall the argumentative roll of her initial diagnosis, then a not insignificant – in the end, even decisive – difference already becomes visible: while Fraser can only consider the introduction of vocabulary of recognition into the categorial framework of a critical social theory justified to the extent that it expresses the normative demands of a new post-socialist conflict scenario, for me, following what has been said so far, there can be no such historical restriction. Quite apart from the fact that the whole idea of a "politics of identity" seems to me a sociological artifact, I instead have to justify the conceptual framework of recognition apart from any reference to social movements. In contrast to Fraser, I assume that it is not the rise of identity-political demands – let alone the goals of multiculturalism – that justifies recasting the basic concepts of critical social theory in terms of a theory of recognition, but rather an improved insight into the motivational sources of social discontent and resistance. For me, in other words, the "recognition-theoretical turn" represents an attempt to answer a theory-immanent problem, not a response to present

social-developmental trends. Because of this systematic difference, in the further course of my argument I will also have to
show that even questions of distributive justice are better
understood in terms of normative categories that come from a
sufficiently differentiated theory of recognition. And, in the
end, even the problem of the normative justification of critical
theory of society as a whole cannot remain unaffected by this
distinction.

First of all, however, an explanation is required of the set of
problems that introducing a conception of recognition is meant
to solve. For this I need only continue the line of argument
already laid out in my remarks on the precarious role of the
"new social movements" within the framework of critical social
theory. As should already have become clear there, a normative
orientation toward the social movements that happen to be
dominant represents precisely the wrong response to a question
that has become increasingly urgent since the collapse of the
historical-philosophical premises of Marxism: if the proletariat
can no longer represent the pretheoretical instance which
theory can self-evidently call upon, how then is a form of social
discontent to be determined as constituting the necessary reference point for empirically justifying critique? It is probably
better, however, to free this question from its hermeneutic
context and first formulate it independently of its specific role
within Critical Theory in order to be as clear as possible about
its substantive core. With what conceptual tools, then, can a
social theory determine what in social reality is experienced by
subjects as socially unjust?

It is clear that no definitive answer to this question of
feelings of injustice is possible without first establishing the
actual reactions of those affected with the tools of empirical
social research. Since, however, all investigations of this kind
are informed, via categories and criteria of relevance, by a
theoretical pre-understanding, it is necessary to treat this problem on a conceptual level. What is at issue here are the basic
concepts to be used to inform us beforehand about the respects

in which subject's expectations can be disappointed by society. Thus, it is a matter of a conceptual pre-understanding of those normative expectations we must assume for the members of a society if forms of social discontent and suffering are to be investigated at all. With respect to this problem, it may be helpful first to recall somewhat more precisely two figures of thought already at work in our opposed positions. This will make clear that the level in question – that of the categorial determination of moral vulnerabilities – need not be entered at all, since, according to prior decisions on matters of principle, they pass either above or below it.

This is not difficult to show for the tradition of critical social theory that remained largely confined to the premises of the Marxist history of philosophy. Where the proletariat was not, following Lukács, endowed with the traits of Absolute Spirit from the start, this was argued on the basis of the sociological figure of ascribable interest, which so to speak gave it a historical-materialist twist. A unified interest was to be ascribed to the working class as a collective subject according to instrument-rational considerations – which, it could then be shown in a second step, would be forever disappointed by capitalist relations. Even if the content of any "ascribable" interest could vary depending on the underlying position and could even include normative goals, the theoretical research could for good reason be broken off before the level that concerns us here. There was no need for a separate explanation of subjects' moral expectations of society, since the place of such expectations was taken by completely instrument-rational interests. Hence, the normative dimension of social discontent was never able to come into view at all in Marxism because of the implicit assumptions of a more or less utilitarian anthropology: socialized subjects were basically regarded not as moral actors, marked in advance by a number of normative claims and corresponding vulnerabilities, but as rational-purposive actors, whose particular interests could be ascribed accordingly.[16]

Now, in my view, the second of the positions discussed above, which is normatively oriented by the empirical indicator of the "new" social movements, relates to this failed intellectual tradition by simply making the opposite mistake. Whereas earlier too much was presumed about subjects' predetermined interests, here there is too little prior orientation to be able to perceive any stratum of normative expectations whatsoever. What predominates in these newer versions of critical social theory is the conviction that further clarification of this kind is not required, since the objectives articulated by social movements already tell us enough about existing forms of social injustice. Any additional experiences of suffering that we may suspect lie beyond such publicly articulated discontent belong instead to the field of theoretical speculation, where sociological ascription prevails over empirical indicators. The consequence of this kind of short-circuit between "social movements" and social discontent as a whole is not simply the already criticized tendency merely to theoretically confirm a society's politically established level of conflict. Graver still, in my view, is the fact that all conceptual efforts to make sense of possible forms of social suffering are nipped in the bud. While within Marxism a certain tendency toward utilitarian anthropology always predominated, allowing a unified interest to be collectively ascribed to a social class, the second position lacks any conceptual tools for hypothesizing about the potential causes of feelings of social injustice. Subjects remain, as it were, unknown, faceless beings until precisely such time as they unite in social movements whose political goals publicly disclose their normative orientations.

With these historical-theoretical reflections we begin to see in outline why the attempt has never really been undertaken within the tradition of critical social theory to come to a preliminary conceptual understanding of the normative sources of social discontent. With the great exception of Jürgen Habermas – alongside whom Antonio Gramsci should perhaps be placed – for various reasons a certain tendency to anti-normativism has prevailed, which essentially prohibited subjects from being endowed with normative expectations vis-à-vis society. For this reason, what must be considered a kind of social-theoretical premise for categorial reflection on possible forms of social discontent could never even come into view: namely, that every society requires justification from the perspective of its members to the extent that it has to fulfill a number of normative criteria that arise from deep-seated claims in the context of social interaction. If the adjective "social" is to mean anything more than "typically found in society," social suffering and discontent possess a *normative* core. It is a matter of the disappointment or violation of normative expectations of society considered justified by those concerned. Thus, such feelings of discontent and suffering, insofar as they are desig-nated as "social," coincide with the experience that society is doing something unjust, something unjustifiable.

The decisive question now, of course, is whether this core of normative expectations amounts to more than what is already contained in the formal criteria of the concept of justification itself. On this minimal interpretation, the experi-ence of social injustice would always be measured by whether the procedural criteria built into established principles of public legitimation or justification are considered sufficient for insti-tutional regulation. What is ascribed to the participants here is thus a kind of conviction of legitimacy oriented by the moral implications of the existing procedures for justifying political decisions. Suggestions for such a procedural model are of course to be found above all in the Habermasian idea that every form of political legitimation must satisfy specific standards of discur-sive rationality;[17] but Joshua Cohen, too, following John Rawls, has more recently tried to show by examining historical accounts that the violation of institutionally expected justifica-tions leads to morally motivated protest.[18] From a sociological perspective, such reflections generally amount to the empirical hypothesis that social feelings of injustice primarily arise when individually understandable reasons for particular institutional measures and rules are lacking. And it must further be assumed that, by virtue of moral socialization processes, these reasons available to individuals make up the elements of public practices of justification that are valid in a given society. In other words, social injustice is experienced the moment it can no longer be rationally understood why an institutional rule should count on agreement in accordance with generally accepted reasons. It is true that this line of thinking takes into account the fact that the individual evaluation of social processes possesses a formal structure that cannot be completely independent of the structure of public practices of justification: what counts as a good argument for general recognition will also sooner or later achieve validity and shape subjective standards. But, on the other hand, this restriction to only a form of justification seems to entirely lose sight of the normative perspectives from which individuals decide how far they can follow the established principles of public justification in the first place. It is as if the generally accepted reasons need not correspond to the normative expectations that the subjects bring – in a certain way on their own – to the social order. Sociologically applied proceduralism thus lacks a counterpart to individual claims and vulnerabilities, which for those affected form the moral substance through which the legitimacy of institutional rules is refracted. What counts as a "good" reason in the legitimation of institutional rules, then, depends for individuals on whether their moral expectations of society as such find appropriate consideration. Thus, when it comes to understanding the experience of social injustice categorially, the material horizons of expectation that make up the "material" of all public processes of justification must also be taken into account. For an institutional rule or measure that, in light of generally accepted grounds, violates deep-seated claims on the social order, is experienced as social injustice.[19]

With this turn against sociologically-oriented proceduralism, however, comes the not unreasonable demand that we be able to say something theoretically convincing about the normative expectations that subjects generally have of the social order. The most serious problem here, of course, turns out to be arriving at determinations that are abstract enough to grasp the multitude of different claims and, if possible, tie them to a normative core. Such an endeavor is not, however, completely hopeless, since over the last two or three decades a number of studies in different disciplines have all pointed in one and the same direction. And, in light of what has been said so far, it should not be surprising that this common goal consists in the idea that what subjects expect of society is above all recognition of their identity claims. This idea becomes clearer if we briefly name the stages through which this research gradually reached a breakthrough.

In the beginning it was historical research on the labor movement that first made clear the extent to which goals of recognition had already marked the social protest of the lower classes in emerging and gradually prevailing capitalism. Taking aim at the tendency to consider only economic interests, historians like E.P. Thompson and Barrington Moore were able to show that, when it came to the motivational sources of resistance and protest, the experience of the violation of locally transmitted claims to honor was much more important.[20] In surprising proximity to this line of research, a broad field of investigation soon opened up in sociology which pursued the question of what members of the lower social classes saw as the core of their experiences of oppression and injustice. And here too it emerged that motivationally what weighed much more heavily than their material plight was that ways of life and achievements, which in their eyes were worthy of respect, were not recognized by the rest of society.[21] But while this provided preliminary evidence that social injury to one's integrity, honor, or dignity represents the normative core of the experience of injustice, these results remained limited for the time being to the lower classes of capitalist societies. Generalizing reflections could thus only come when these findings were placed in a broader context, where their convergence with completely different life-situations and constellations of experience could come into view. Comparison with the social resistance of colonized groups or the subterranean history of women's protest then showed that the proletarian struggle for respect for claims to honor was by no means a special case, but only a particularly striking example of a widespread experiential pattern: subjects perceive institutional procedures as social injustice when they see aspects of their personality being disrespected which they believe have a right to recognition.

Even these empirical findings provided little more than illustrative raw material requiring conceptualization to serve as a tenable basis for a generalizable thesis. Referring back to the problem under discussion here, the mutually reinforcing findings said no more than that perceptions of social injustice depend not only on established principles of legitimation, but also on different expectations of social recognition. But how a social order's standards of public justification were specifically connected with these relatively stable claims – how the moral form of justification was to be thought together with ideas of integrity and worth – largely evaded clarification in this empirically and historically focused discussion. Further progress could only come when, under the impact of research that had accumulated in the meantime, social theory and political philosophy began to open up to the theme. Alongside work that further developed Hegel's theory of recognition, studies by Tzvetan Todorov, Michael Ignatieff, and Avishai Margalit are especially noteworthy here.[22] Despite their different methods and aims, their efforts are nevertheless united by the initial premise that the experience of a withdrawal of social recognition – of degradation and disrespect – must be at the center of a meaningful concept of socially caused suffering and injustice. With this, what had previously only had the status of generalized empirical findings was raised to the level of a normatively substantive social theory: the basic concepts through which social injustice comes to bear in a theory of society must be tailored to subjects' normative expectations regarding the social recognition of their personal integrity.

Of course, this finding is still a far from satisfactory answer to the question of how such deep-seated claims to recognition are influenced by the forms of justification that inform subjects' evaluative standards by way of social discourses of justification. Moreover, it is not yet entirely clear what is meant by the personal integrity which people generally expect their society to recognize. But the research just described already provides the initial outline of a thesis that lends additional weight to the objection I made against Fraser: the conceptual framework of recognition is of central importance today not because it expresses the objectives of a new type of social movement, but because it has proven to be the appropriate tool for categorially unlocking social experiences of injustice as a whole. It is not the particular, let alone new, central idea of oppressed collectives – whether they are characterized in terms of "difference" or "cultural recognition" – that is now to provide the basis for the normative framework of a theory of recognition. Rather, what gives rise to – indeed compels – such a categorial revision are the findings that have been compiled concerning the moral sources of the experience of social discontent. Barrington Moore's path-breaking investigation of proletarian resistance; the scattered studies of the significance of damaged self-respect among colonized peoples; the growing literature on the central role of disrespect in women's experiences of oppression; Avishai Margalit's systematic treatise on the key place of "dignity" in our ideas of justice – all point in the same direction: to the necessity of adopting the terms of recognition. According to the knowledge now available to us, what those affected regard as "unjust" are institutional rules or measures they see as necessarily violating what they consider to be well-founded claims to social recognition.

For the project of a critical social theory Nancy Fraser and I seek to renew, a consequence follows from this line of thinking that diverges significantly from her own strategy. More theoretical innovation is needed today than Fraser has in mind when she tries to categorially expand theory's normative frame of reference so that both the older and the newer objectives of emancipatory movements can find appropriate expression. Quite apart from the above-mentioned risk of merely affirming the existing level of conflict, such an approach fails even to touch on the problem of systematic lack of access to everyday experiences of injustice. This difficulty – a legacy of the sociological anti-normativism that also prevailed in the older Frankfurt School – must now stand at the beginning of any renewal of critical social theory. For without a categorial opening to the normative standpoint from which subjects themselves evaluate the social order, theory remains completely cut off from a dimension of social discontent that it should always be able to call upon. Neither the idea of ascribable interests, stemming from Marxism, nor an atheoretical attachment to "new" social movements, is of any help here. Rather, in accordance with the research I have briefly summarized, what is needed is a basic conceptual shift to the normative premises of a theory of recognition that locates the core of all experiences of injustice in the withdrawal of social recognition, in the phenomena of humiliation and disrespect. In this way, the "recognition-theoretical turn" I am recommending for critical social theory moves one level beneath Fraser's argument. Such a categorial transformation would not serve to include emancipatory movements that have thus far been insufficiently thematized, but to solve problems having to do with the thematization of social injustice as such. To be sure, pursuing this more comprehensive strategy also entails taking the second step that arises from the basic recognition-theoretical shift: even the "material" inequalities that most concern Fraser must be interpretable as expressing the violation of well-founded claims to recognition.

II.   The Capitalist Recognition Order and Struggles over Distribution

In the first round of my debate with Nancy Fraser, I wanted to call into question two connected premises that tacitly underlie her determination of the relation between conflicts over recognition and distribution. First, it seems highly implausible to me to interpret the history of political conflict within capitalist societies according to a schema that asserts a transition from interest-based to identity-oriented social movements, and hence a shift in normative semantics from "interest" to "identity," or from "equality" to "difference." If we take into account reports of moral discontent and social protest in earlier times, it quickly emerges that a language is constantly used in which feelings of damaged recognition, respect, or honor play a central semantic role. The moral vocabulary in which nineteenth-century workers, groups of emancipated women at the beginning of the twentieth century, and African-Americans in big US cities in the 1920s articulated their protests was tailored to registering social humiliation and disrespect. True, this does not yet tell us anything about how they saw themselves as disrespected or not recognized, but the evidence nonetheless shows unmistakably that injustice is regularly associated with withheld recognition. To this extent, it seems to me inadvisable simply on the descriptive level to divide experiences of injustice into two diametrically opposed classes, the first comprising questions of distribution, the second questions of "cultural recognition." Not only is the spectrum of moral discontent not exhausted by this simple opposition; it would also suggest that experiences of "material" disadvantage can be described independently of individuals' and groups' problems with social recognition. It therefore seems more plausible to me that experiences of injustice be conceived along a continuum of forms of withheld recognition – of disrespect – whose differences are determined by which qualities or capacities those affected take to be unjustifiably unrecognized or not respected. Such an approach also allows us to consider that differences in the experience of injustice can be determined not only with regard to the object, but also by the form of the missing recognition. Thus, when it comes to the sorts of "identity conflicts" Fraser stresses, it makes a fundamental difference whether the culturally defined groups are demanding a kind of social appreciation or the legal recognition of their collective identity. In any case, simply mentioning these two alternatives gives rise to the suspicion that, because of the rigid distinction between "redistribution" and "cultural recognition," Fraser simply does not have the categorial tools to take adequate account of this "legal" form of recognition. Her argument creates the impression that social groups basically struggle for material resources or cultural recognition, while the struggle for legal equality surprisingly finds no systematic expression at all.[23]

These preliminary considerations, which I will explain further in the course of my response, give rise to the second of Fraser's conceptual premises I wish to call into question. Those who argue along the lines I have just indicated cannot historically restrict the concept of recognition to a new phase of social "identity conflicts." Rather, this framework should serve to make visible a deep layer of morally motivated conflicts that the tradition of critical social theory has not infrequently misrecognized, owing to its fixation on the concept of interest. To be sure, such a recognition-theoretical reconceptualization requires more than opposing, as if from the outside, a series of recognition expectations which can potentially produce social conflicts to an otherwise conceptually unaltered social reality. Those who proceed this way have not sufficiently appreciated that forms of reciprocal recognition are always already institutionalized in every social reality, whose internal deficits or asymmetries are indeed what can first touch off a kind of "struggle for recognition." What is therefore required first of all is an attempt to explicate the moral order of society as a fragile structure of graduated relations of recognition; only then can it be shown in a second step that this recognition order can touch off social conflicts on various levels, which as a rule refer to the moral experience of what is taken to be unfounded disrespect. With such an approach it is moreover clear from the start that the expectations of recognition attributed to subjects cannot be treated like a kind of anthropological yardstick, as Fraser seems to reproach me for in some places. Rather, such expectations are the product of the social formation of a deep-seated claim-making potential in the sense that they always owe their normative justification to principles institutionally anchored in the historically established recognition order. Once we see this internal entwinement of expectations of recognition – or, put negatively, experiences of disrespect – and historically institutionalized principles of recognition, we also see the initial outlines of how the so far unexplained connection between social discourses of recognition and justification must be construed.

This short summary of the conclusions of the first part of my response theoretically anticipates the direction I will pursue in continuing the argument. Before I can attempt to interpret distribution conflicts according to the "moral grammar" of a struggle for recognition, a short explanation is required of what it can mean to speak of capitalist society as an institutionalized recognition order. To this end, in a first step I will explain how the development of bourgeois-capitalist society can be understood as the result of the differentiation of three social spheres of recognition (1). Only then can I set myself the task of interpreting distribution conflicts – *contra* Fraser's proposal – as the expression of a struggle for recognition; this morally motivated struggle takes the specific form of a conflict over the interpretation and evaluation of the recognition principle of "achievement" (2).

1. *On the historical differentiation of three spheres of recognition:*
   Love, law, achievement

In light of the merely preparatory aims of the first part of my
remarks, in the following I will have to content myself with
only a rough sketch of the argument. I thus rely for the most
part on research that at least implicitly attempts to interpret
bourgeois-capitalist society as an institutionalized recognition
order. In this way, it should not only become clear in which of
the particular spheres of recognition what are traditionally and
in shorthand termed "conflicts of distribution" take place.
Beyond this, I am also concerned to show that the distinctively
human dependence on intersubjective recognition is always
shaped by the particular manner in which the mutual granting
of recognition is institutionalized within a society. From a
methodological point of view, this consideration has the consequence that subjective expectations of recognition cannot
simply be derived from an anthropological theory of the person.
To the contrary, it is the most highly differentiated recognition
spheres that provide the key for retrospective speculation on
the peculiarity of the intersubjective "nature" of human beings.
Accordingly, the practical self-relation of human beings – the
capacity, made possible by recognition, to reflexively assure
themselves of their own competences and rights[24] – is not
something given once and for all; like subjective recognition
expectations, this ability expands with the number of spheres
that are differentiated in the course of social development for
socially recognizing specific components of the personality.

Following these preliminary reflections, it seems to make
sense to understand the breakthrough to bourgeois-capitalist
society as the result of a differentiation of three spheres of
recognition. In order to allow for the socialization of progeny,
the estate-based order of premodern society must already have
rudimentarily developed the attitudes of care and love – without which children's personalities cannot develop at all – as a
separate form of recognition.[25] But this practice of affective

recognition, through which growing individuals acquire trust in the value of their own bodily needs, went on only implicitly until childhood was institutionally marked off as a phase of the life process requiring special protection.[26] Only then could awareness develop within society of the special duties of care that parents (historically, of course, at first only the mother) have to assume with respect to the child in order to prepare the way from organic helplessness to the development of self-confidence. Parallel to this process, the recognition form of love similarly became independent: the relations between the sexes were gradually liberated from economic and social pressures and thus opened up to the feeling of mutual affection. Marriage was soon understood – albeit with class-specific delays – as the institutional expression of a special kind of intersubjectivity, whose peculiarity consists in the fact that husband and wife love one another as needy beings.[27] With these two processes of institutionalization – the marking off of childhood and the emergence of "bourgeois" love-marriage – a general awareness gradually arose of a separate kind of social relation, which, in contrast to other forms of interaction, is distinguished by the principles of affection and care. The recognition that individuals reciprocally bring to this kind of relationship is loving care for the other's well-being in light of his or her individual needs.

Of course, another developmental process was incomparably more important for the emergence of the core institutions of capitalist society, since it laid the foundation for their moral order. Not only in the estate-based social constitution of feudalism but in all other premodern societies, the legal recognition of the individual – his or her recognized status as a member of society protected by certain rights – was directly connected to the social esteem he or she enjoyed by reason of origin, age, or function. The scope of the rights legitimately at a person's disposal arose in a sense directly from the "honor" or status conferred on him or her by all other members of society within the framework of an established prestige order. This alloy of legal respect and social esteem – the moral fundament of all traditional societies – broke up with the emergence of bourgeois capitalism. For with the normative reorganization of legal relations that developed under the pressure of expanding market relations and the simultaneous rise of post-traditional ways of thinking, legal recognition split off from the hierarchical value order insofar as the individual was in principle to enjoy legal equality vis-à-vis all others.[28] The normative structural transformation that went along with this institutionalization of the idea of legal equality should not be underestimated, since it led to the establishment of two completely different spheres of recognition, revolutionizing the moral order of society: the individual could now – certainly not in actual practice, but at least according to the normative idea – know that he or she was respected as a legal person with the same rights as all other members of society, while still owing his or her social esteem to a hierarchical scale of values – which had, however, also been set on a new foundation.

The transformation that occurred in the social status order with the transition to bourgeois-capitalist society was no less subversive – indeed revolutionary – than what happened at the same time within the autonomized sphere of legal respect. With the institutionalization of the normative idea of legal equality, "individual achievement" emerged as a leading cultural idea under the influence of the religious valorization of paid work.[29] With the gradual establishment of the new value model asserted by the economically rising bourgeoisie against the nobility, the estate-based principle of honor conversely lost its validity, so that the individual's social standing now became normatively independent of origin and possessions. The esteem the individual legitimately deserved within society was no longer decided by membership in an estate with corresponding codes of honor, but rather by individual achievement within the structure of the industrially organized division of labor.[30] The entire process of transformation triggered by the normative reorganization of legal status and the prestige order can thus be vividly described as a splitting of the premodern concept of honor into two opposed ideas: one part of the honor assured by hierarchy was in a sense democratized by according all members of society equal respect for their dignity and autonomy as legal persons, while the other part was in a sense "meritocracized": each was to enjoy social esteem according to his or her achievement as a "productive citizen."

Of course, the latter kind of social relation – which represented a third sphere of recognition alongside love and the new legal principle in the developing capitalist society – was hierarchically organized in an unambiguously ideological way from the start. For the extent to which something counts as "achievement," as a cooperative contribution, is defined against a value standard whose normative reference point is the economic activity of the independent, middle-class, male bourgeois. What is distinguished as "work," with a specific, quantifiable use for society, hence amounts to the result of a group-specific determination of value – to which whole sectors of other activities, themselves equally necessary for reproduction (e.g. household work), fall victim. Moreover, this altered principle of social order at the same time represents a moment of material violence insofar as the one-sided, ideological valuing of certain achievements can determine how much of which resources individuals legitimately have at their disposal. Between the new status hierarchy – the gradation of social esteem according to the values of industrial capitalism – and the unequal distribution of material resources there is, to this extent, more than a merely external relation of "superstructure" and "basis," of "ideology" and objective reality. The hegemonic, thoroughly one-sided valuation of achievement rather represents an institutional framework in which the criteria or principles for distributing resources in bourgeois-capitalist society can meet with normative agreement.[31] This additional consideration gives rise to what Richard Münch has rightly called the intermeshing of payment and respect in the capitalist economic sphere.[32] It would be wrong to speak, with Luhmann and Habermas, of capitalism as a "norm-free" system of economic processes since material distribution takes place according to certainly contested but nevertheless always temporarily established value principles having to do with respect, with the social esteem of members of society. It is not hard to see that these considerations will have far-reaching consequences for defining what have been traditionally termed "distribution struggles."

Summing up these brief remarks on the social-moral development of bourgeois-capitalist society, it turns out that we can speak of a differentiation of three spheres of recognition with some plausibility. These violent transformative processes established three distinct forms of social relations in which members of society can count, in different ways and according to different principles, on reciprocal recognition. In terms of the new kind of individual self-relation made possible by the revolution in the recognition order, this means that subjects in bourgeois-capitalist society learned – gradually, and with many class- and gender-specific delays – to refer to themselves in three different attitudes: in intimate relationships, marked by practices of mutual affection and concern, they are able to understand themselves as individuals with their own needs; in legal relations, which unfold according to the model of mutually granted equal rights (and duties), they learn to understand themselves as legal persons owed the same autonomy as all other members of society; and, finally, in loose-knit social relations – in which, dominated by a one-sided interpretation of the achievement principle, there is competition for professional status – they in principle learn to understand themselves as subjects possessing abilities and talents that are valuable for society. Of course, this does not mean that the developing capitalist social order did not also produce other forms of social relations allowing individuals hitherto unknown types of self-relation. Thus, for example, the increased anonymity of interaction in rapidly growing cities led to a rise in individuals' opportunities to test new patterns of behavior without sanction, experimentally broadening their horizons of experience.[33] But unlike other newly developing patterns of communication, each of the three forms of relation I have outlined is distinguished by internal normative principles that establish different forms of mutual recognition. "Love" (the central idea of intimate relationships), the equality principle (the norm of legal relations), and the achievement principle (the standard of social hierarchy) represent normative perspectives with reference to which subjects can reasonably argue that existing forms of recognition are inadequate or insufficient and need to be expanded. To this extent, unlike other structurally produced social relations in the new society, the three spheres of recognition form normatively substantive models of interaction in the sense that they cannot be practiced if their underlying principles are not somehow respected. Finally, a further difference concerns the fact that only social relations that require an attitude of mutual recognition contribute to the development of a positive self-relation. For only by participating in interactions whose normative preconditions include reciprocal orientation to specific principles of recognition can individuals experience the enduring value of their specific capacities for others. Thus, with the institutional differentiation of spheres of recognition, the opportunity for greater individuality also rises — understood as the possibility of increasingly assuring the singularity of one's own personality in a context of social approval: with each newly emerging sphere of mutual recognition, another aspect of human subjectivity is revealed which individuals can now positively ascribe to themselves intersubjectively.

These additional points should make it clear how much the idea of a social differentiation of three spheres of recognition owes to a kind of social-theoretical transformation of Hegel's *Philosophy of Right*. Just as Hegel spoke with regard to the "ethical" (*sittlich*) order of modern society of three institutional complexes (the family, civil society, and the state), whose internal constitution as spheres of recognition allows the subject to attain the highest degree of individual freedom through active participation, the same basic idea is to be found in my own reflections in the form of a differentiation of three differently constituted spheres of reciprocal recognition. Before I pursue this line of argument to reach another view of "distribution struggles," however, I would like to indicate at least two differences that fundamentally distinguish my project from Hegel's.[34]

a) It is true that in his *Philosophy of Right* Hegel tends to assert a kind of built-in recognition conflict within each of the three complexes, but these essentially function only to motivate the transition to the next level of ethically constituted institutions. In contrast, I have tried to introduce the three spheres of recognition that emerge with capitalism in such a way that it is clear from the start how each must be distinguished by an internal conflict over the legitimate application of its respective principle. With the three new forms of social relations that in my view prepare the way for the moral order of capitalist society, distinct principles of recognition develop in whose light the subject can assert specific experiences of undeserved, unjustifiable disrespect, and thus produce grounds for an expanded kind of recognition. In intimate relationships this internal conflict typically takes the form of bringing forth newly developed or previously unconsidered needs by appeal to the mutually attested love in order to demand a different or expanded kind of care.[35] In the recognition sphere of modern law, in contrast, it normally takes the form of showing how previously excluded groups deserve legal recognition or previously neglected facts require a differentiation of legal principles by appeal to the basic idea of equality.[36] And in the third recognition sphere, individuals or social groups generally bring forth hitherto neglected or underappreciated activities and capacities by appeal to the achievement principle in order to demand greater social esteem and at the same time a redistribution of (material) resources.

With the help of this brief summary we can now also see more clearly how the connection between subjective claims for recognition and existing discourses of justification must be construed. If deep-seated claims of this kind are always socially shaped – in the sense that the content of the expectation is always influenced by institutionally anchored principles of recognition – then these principles always give rise to practical grounds that make up the rational web of sphere-specific discourses of questioning and justification. Thus, the spheres of recognition represent normatively substantive models of interaction in which the intersubjective nature of human beings is expressed in a generalizable way. Owing to these underlying principles, what is socially established here in forms of reciprocal recognition has the character of publicly justified standards whose social application can accordingly be subject to rational objections and doubts. As his reflections on the rational content of "ethical life" (*Sittlichkeit*) shows, Hegel was not far from such an insight; but seeking the harmonious closure of ethical totality, he shrank from seeing a transcending struggle structurally built into each of his spheres of recognition.

b) This tendency of the late Hegel to as it were bring his *Philosophy of Right* to systematic closure, despite all the internal tensions within ethical life,[37] reappears in the second respect in which my proposal differs from the original. Hegel not only tried to deny the built-in structural conflicts that always characterize his three spheres of recognition; he also wanted to equate them with the institutional complexes typical of his time. He thus rashly identified the recognition sphere of love with the institution of the bourgeois nuclear family, that of modern law with the organizational structure of "bourgeois society," and the sphere I have presented under the rubric of "social esteem" with the institution of the state, in accordance

146 REDISTRIBUTION OR RECOGNITION?

with his idea of political standing or honor. The disadvantage of this institutionalist way of thinking is not only that institutions are interpreted much too one-sidedly in terms of a single recognition principle – as emerges, for instance, in the curious absence of any reference to legal recognition in the "family" or "state." Under the pressure of this concretism, the borders between the institutional complexes on the one side, and the spheres of recognition on the other, break down altogether. But an even more serious problem is that Hegel is no longer free to systematically bring other institutional embodiments of the recognition principles into his analysis. Thus, to name only the most striking example, his discussion of the ethical relation of love lacks any reference to the social importance of "friendship," although this would seem to have been strongly suggested by his orientation to classical ideals.

In order to avoid such inconsistencies, it seems much more plausible to me to introduce the different spheres of recognition above the concrete level on which we speak of social or legal institutions: such spheres refer to the forms of socially established interaction that have a normative content insofar as they are anchored in different principles of reciprocal recognition. If the basic idea of the *Philosophy of Right* is taken up again today in this altered form, it is clear from the start that the idea of social *Sittlichkeit* can designate only the most abstract possible idea of an ensemble of historically specific spheres of recognition.[38] And it is also self-evident that institutional complexes represent a single recognition principle only in the rarest of cases; as a rule, they rather result from an intermeshing of several of them. Thus, to take another obvious example, the modern "bourgeois" nuclear family is an institution in which the recognition principle of love has been gradually complemented by the legal regulation of intrafamilial interactions. The introduction of the legal principle of recognition – an external constraint of legal respect among family members – typically has the function of guarding against the dangers that can result from the "pure" practice of only the principle of reciprocal love and concern.[39]

If we consider the possibilities of such institutional interconnections, we also see that the third sphere of recognition I have introduced — the "achievement principle" as a selective embodiment of social esteem — was already complemented early in the history of capitalist society by references to legal recognition. The development of social-welfare measures can be understood such that individual members of society should be guaranteed a minimum of social status and hence economic resources independently of the meritocratic recognition principle by transforming these claims into social rights. And with this suggestion, I can pick up the thread of my argument where I left it before this short excursus on the Hegelian *Philosophy of Right*: we cannot adequately analyze the significance of "distribution struggles" within the framework of a theory of recognition without first briefly describing the social-welfare state's incorporation of the sphere of social esteem.

The individualistic achievement principle, which emerged as a new criterion of social esteem after the dissolution of the estate-based status hierarchy, was from the beginning a double-edged source of legitimacy. On the one hand, as mentioned, it represented little more than part of an influential ideology insofar as it simply expressed the one-sided value horizon of those social groups which, because they possessed capital, had the means to reorganize economic reproduction. Thus, what "achievement" means, and what guarantees a just distribution of resources, was measured right from the start against an evaluative standard whose highest reference point was investment in intellectual preparation for a specific activity. But this characterization is in a certain way already misleading, since hardly any of the criteria used beneath the surface is free from one-sided evaluation — as is shown, for example, by the definition of individual risk-taking by the investment risk of the owner of capital.[40] Beyond this, the whole way of evaluating achievement was also influenced from the start by encompassing horizons of interpretation whose origins lie not in the evaluations of the capitalist elite, but in much older worldviews that nonetheless help determine what counts as an expression of individual effort. Naturalistic thinking, which attributes essentialist collective properties to social subgroups so that their practical efforts are not viewed as "achievement" or "work," but merely as the realization of an "innate" nature, plays an especially big role here. Within the social–ontological horizon of this naturalism, the activities of the housewife or mother, for instance, are never viewed as a "productive" contribution to social reproduction that would justify any form of social esteem, while women's work in the formally organized sector is not believed to be as productive as that of men, since according to women's nature it involves less physical or mental exertion.[41] Once we become cognizant of the many superimpositions and distortions inherent in the capitalist achievement principle, it is hard to see any normative principle of mutual recognition in it at all. Nevertheless, putting the new idea into social practice indeed did away with the estate-based form of social esteem, and at least normatively sustains the demand that the contributions of all members of society be esteemed according to their achievements.

On the other hand, then, for the time being the individualist achievement principle is also the one normative resource bourgeois-capitalist society provides for morally justifying the extremely unequal distribution of life chances and goods. If social esteem as well as economic and legal privileges can no longer be legitimately governed by membership in a certain estate, then the ethico–religious valorization of work and the establishment of a capitalist market suggest making social esteem dependent on individual achievement. To this extent, the achievement principle henceforth forms the backdrop of normative legitimation which, in case of doubt, has to provide rational grounds for publicly justifying the privileged appropriation of particular resources like money or credentials. And the fact of social inequality can only meet with more or less rational agreement because, beyond all actual distortions, its legitimating principle contains the normative claim to consider the individual achievements of all members of society fairly and appropriately in the form of mutual esteem. To be sure, the unequal distribution of resources also found normative support from another side, which would serve as the gateway for a far-reaching restructuring of the capitalist social order. For alongside the newly-created achievement principle, it was the modern legal order, with its inherent claim to equal treatment, that saw to it that the state-approved, and hence sanction-supported, appropriation of resources by structurally advantaged groups could be considered legitimate.[42] But it was also precisely this principle of equal legal treatment that could be mobilized in countless social struggles and debates, especially by the working class, to establish social rights. Thus, the recognition sphere of the achievement principle was in a certain way contained by the social-welfare state by making a minimum of social esteem and economic welfare independent of actual achievement and transforming them into individual rights claims.[43]

The changes that take place in the capitalist recognition order with the emergence of the welfare state can perhaps best be understood as the penetration of the principle of equal legal treatment into the previously autonomous sphere of social esteem. For the normative argument which made social welfare guarantees in a certain sense "rationally" unavoidable is essentially the hardly disputable assertion that members of society can only make actual use of their legally guaranteed autonomy if they are assured a minimum of economic resources, irrespective of income.[44] Here we have an especially vivid example of how historical changes can be brought about by innovations whose origins lie in nothing other than the persuasive power – or better, the incontrovertibility – of moral reasons[45]: thanks to their underlying principles, the social spheres of recognition that together make up the socio-moral

order of bourgeois-capitalist society possess a surplus of validity, which those affected can rationally assert against actual
recognition relations. The social-welfare innovations that were
achieved in this way in at least some western capitalist
countries placed social stratification on an altered moral basis,
inasmuch as the group-specific appropriation of resources is in
a certain way normatively divided and subjected to two different principles: a lesser share of socially available goods is now
guaranteed to individuals as legal persons in the form of social
rights, while the far greater share continues to be distributed
according to the capitalist achievement principle. But with
this, the social conflicts designated as "distribution struggles"
take on a double form, since they can occur either by mobilizing legal arguments or by revaluing prevailing definitions of
achievement.

2. *Distribution conflicts as struggles for recognition*

As is well known, Marx already expressed a number of grave
reservations about the political idea of distribution struggles, as
advocated in his time mainly by Social Democrats. Essentially,
his objections were based on the conviction that the goal of
merely redistributing economic resources leaves untouched the
asymmetry between capital and labor, the real cause of social
inequality.[46] Now, I have no intention of dusting off this
criticism in my debate with Fraser, since I share with many
others the conviction that Marx makes some serious mistakes
in his analysis of capitalist society. The central objection here
concerns his unmistakable propensity to dismiss the moral
power of the equality and achievement principles as cultural
superstructure, although they provided the newly emerging
market society with its legitimating framework in the first
place.[47] Nevertheless, a reflex resembling the Marxist reser-
vation kicks in when I see Fraser attempting to politically
valorize distribution struggles against the (putative) predomi-
nance of identity struggles. Are not the social phenomena the

latter category is meant to designate far from transparent, since neither their moral-motivational backdrop nor the standards of legitimation connected to them are adequately grasped? True, there has been a pronounced tendency in the debate sparked not least by Fraser to consider distribution struggles, as against the newly emerging cultural conflicts of the 1990s, as unproblematically given.[48] But this often amounts to merely projecting principles of justice based on distribution theory onto social reality, as if this type of moral consideration would self-evidently play a motivating role. In the end, therefore, often little more remains of the phenomenon of distribution struggles than the redistributional measures negotiated in public wage bargaining or parliamentary debates over tax policy. There can, to be sure, be little talk here of social struggle in the real sense of the term, i.e., everyday conflicts in which those affected attempt by their own symbolic and practical efforts to alter a distribution order they feel is unjust.[49] To this extent, a concept of distribution struggles must be reconstructed that is not tailored to the level of state redistributional measures, but rather takes into account the non-state spaces where the initial efforts to delegitimize the prevailing distribution order are undertaken. Only then will it emerge whether Fraser is right to establish an unbridgeable chasm between these conflicts and so-called identity struggles.

My account of the capitalist recognition order so far should have made it clear that I regard the restriction of social recognition to just one form – the "cultural" – as seriously misleading. Rather, there are three recognition spheres embedded in the moral order underlying capitalism at least in western societies, whose respective "surplus of validity" produces different experiences of injustice or unwarranted disrespect. Here one dimension – which Fraser surprisingly leaves out of her critical diagnosis of the times altogether – plays an absolutely central role in the history of these societies: a conflict dynamic runs through the history of capitalism up to the present day over the appropriate interpretation of the principle

of legal equality, starting with Marx's account of the debates
over the justification of stealing wood and continuing today,
for instance, in women's struggle for special pregnancy provi-
sions in labor law.[50] The medium through which this sort of
social struggle unfolds is modern law, which promises all
members of society equal respect for their individual autonomy.[51] It may be that Fraser was misled into leaving out the
legal form of recognition by Charles Taylor's suggestive presentation, according to which the struggle for equality in a
certain way belongs to a now superseded phase of historical
development that was still free from demands for the recognition of cultural "difference." This seems to me to be mis-
taken, however, beyond the above-mentioned grounds,
because the battle for legal recognition itself never occurs
except by asserting a specific "difference" in life-situation,
which so far has not received legal consideration, with normative reference to the equality principle. All struggles for
recognition, it could be more pointedly said, progress through
a playing out of the moral dialectic of the universal and the
particular: one can always appeal for a particular relative difference by applying a general principle of mutual recognition,
which normatively compels an expansion of the existing relations of recognition.[52]

Now, the conflictual playing out of this moral dialectic
takes an especially capricious and opaque form within those
recognition spheres that normatively underlie the social stratification of capitalist society; for here there are in a sense two
ways in which subjects can demand recognition of their particular life-situations or personalities in order to struggle for
greater social esteem and hence more resources. On the one
hand, up to a certain, politically negotiated threshold, it is
possible to call for the application of social rights that guarantee every member of society a minimum of essential goods
regardless of achievement. This approach follows the principle
of legal equality insofar as, by argumentatively mobilizing the
equality principle, normative grounds can be adduced for

making minimum economic welfare an imperative of legal recognition. On the other hand, however, in capitalism's everyday social reality there is also the possibility of appealing to one's achievements as something "different," since they do not receive sufficient consideration or social esteem under the prevailing hegemonic value structure.[53] To be sure, a sufficiently differentiated picture of this sort of recognition struggle is only possible when we take into account the fact that even the social demarcation of professions – indeed, the shape of the social division of labor as a whole – is a result of the cultural valuation of specific capacities for achievement. Today it is becoming especially clear that the social construction of professional fields is shot through with prejudices about the limits of women's capabilities.

An examination of the relevant research quickly shows that the undervaluing of predominately female professions is not due to the actual content of the work. Rather, it is the other way around: every professionalized activity automatically falls in the social status hierarchy as soon as it is primarily practiced by women, while there is a gain in status if the gender reversal goes the other way.[54] Gender functions here in the organization of the social division of labor as a cultural measure that determines the social esteem owed a particular activity independent of the specificity of the work. Only this cultural mechanism, the (naturalistically grounded) denigration of female capacities for achievement, can explain how it is that that, on bourgeois-capitalist society's understanding of its own premises, the *de facto* women's activities of housework and childcare do not conceptually register as "work" at all. And the same mechanism must be invoked to explain why there is always a pronounced loss of status when a profession shifts from male to female.[55] All this shows how much the legitimation of the social distribution order owes to cultural views of the contribution of different status groups or strata to social reproduction. Not only which activities can be valued as "work," and hence are eligible for professionalization, but also how high the social return should be for each professionalized activity is determined by classificatory grids and evaluative schemes anchored deep in the culture of bourgeois-capitalist society. If, in light of this finding, we also consider that experiences of injustice are generally sparked off by the inadequate or incomplete application of a prevailing legitimation principle, we arrive at a thesis that seems to me appropriate for interpreting distribution struggles under capitalism: such conflicts typically take the form of social groups, in response to the experience of disrespect for their actual achievements, attempting to throw the established evaluative models into question by fighting for greater esteem of their social contributions, and thereby for economic redistribution. Thus, when they do not take the form of mobilizing social rights, redistribution struggles are definitional conflicts over the legitimacy of the current application of the achievement principle.[56]

Now, this thesis's claim to universality may come as a surprise at this point, since so far I have shown how strong the influence of cultural evaluative models is on status distribution only in the case of the gendered division of labor. The feminist struggle to socially valorize "female" housework is so far the clearest example of how, within the framework of the capitalist achievement principle, social redistribution can be brought about primarily by delegitimizing prevailing assessments of achievement. When threatened by a lack of status, writes Reinhard Kreckel, women today can respond only by either themselves joining the labor market or "struggling for social recognition of their own reproductive activity within the household as equally valuable social labor."[57] If we socially generalize this especially vivid example and make it the paradigm of distribution struggles, we arrive at the argumentative logic of most such conflicts: time and again, an already professionalized or even unregulated activity must be symbolically presented in a new light − a new value horizon − in order to establish that the institutionalized evaluative system is one-sided or restrictive, and thus that the established distribution order does not possess sufficient legitimacy according to its own principles. The full extent of such struggles only emerges, however, when we consider at the same time that the question of appropriate esteem for various activities is itself the stuff of everyday conflict in the reproduction of the capitalist division of labor. Whether in the industrial or the service sector, in administration or, increasingly, in the family, not only the "just" valuation but also the demarcation and connection between activities are always subject to a conflictual process of negotiation, since there is no adequate way of anchoring them in something like a value-neutral, purely "technical" functional order. And precisely to the extent that the redistribution of material goods is directly or indirectly connected to the outcomes of such conflicts, these are first and foremost distribution conflicts in the entirely unspectacular, even prepolitical sense. But of course these ubiquitous conflicts only become "struggles" in a more exacting political sense when a sufficiently large number of those affected come together to convince the broader public of the general, exemplary significance of their cause, thereby calling into question the prevailing status order as a whole.

The argument just outlined contains two social-theoretical implications I would now like to reformulate more sharply, since they directly contradict central premises of Nancy Fraser's position. In both cases, our disagreement concerns the relation between the economy and culture, or between the capitalist economic order and cultural values.

a) My reflections so far have led to the conclusion that a satisfactory conception of the capitalist social order requires not only including the three spheres of social recognition, to whose normative principles subjects can connect their legitimate expectations of reciprocal recognition. Rather, we must also consider the cultural values involved in the institutional constitution of the economic sphere through interpretations of the achievement principle, which give it a particular shape in the

form of a division of labor and a distribution of status. To this
extent, as has been shown not only by feminist studies on the
constitutive role of gender dualism but also by a number of
earlier anthropologists, it is not advisable to theoretically isolate
purely economic or systemic factors from cultural elements
with regard to the capitalist economic order.[58] All the changes
in professional organization or remuneratory rules that take
place within the borders of these spheres are due to efficiency
considerations that are inextricably fused with cultural views of
the social world. Fraser is of course free to account for this fact
of the "interpenetration" of culture and the economy through
a procedure of "perspective dualism," which methodologically
allows one and the same object domain to be analyzed alternatively from the perspective of economic utility or cultural
hegemony. But there is something arbitrary about this proposal
insofar as one finds no argument for why, if we are to combine
two merely analytical perspectives, they should be those of
"economy" and "culture."

     In all classical versions of methodological dualism – like that
we find in Habermas's early writings, following David Lockwood's famous distinction[59] – the methodological admission of
two complementary perspectives is justified by considerations
that refer to the structure of the object domain itself: the
standpoints of "social integration" and "system integration" are
to be understood as aspects of the coordination of social action
that are essential to or constitutive of the reproduction of late-
capitalist societies. Whatever one makes of this argument, its
significance here is that nothing analogous is to be found in
Fraser's reflections: it remains completely unclear why the
capitalist social order is now to be investigated specifically from
the two perspectives of "economy" and "culture," when it
would seem equally possible to analyze the object field from
other perspectives, such as "morality" or "law." In short, any
kind of methodological perspectivism remains empty as long as
it is not anchored in social-theoretical views about how social
reproduction in capitalist societies is to be understood. Now, as

far as this last question is concerned, in contrast to Fraser's (on this point) unclear conception, I advocate a position that leads not, for instance, to a "culture-theoretical," but – if we are going to use such formulations – to a "moral-theoretical monism." Since the central institutions of even capitalist societies require rational legitimation through generalizable principles of reciprocal recognition, their reproduction remains dependent on a basis of moral consensus – which thus possesses real primacy vis-à-vis other integration mechanisms, since it is the basis of the normative expectations of members of society as well as their readiness for conflict.

b) As my remarks in this section have shown, I always introduce the conflicts and struggles of capitalist social formations with reference to those principles of mutual recognition that are considered legitimate by the members of society themselves. What motivates individuals or social groups to call the prevailing social order into question and to engage in practical resistance is the *moral* conviction that, with respect to their own situations or particularities, the recognition principles considered legitimate are incorrectly or inadequately applied. It follows from this, first of all and *contra* Fraser, that a moral experience that can be meaningfully described as one of "disrespect" must be regarded as the motivational basis of all social conflicts: subjects or groups see themselves as disrespected in certain aspects of their capacities or characteristics because they have become convinced that the institutional practice of a legitimate principle of recognition unjustifiably fails to reflect these dispositions.[60] In contrast, the opposition between "economic" and "cultural" conflicts could at most have a secondary significance, since it more precisely designates the respects in which disrespect is experienced.

But this way of speaking would again be misleading insofar as it suggests that today questions of cultural interpretation and evaluation are only of decisive relevance in particular types of social conflict. As my reinterpretation of "distribution struggles" should have made clear, such an assertion is inappropriate even for those conflicts seen by their participants as aiming at a redistribution of material resources. Here too, cultural interpretations play a constitutive role: what is contested is precisely whether, with regard to the actual division of tasks, the prevailing evaluative schemata for social achievements and contributions are in fact just. But this observation can now be generalized beyond the narrow framework of distribution struggles in the sense that cultural questions are internally relevant to all struggles for "recognition," inasmuch as the application of principles of recognition always takes place in light of cultural interpretations of needs, claims, or abilities. Whether in contemporary conflicts around the socio-moral implications of love, the appropriate exercise of the principle of legal equality, or the just interpretation of the achievement principle, specific problematizations of traditional evaluative models always play a central role. It would be misleading here to restrict the influence of "culture" to just one type of social conflict.[61] In fact, I have always understood Fraser's influential earlier article on the "struggle over needs" as arguing that precisely this constitutive significance of cultural prejudices and interpretive schemata should be emphasized in all social conflicts.[62]

I hope these reflections have made it clear that an adequate social-theoretical approach to social conflicts can only be found if, starting from institutionalized, legitimating principles of recognition, attention is paid to moral disappointments and experiences of injustice. Two problem areas, which will be the subject of the third section, now remain in my debate with Nancy Fraser. First of all, following my proposed interpretation of the moral content of "distribution struggles," it remains unclear how the conflicts now generally designated as "identity struggles" are to be fit into the resulting spectrum of social conflict. Even if Fraser and I have different views about the novelty and social relevance of these struggles for "cultural recognition," their contemporary significance is hardly contested and the question of their interpretation is pressing. Here, against the background of my remarks to this point, two answers seem to me possible in principle. They can be distinguished by their different reference to the dominant system of recognition principles: either these "cultural" conflicts are interpreted within the horizon of the principle of legal equality, so that they essentially have to do with an expansion of our liberal understanding of individual autonomy; or they are described as something novel, in the sense that they pave the way for the epochal emergence of something like a fourth recognition principle in liberal-capitalist societies, which would revolve around mutual respect for the cultural particularities of groups or collectivities (III, 1).

The second unanswered question concerns the problem of the normative standards by which demands made in social conflicts are to be judged morally. Indeed, I see it as a great advantage of an adequately differentiated theory of recognition that social experiences of injustice can be described in the same language in which the demands are to be justified: experiences of unfounded bias in the application of recognition principles are assumed as "motives" of social resistance and conflict, and these experiences can then be invoked on the normative level in the moral justification of the corresponding demands. But of course this says nothing about either the morally "correct" implementation of these principles or their moral legitimacy as a whole. I would like to take this step in rough outline in the last part of my response (III, 2). In so doing, I will try to bring together my earlier reflections into a recognition-theoretical conception of justice, clarifying in which respects this differs from the idea of "participatory parity."

III.   Recognition and Social Justice

For all the reservations and misgivings I have expressed about
Fraser's opposition between "distribution" and "cultural recognition," I have not yet discussed how I would describe the
new tendencies of a "politics of identity" within the framework
of my alternative schema. True, from the first step of my
argument I have made it clear that I take the restriction of the
concept of "recognition" to demands now made by cultural
minorities to be highly problematic: this systematically obscures
the fact that resistance to an established social order is always
driven by the moral experience of in some respect not receiving
what is taken to be justified recognition. I then tried to explain
the ways in which social disrespect can be experienced in
contemporary societies with the help of three principles of
recognition, which are institutionally anchored in modern
capitalist societies. This should have established not only that
experiences of social disrespect are relative to historically developed recognition norms, but above all that distribution conflicts
must be understood to a large extent as struggles for recognition
insofar as they relate to the appropriate interpretation of the
achievement principle. But to this point, I have not yet myself
offered any answer to the question of how the political-moral
demands now made by cultural minorities for the "recognition"
of their (collective) identities should be understood on the basis
of a differentiated concept of recognition. It is precisely such
political objectives for which Fraser reserves her concept of
"cultural recognition"; whereas this concept seems to me to be
just as much in need of normative explanation as the earlier
umbrella concept of "distribution." I want to proceed by asking
with regard to the complex phenomenon of "identity politics":
which normative principle can the different groups in question
lay claim to in order to publicly justify their demands for
"cultural" recognition? It turns out that the adjective "cultural"
tells us very little, since it does not explain whether the means

of fulfilling such identity-political demands are legal, political, or cultural.

1. Cultural identity and struggles for recognition

At present, the concept of "identity politics" describes the tendency of a great many disadvantaged groups not only to call for the elimination of discrimination through the exercise of universal rights, but also to demand group-specific forms of preference, recognition, or participation. Only with this turn toward demands for the public recognition of collective identities has there been a "culturization" of social conflicts, in the sense that membership in a particular minority "culture" can be used to morally mobilize political resistance. Even if we already saw in section one that today such forms of political resistance should by no means be sociologically overestimated, since their public prominence is often only due to mass media stylization, they nevertheless remain a not insignificant challenge for a normatively-oriented social theory. For the question arises of whether the politicization of cultural identity is only another mode of the identity conflicts sketched above, or whether, conversely, we have reached a new threshold in the conflict history of liberal-capitalist societies. If this is the correct way of setting out the challenges connected to the "politics of identity," it means considering the possibility of the emergence of a new fourth principle of recognition within the normative infrastructure of capitalist societies. In the present interplay of transformed value horizons and social demands, are the normative contours emerging of a recognition principle that cannot be neatly translated back into the already established principles, since it requires social recognition not of the singular needy subject (love), the autonomous legal person (law), or the cooperative member of society (esteem), but of members of a cultural group? Or can the demands for the public recognition of collective identities be meaningfully responded to within the normative horizon of the existing recognition culture insofar as they can be understood as either applications of the equality principle or reinterpretations of the achievement principle?

An observation by Will Kymlicka offers a suitable entry into this set of problems. According to Kymlicka, the current tendency toward "identity politics" is due to a cultural upheaval that has led in recent decades to a gradual self-redefinition by social minorities. While groups such as homosexuals or the disabled previously defined their own identities through concepts of sexual or biological deviation, so that that they had to understand themselves as contingent collections of individuals, today they characterize themselves to a much greater extent as culturally integrated communities with a common history, language, and sensibility.[63] Only with this construction of a cultural identity have groups suffering social discrimination developed a self-understanding that now allows them to see themselves in something like a common front with ethnic groups struggling for respect for their cultural independence. The same can of course be said for those parts of the women's movement that try to make the fact of sexual difference the reference point for a cultural redefinition in which "femininity" becomes the basis for a common culture. Here too, in a certain way adopting the example of ethnic minorities with a common language, origin, and everyday culture, a transformation of collective self-understanding is taking place that could lead to the claim for recognition of one's own culture. Thus, a great many social groups whose commonalty initially consisted only in the negative experience of social discrimination have recently undergone such a process of gradual redefinition whereby the necessity of exclusion is made into the virtue of constructing of an independent culture.[64] The result of this change in the form of collective identities is the emergence of a whole spectrum of culturally defined communities, extending from "gay communities" to initiatives by the disabled to ethnic minorities. The concept of "identity politics" captures the idea that all of these newly emerged – or better, "construed" – collectivities struggle for the recognition of their culturally defined independence.

Of course, concealed behind this common rhetoric – the demand for the recognition of cultural identity – are a multiplicity of different objectives, and distinguishing between them is central to normatively evaluating them. On the highest level, such demands for recognition can first of all be distinguished according to whether the objectives they articulate have an individual or an originally "communal" or collective character. Here, following a suggestion by Bernhard Peters, those collective demands for recognition that aim at improving the situation of the group's individual members will be called "individualistic," while those that aim in an essential sense at the common life of the group will be called "communal."[65] Against the background of this distinction, it quickly becomes clear that a number of demands for recognition made in the name of a cultural group possess a hidden individualistic character, since they concern the situations of individual members. Thus, the appeal to such recognition often only serves the aim of eliminating social discrimination that prevents the group's members, as members of their specific group, from making use of universal basic rights. When it comes to this type of collectively raised objective, there can be no doubt that the "identity-political" demands remain within the normative framework of a struggle for equal legal treatment: what is demanded by appeal to the equality principle is the elimination of obstacles or disadvantages relating to a social group's cultural characteristics such that they put its members at a disadvantage vis-à-vis the majority.[66] Because it is a matter here of demands that become, as it were, sublated within the normative recognition order of liberal-capitalist society, those objectives with an originally communal character are of much greater interest for our present question.

Objectives of this type, as I said, make the well-being of the social group as such the reference point of collective demands. What is demanded when a community that understands itself as cultural appeals for the recognition of its cultural independence is not the improvement of the situations of its members, but rather the protection or improvement of its common life as a group. Here too, Peters has suggested a series of further differentiations that are helpful for our purposes. Following his analysis, there are three different objectives with a communal character that can be sought by social groups in rhetorical appeals to the concept of recognition.[67] The first type of demand has to do with obtaining protection from external encroachments that could negatively influence the group's cultural reproduction. Here we need only think of the innocuous case of the basic freedoms of speech, assembly, and religion as they are for the most part protected in democratic constitutional states, where serious conflicts generally arise when the continuation of certain practices of a cultural community (e.g. injunctions regarding clothes or slaughter) require an exemption from existing laws. But even complications of this kind leave no doubt that, in this first case, the group's struggle takes place within the normative framework staked out by the equality principle of legal recognition: the exemptions demanded by a group to protect its cultural integrity are grounded in an appeal to legal equality insofar as they claim the same legal protection for a minority that is actually guaranteed the majority. Where demands for the recognition of cultural identity aim at protecting the integrity of group life, they necessarily pass through the needle's eye of the equality principle. For everything to which objectives of this kind can normatively appeal in the end derives from the idea that legal equality requires abstraction from cultural differences.

If this type of demand can be understood as a kind of negative objective, since it has to do with defense against culture-threatening encroachments, the second type examined by Peters has an unambiguously positive character. Here social groups appeal for recognition of their cultural identity in that they require resources or preventive measures to promote and develop the cohesion of the community. The spectrum of means that can in principle be called for in this context extends from economic support to instruction in the native language to adequate representation in the mass media; but in each case the group in question must first publicly establish that it will not be possible for them to maintain their culture and way of life without such resources or preventative measures. Here too, one of the possibilities of normative justification consists in laying claim to the principle of legal equality by pointing to past or present disadvantages. What is then appealed to is the state's elimination of obstacles that unjustifiably disadvantage or have disadvantaged a social group in carrying on its cultural life relative to the majority culture. To be sure, only demands with a temporally limited character can be made in this way, since they lose their normative force with the elimination of the disadvantage.[68] As soon as long-term means for furthering a communal culture are demanded, other arguments must come into play, whose normative peculiarity points to a third type of "communal" objective.

As a third type of demand that social groups make with a view to their common well-being as a group, Peters names the goal of recognition or respect from a society's majority culture. Here "recognition" no longer seems to have the merely indirect sense of ensuring a community's continued existence by either non-interference in or promotion of its cultural practices, but rather the entirely direct sense of acceptance of – or indeed esteem for – its objectives or value orientations as such.[69] It is probably only this third level that reaches what is today first and foremost designated by the idea of the "recognition" of cultural differences, and I suppose is primarily intended by Nancy Fraser with the concept of "cultural recognition." In other words, it could be said that here the demand for the non-consideration of difference gives way to the demand for the consideration of difference. Of course, more than a few difficulties are involved in clarifying the meaning of this kind of objective if it cannot mean the above-mentioned means of indirect, legal protection of the continued existence of a

cultural community. We can here once more follow the
suggestions of Peters, who tries to distinguish between a
number of such direct applications of "recognition." First of
all, this objective can include the demand that, as a member of
a cultural minority, one not only enjoy equal political rights,
but also the real opportunity to gain public attention for one's
group-specific value convictions. What this could mean can
best be explained in terms of a procedural virtue of democratic
institutions that is measured by their capacity for respectful
interaction with cultural minorities.[70] The direct demand for
cultural recognition appears to have another meaning when it
aims to protect a group from forms of cultural degradation,
disrespect, and humiliation; here one can think, for example,
of cases in which feminist organizations have called for a
prohibition of or restriction on pornography because they saw
it as a degrading representation of women. But closer consideration of this example quickly makes it clear that objectives
of this kind once again involve an attempt to normatively
reactivate the equality principle of modern law in order to
present recurring experiences of degradation as the cause of a
group-specific disadvantage. Here, depending on the constitutional order, two possibilities are generally available to
those affected: depending on the facts of the case, they can
define the disadvantaging effect of cultural humiliation in terms
of either a violation of their dignity or a limitation on their
freedom.[71]

As soon as such demands for recognition no longer take the
merely negative form of protection from group-specific degradation but shift to seeking esteem for one's own goals and
values, the normative framework of the legal equality principle
is finally exceeded. For now we face the idea that the cultural
community's constitutive practices, way of life, and value
orientation deserve a special form of appreciation that cannot
be derived from the principle of equal treatment. One's culture
should enjoy social esteem not because it should not be
disadvantaged vis-à-vis the majority culture, but because it in

itself represents a good the society should acknowledge. Of course, here too there are once again two conceivable alternatives, whose differences stem from the different standards according to which the demand for social esteem is made. On the one hand, it would be in principle possible to stress or appeal to the value of one's own culture with reference to the normative idea by which esteem for individuals or groups is generally measured in liberal capitalist society, i.e., the merit principle. For the cultural community, however, the consequence of this would be that it would have to present its own practices and way of life as representing an essential contribution to the reproduction of society, and in this sense offering an indispensable "achievement." Leaving aside the possibility that this forced presentation already involves an unreasonable demand that contradicts the group's demands, this form of esteem would presuppose expanding the achievement principle to the point of exceeding its remaining "material" substance in a way that could hardly be justified. It therefore seems more promising for cultural minorities to adopt an alternative way of grounding their demands: the value of their culture would be appealed to not relative to an accepted recognition principle, but independently of all previously institutionalized value references, and in this sense "absolutely." However, what this could mean in the contemporary debate is anything but clear.

With the demand that a minority communal culture be socially esteemed for its own sake, the normative horizon of both the equality principle and the achievement principle is definitively exceeded. For it is no longer a matter of either ensuring, with the greatest possible value-neutrality, the equal opportunity of all subjects to realize their life goals, nor of as fairly as possible esteeming particular contributions to society as "achievements," but rather the far more sweeping goal of respecting the cultural practices of a minority as something socially valuable in itself – as a social good. If the idea of recognizing cultural difference is connected to this radical demand, then, even before all the justificatory problems, it is unclear what political measures would go along with it in particular cases. The spectrum of possible alternatives here might extend from inclusion in the practice of bestowing public honors, to the pedagogic transmission of cultural achievements, to consideration of important ritual holidays in a political community's public calendar. Beyond this, it should not be ruled out that a society is in a position to increase its institutional imagination concerning arrangements of this kind to the extent that it can give an account of the value-bounded nature of its own practices and rituals. But the central problem in this context is certainly not the appropriate form of institutional implementation, but rather the normative character of the demand itself. The sort of social esteem that would be entailed in recognizing a culture as something valuable is not a public response that could be appealed for or demanded, since it could only arise spontaneously or voluntarily according to standards of evaluative examination.[72] In contrast to the esteem normatively required by the institutionalized merit principle, there is no possibility of normatively demanding the positive evaluation of cultural ways of life. At best, we can here speak only of the readiness to take note of the specific qualities of other cultures such that their value can then be examined.

This last circumstance makes it clear that we cannot meaningfully speak of a "demand" for social esteem for one's culture. Certainly, cultural minorities can nurture hopes or have expectations of being especially valued by the majority for the achievements reflected in the fact of developing a distinct language and value orientation. But there can be no legitimate claim to this sort of esteem, since it can only be the result of a process of judgment that escapes our control, just as sympathy or affection does. It may, however, make perfect sense to speak in this context of an indirect, secondary claim to well-meaning attention and consideration by the majority, so that the process of intercultural communication can get started in the first place. Here we might even speak in a weak sense of a right owed to cultural minorities to be judged according to an "anticipation of completeness" (Gadamer) of their value. But in the end this way of speaking says nothing more than that a liberal democratic society must possess the procedural virtue of being able to treat its minorities as candidates for the same social esteem it shows its own culture. Whether this candidate status regarding "cultural" esteem is already tied to a new fourth recognition principle, which is gradually starting to join the previously institutionalized principles, is a very difficult question. If so, then the cultural conflicts of the present could produce a normative principle whose moral consequences do not complement the traditional offering of tolerance, but move beyond it. For such a fourth recognition principle would mean that we also have to recognize one another as members of cultural communities whose forms of life deserve the measure of well-meaning attention that is necessary to judge their value.

These speculative reflections should not, however, conceal the basically negative result of our systematic examination of the idea of recognizing cultural differences: the overwhelming majority of demands now being made by means of this rhetorical formula do not really transcend the normative horizon of the dominant recognition order. The groups involved may in fact have a far more radical self-understanding of their own objectives, but more soberly regarded, their normative content can usually be understood as an innovative application of the equality principle. The moral grammar of the conflicts now being conducted around "identity-political" questions in liberal-democratic states is essentially determined by the recognition principle of legal equality. Whether the demands refer to protection from culture-threatening encroachments, the elimination of group-specific discrimination, or support for the maintenance of particular ways of life, their public justification must always mobilize moral arguments somehow tied to the equality principle, often bolstered by additional assumptions.[73] Of course, this does not yet answer the really challenging normative question of which cultural minorities can legitimately raise which demands by enlisting such arguments. But a clarification of the multiple distinctions that would be required just on empirical grounds[74] is not necessary here, since we are now concerned only with locating "identity-political" demands within the normative horizon of contemporary society. When it comes to these fronts of cultural conflict, the concept of "cultural" recognition as it is used by Nancy Fraser leads to confusion rather than clarification. For it fails to recognize that the majority of identity-political demands can be meaningfully grasped only as expressions of an expanded struggle for legal recognition.

2. Perspectives for a recognition-theoretical concept of justice

Thus far in my reply to Nancy Fraser I have used a purely descriptive language to show that appropriate access to the moral content of social conflicts is only possible using a sufficiently differentiated concept of recognition. A first step toward this goal drew on a number of recent studies to show that the experience of social injustice always corresponds to the withholding of what is taken to be legitimate recognition. To this extent, the distinction between economic disadvantage and cultural degradation is phenomenologically secondary and rather signifies a difference in the perspective from which subjects experience social disrespect or humiliation. In order to be able to make these intuitions fruitful for social theory, in a second step I then tried to describe the rise of a liberal-capitalist social order as the differentiation of three spheres of recognition. Accordingly, in contemporary societies we can expect various types of morally substantive struggles or conflicts whose differences correspond to whether what is contested is the "just" application of the recognition principle of love, legal equality, or the merit principle. Of course, a direct consequence of this consideration is that the opposition of "distribution conflicts" and "struggles for recognition" is not very helpful, since it creates the impression that demands for economic redistribution can be understood independently of any experience of social disrespect. It seems much more plausible to me, to the contrary, to interpret distribution conflicts as a specific kind of struggle for recognition in which the appropriate evaluation of the social contributions of individuals or groups is contested. But in drawing this conclusion, I have not yet offered a single argument that would possess any kind of normative character. Rather, my intent being purely descriptive, my response has been limited to explaining the normative infrastructure of the capitalist constitutional state, so as to delineate the broad contours of the struggle for recognition.

Now, Nancy Fraser justifies her distinction between "distribution" and "cultural recognition" not only in terms of social theory but also with normative considerations. Her central argument here is that only the combination of economic and cultural justice can guarantee "participatory parity," which is to be understood as the highest moral principle of liberal societies; and she then links the development of such a conception of justice with a critique of recognition theory, which she takes to be too closely tied to the ethical idea of individual self-realization. My approach up to now appears to have no ready answer to the complex questions opened up by this normative turn in the argument. True, the entire project of a differentiated recognition theory is of course based on a certain moral intuition, but it has remained completely unarticulated as such. For the sake of a better overview, I would now like to systematically arrange the problems on the agenda in order to consider each of them in turn.

The shift to the normative becomes necessary as soon as we are no longer discussing the question of how the social struggles of the present are to be theoretically analyzed, but instead turn to the question of their moral evaluation. Of course, it is obvious that we cannot endorse every political revolt as such – that we cannot consider every demand for recognition as morally legitimate or acceptable. Instead, we generally only judge the objectives of such struggles positively when they point in the direction of social development that we can understand as approximating our ideas of a good or just society.[75] In principle, of course, other criteria, which instead have to do with goals of social efficiency or stability, could also play a deciding role here; but these, too, simply mirror value decisions, made on a higher level, concerning the normative meaning and purpose of a social order. To this extent, every evaluation of a social conflict situation depends upon showing the normative principles in which social morality or political ethics are anchored and by which they are guided beneath the surface. From this preliminary consideration arises the particular tasks whose execution Nancy Fraser and I must agree on if we wish to clarify our differences on the normative level. First of all, we need to spell out the principles we take to make up the normative kernel of the idea of a just and good society. Here the debate will lead to the question of how the principle of participatory parity relates to the normative ideas contained in the concept of "recognition" from a moral point of view (a). Once we clarify these differences, the next question would be how we think our different conceptions of a good or just social order can be justified. In this context, the problem thematized by Nancy Fraser will become acute: whether such a justification must have recourse to the ethical idea of the good life, or whether it can make do without any anchoring of this kind (b). Finally, out of this last problem emerges the question of how each of the differently formulated guiding principles is to be applied to social reality such that it can be called upon in moral judgments of social conflict situations. My suspicion is that the full extent of the differences between our positions will only become fully clear at this point (c). Naturally, a sufficiently differentiated concern with these three problem areas would require more space than is available to me here. For this reason, I must limit myself to abbreviated remarks on the debate's main points, in the hope that we will at least agree on the difficulty of the problems to be solved.

a) As indicated, in different parts of my response I have made use of the normative idea of recognition in a purely descriptive sense. My basic concern was to defend the thesis that the normative expectations subjects bring to society are oriented toward the social recognition of their capabilities by various generalized others. The implications of this moral-sociological finding can be further developed in two directions: the first concerning the subject's moral socialization, the second concerning the moral integration of society. As far as the theory of the subject is concerned, we have good reasons to assume that individual identity-formation generally takes place through stages of internalizing socially standardized recognition responses: individuals learn to see themselves as both full and special members of the community by gradually being assured of the specific capabilities and needs that constitute them as personalities through the supportive reaction patterns of their generalized interaction partners.[76] To this extent, every human subject depends essentially on a context of forms of social interaction governed by normative principles of mutual recognition; and the disappearance of such relations of recognition results in experiences of disrespect or humiliation that cannot fail to have damaging consequences for the individual's identity-formation. But this tight intermeshing of recognition and socialization gives rise in the opposite direction to an appropriate concept of society, which allows us to see social integration as a process of inclusion through stable forms of recognition. From the perspective of their members, societies only represent legitimate ordering structures to the extent they are in a position to guarantee reliable relations of mutual recognition on different levels. To this extent, the normative integration of societies occurs only through the institutionalization of recognition principles, which govern, in a comprehensible way, the forms of mutual recognition through which members are included into the context of social life.[77]

If we allow ourselves be led by these social-theoretical premises, they seem to me to have the consequence that a political ethics or social morality must be tailored to the quality of the socially guaranteed relations of recognition. The justice or well-being of a society is proportionate to its ability to secure conditions of mutual recognition under which personal identity-formation, hence individual self-realization, can proceed adequately. Of course, we should not think of this normative turn as a simple inference from the objective functional requirements of an ideal form of social coexistence. Rather, the demands of social integration can only be understood as referring to the normative principles of a political ethics because, and to the extent that, they are mirrored in the expectations of socially integrated subjects. But if this assumption is valid – and I am convinced that a great deal of evidence speaks for it, some of which I referred to in section one – then such a transition seems to me justified: in the choice of the basic principles by which we want to orient our political ethic, we rely not merely on empirically given interests, but rather only on those relatively stable expectations that we can understand as the subjective expression of imperatives of social integration. It is perhaps not entirely wrong to speak here of "quasi-transcendental interests" of the human race;[78] and possibly it is even justified to talk at this point of an "emancipatory" interest that aims at dismantling social asymmetries and exclusions.

Now, it has also become clear that the content of such expectations of social recognition can change with a society's structural transformation: only their form represents an anthropological constant, while they owe their specific direction and orientation to the established type of social integration. Here is not the place to defend the more far-reaching thesis that the normative structural change of society can for its part also be traced back to the impetus of a struggle for recognition. All in all, my idea is that, with regard to social development, we should be able to speak of moral progress at least to the extent that the demand for social recognition always possesses a surplus of validity and therefore in the long run brings about an increase in the quality of social integration. But for the purposes of my response to Nancy Fraser, it is only necessary to assert here that the fundamental interest in social recognition is always substantively shaped by the normative principles determined by the elementary structures of mutual recognition within a given social formation. From this follows the conclusion that at present we should orient a political ethics or social morality by the three principles of recognition that, within our societies, govern what legitimate expectations of recognition there can be among members of society. Hence, it is the three principles of love, equality, and merit that together determine what should now be understood by the idea of social justice. But before I develop the main features of this plural conception of justice, I need to clarify its relation to the conception outlined by Fraser.

At first sight, Fraser seems to favor a conception of social justice that bears the features of a pluralism of various principles or aspects. For her central idea on the normative level is indeed that only the elimination of both economic inequality and cultural humiliation can contribute to establishing a just society. However, with a second look it quickly becomes clear that it is really not a matter of a pluralism of principles, but rather only of two different fields of application of one and the same basic principle: economic redistribution and cultural recognition are measures that owe their normative justification to the fact that both represent means for realizing the single goal of "participatory parity." This goal is the highest principle in Fraser's approach, while the determination of two types of injustice is only the result of its application to the institutional conditions of our societies. Once we have clarified the related architectonic distinctions, the first question that arises is how the two approaches' normative intuitions are related: on the one hand, there seems to be the idea here that subjects are entitled to equal opportunities to participate in social life; on the other hand, there is the idea that subjects as it were deserve the amount of social recognition required for successful identity-formation. In one respect, these two intuitions are very similar, since the concept of recognition indeed links the possibility of identity-formation to the presupposition of participating in social interaction, thus giving participation great importance: only the subject who has learned, through the acknowledging responses of his or her social environment, "to appear in public without shame"[79] is able to develop the potential of his or her own personality free from coercion, and hence to build a personal identity. But this agreement – which in fact stems only from the vagueness of the concept of "social participation" – can in no way conceal the deeper differences. Even if the idea of uncoerced participation in public life plays a prominent role in both intuitions, for Fraser it serves above all to explain what it now means to speak of social justice, while for me it serves to explain the fact that successful identity-formation has a social, "public" side.

Perhaps it is best first to clarify this difference indirectly. It is the case that both Fraser and I proceed from the idea that, under the conditions of modern societies, every conception of justice must have an egalitarian character from the start, in the sense that all members of society regard one another as having equal rights and each is therefore accorded equal autonomy. But the difference between our approaches consists essentially in the fact that Fraser moves immediately from this starting point in individual autonomy to the idea of social participation, while I move from individual autonomy first to the goal of the most intact possible identity-formation, in order to then bring in principles of mutual recognition as that goal's necessary presupposition. To this extent, the two normative conceptions are based on different answers to the question of what we should refer to when we speak of the equality of all citizens. Put in terms of an ethics of particular goods, Nancy Fraser defines the "why" or "what for" of equality with reference to the good of participation, whereas I understand this "what for" as the good of personal identity-formation, whose realization I see as dependent on relations of mutual recognition. Now, as a result of these differences concerning the aim of equality, a second step would appear to involve examining the differences that open up between our approaches with regard to the sources or resources of equality. Here it would need to be shown why, in distinction to Fraser, I consider it correct to proceed from a plural conception of social justice. But before I can turn to this question, I must first address the problem of how we can each justify our different starting points. This is the point at which Nancy Fraser raises vehement objections against the attempt to tie the idea of social justice to a conception of the good life.

b) In what has been said so far I have already indirectly suggested how I conceive the normative justification of the idea that the quality of social relations of recognition should be the reference point of a conception of social justice. Thus, for modern societies I proceed from the premise that the purpose of social equality is to enable the personal identity-formation of all members of society. For me this formulation is equivalent to saying that enabling individual self-realization constitutes the real aim of the equal treatment of all subjects in our societies. Now, the question is how to get from such a (liberal) starting point to the normative conclusion that the quality of social relations of recognition should represent the central domain of a political ethics or social morality. Here we come to my idea outlined above that we should generalize our knowledge of the social preconditions of personal identity-formation into a conception that has the character of a theory of egalitarian ethical life (*Sittlichkeit*). Within such a conception, we express the conditions that, to the best of our knowledge, are indispensable to giving every individual an equal chance to realize his or her personality. The early Rawls puts assumptions of this (ethical) kind in his list of "basic goods," Joseph Raz in his explication of the preconditions of human well-being, the Hegel of the *Philosophy of Right* in his communication-theoretical determination of the existential conditions of the "free will."[80] All three authors tie a justification of their conceptions of social justice to an ethical theory that defines the socially influenced preconditions that must be available for individual subjects to realize their autonomy. And, on the basis of this connection to ethical premises, these approaches are now assigned to a tradition of "teleological liberalism." The advantage I see in such a conception is that it tries to spell out and justify what for the most part only ashamedly forms the hidden basis of procedural versions of liberalism: a normative idea of the goals for whose sake the establishment and realization of social justice represent a political task that we consider ethically well-grounded.

Now, in my view, Nancy Fraser takes an unclear in-between position within the spectrum of these two alternatives. On the one hand, she seems to want to tie the idea of social equality to a goal she refers to with the concept of "participation"; here realizing equality corresponds to the goal of putting all members of society in a position to take part in social life without disadvantage. But on the other hand, Fraser does not want this goal to be understood as the result of a conception of the good life, but simply as an explanation of the social implications of the idea of individual autonomy. Thus, she can attack the ethical overload of recognition theory without being forced herself to call upon ethical elements. What is unclear in this strategy is not only whether it is proceduralistic, in the sense that the idea of "participation" is regarded as a mark of precisely the public procedure by means of which autonomous subjects are to coordinate their individual freedom in a fair way. Such a Habermasian conception would, however, require a considerably thinner, more formal concept of public life than Fraser seems to have in mind with her idea of participation, which is clearly to include all dimensions of people's appearance in the public sphere. The democratic will-formation Habermas has in mind with his concept of "popular sovereignty" encompasses less than can suit Fraser's normative intuitions.[81] But if the idea of social participation is to be more comprehensive than the minimum accommodated by the procedural concept of democratic will-formation, then the question cannot be avoided of how it is to be filled in without recourse to ethical considerations. For we only learn which aspects of public life are important for realizing individual autonomy from a conception of personal well-being, however fragmentarily developed.

Because Nancy Fraser does not see this internal imbrication, there is something inherently arbitrary about her idea of participatory parity. We do not learn precisely why the right to equal participation in public life presupposes only the elimination of economic inequality and cultural humiliation, but not also self-respect with reference to individual achievements or ego strength acquired through socialization. And, on the same level, it is also uncertain why the economy and culture, but not the spheres of socialization or law, appear as possible obstacles to participation in social interaction. All these questions impose themselves because Fraser introduces her concept of "participation" without considering the functions it has to fulfill in view of the social preconditions of individual autonomy. Only a careful analysis of the connection between the realization of autonomy and forms of social interaction could have prevented this under-specification of her central normative concept. We need only recall the moral-psychological lengths John Rawls goes to when introducing the basic good of "self-respect" in his *Theory of Justice* to show the full extent to which normative theory depends on precisely the kinds of identity- and personality-theoretical set-pieces Fraser calls into question.[82] As soon as a theory of justice, starting from an egalitarian idea of individual autonomy, is to be developed that also includes substantive principles, we depend upon theoretical bridging arguments, with which either stipulated goals or conditional relations can be systematically justified. And if the corresponding solution amounts only to the idea of social participation, then general assumptions are necessary concerning the extent and forms of participation in social interaction that are helpful or conducive to individual autonomy.

In contrast to the early Rawls, however, I am convinced

that compiling so many theoretical arguments cannot replace the generalization of our knowledge into an always anticipatory conception of the good life. While it is true that we devise such a theory in light of all the knowledge at our disposal, we cannot hope to ever see it exhausted by empirical findings or theoretical assumptions. To this extent, even recognition theory – insofar as it is now understood as a teleological conception of social justice – only has the status of a hypothetically generalized outline of the good life: informed by converging funds of knowledge, such an outline determines the forms of mutual recognition subjects now need in order to develop the most intact possible identities.

c) Having outlined these reflections on the normative status of recognition theory with regard to the question of justice, the not inconsiderable task still remains of defining the guiding principles of social justice. And the question of how the corresponding principles can be brought to bear in judging social struggles also requires at least the rough outlines of an answer. In contrast to Nancy Fraser, who understands her principles of economic equality and the avoidance of social degradation as instrumental means for realizing participatory parity, I proceed from a plurality of three equally important principles of social justice. This tripartite division arises from the consideration that subjects in modern societies depend for their identity-formation on three forms of social recognition, based in the sphere-specific principles of love, equal legal treatment, and social esteem. I would like first to justify the idea of such a tripolar theory of justice, before addressing the question of its application to present-day conflict scenarios.

Until now, I have only outlined my reflections to the point where it became clear why a social morality needs to refer to the quality of the relations of social recognition. I see the decisive argument for this in the sufficiently justified thesis that, for the individual subject, the possibility of realizing individual autonomy depends on being able to develop an intact self-relation through the experience of social recognition. The connection to this ethical assumption in the outline of a social morality now makes room for a temporal element, insofar as the structure of the required recognition conditions continues to change with the historical process. What subjects can regard as dimensions of their personality for which they can legitimately expect social recognition at any given time depends on the normative mode of their inclusion into society, and hence on the differentiation of the spheres of recognition. Thus, the corresponding social morality can also be understood as a normative articulation of the principles that govern the way subjects recognize each other in a given society.[83] This initially only affirmative or perhaps even conservative task includes the idea that, at present, a theory of justice must encompass three equally important principles, which can together be understood as principles of recognition. In order to be able to actually make use of their autonomy, individual subjects are in a certain way entitled to be recognized in their neediness, their legal equality, or their social contributions, according to the kind of social relation at issue. As this formulation indicates, the content of what we call "just" is measured here in each case by the different kinds of social relations among subjects: if what is involved is a relation shaped by an appeal to love, then the neediness principle has priority; in relations shaped by law, the equality principle gets priority; and in cooperative relations, the merit principle holds. To be sure, in contrast to David Miller, who wants to proceed from a comparable pluralism of three principles of justice (need, equality, desert),[84] the tripartite division I propose arises neither from mere agreement with the empirical results of research on justice, nor from a social-ontological distinction between patterns of social relations, but rather from reflection on the historical conditions of personal identity-formation. Because we live in a social order in which individuals owe the possibility of an intact identity to affective care, legal equality, and social esteem, it seems to me appropriate, in the name of individual autonomy, to make the three corresponding recognition principles the normative core of a conception of social justice. A further difference from Miller's approach concerns the fact that he wants to understand his three principles solely as distributional principles, regulating how socially valued goods are to be distributed within each sphere, whereas I try to grasp the three principles first and foremost as forms of recognition linked to specific attitudes and moral considerations. And I would also only speak of distributional principles in an indirect sense, where these types of moral respect have consequences for the distribution of particular goods.

Despite all these difference, however, the essential commonalities between the two approaches should not be missed. Without recourse to teleological or ethical assumptions, Miller also proceeds from the conviction that the modern idea of social justice should be divided into three facets, each of which names one of the respects in which individuals are to be treated equally. Accordingly, he distinguishes between the principles of need, equality, and desert in the same way I have spoken of the differentiation of three recognition principles of love, legal equality, and social esteem. It should not be surprising that, in both cases, the term "equality" turns up simultaneously in two places, since this touches on the distinction between two levels of the conception of justice. On a higher level, it holds that all subjects equally deserve recognition of their need, their legal equality, or their achievements, according to the type of social relation. And, on a subordinate level, it then holds that the principle of legal autonomy implies the idea of equal treatment and thus in a strict sense has an egalitarian character.[85] So, to formulate it paradoxically, in the name of a higher-level equality, it is possible to appeal for the application of either the equality principle or the two other, not strictly egalitarian recognition principles, according to the sphere under consideration.

But the decisive question concerns the problem of how, beyond mere affirmation, such a recognition-theoretical conception of justice can take on a role that is critical and indeed progressive. For what above all is at issue between Fraser and myself is the extent to which, with the help of an appropriate theory, something normative can be said about the developmental direction present-day social conflicts should take. So far I have only spoken of the affirmative role the idea of justice I have outlined must be able to play, insofar as it tries to maintain an awareness of the irreducible plurality of principles of justice in modernity. As I have tried to make clear, here there are three independent, sphere-specific principles of recognition that must be affirmed as distinct standards of justice if the intersubjective conditions for the personal integrity of all subjects are to be equally protected. To be sure, this ability to differentiate – which could perhaps be called, following Michael Walzer, a justice-immanent "art of separation"[86] – does not yet address the critical role that such a conception of justice has to assume when it comes to the moral evaluation of social conflicts. In this second case, it can no longer simply be a matter of spelling out already-existing, socially anchored principles of justice in all their plurality; rather, what is at stake is the central, far more difficult task of developing normative criteria out of the plural concept of justice, by means of which contemporary developments can be criticized in light of future possibilities. If we do not want to get caught in a shortsighted presentism that proceeds only on the basis of the objectives of momentarily influential social movements,[87] we cannot avoid developing such criteria in connection with theses about the moral progress of society as a whole. For the evaluation of contemporary social conflicts requires, as Maeve Cooke has recently shown very clearly, a judgment of the normative potential of particular demands with regard to transformations that promise not only short-term improvement, but also allow us to expect a lasting rise in the moral level of social integration.[88] To this extent, the so far only crudely sketched theory of justice must be embedded within the comprehensive framework of a conception of progress that is in a position to determine a directed development in the moral constitution of society. Only on this basis can it be shown with more than a merely relativistic claim to justification to what extent certain social demands can be regarded as normatively justified.[89]

Now, these final pages cannot even present a bare outline of such a conception of progress. Indeed, throughout my reply I have given scattered indications of the necessity and at the same time the possibility of a conception of the directed development of the social relations of recognition; but here I can deliver nothing more than an abbreviated summary that essentially has the function of putting the recognition-theoretical conception of justice in a position to be able to make normatively justified judgments about present-day social conflicts.

In my overview of the recognition relations of liberal-capitalist societies, I already had to make a number of implicit assumptions about the moral direction of social development. For only on the assumption that the new order involves a morally superior form of social integration can its internal principles be considered a legitimate, justified starting point for outlining a political ethic. Like all internally situated social theorists who proceed from the legitimacy of the modern social order − be it Hegel, Marx, or Durkheim − I had to first presume the moral superiority of modernity by assuming that its normative constitution is the result of past directed development. This gave me criteria that allowed me to describe the differentiation of three distinct spheres of recognition as moral progress, albeit only in passing. With the development of the three separate spheres, I said, the opportunities increase for all members of the new type of society to achieve a higher degree of individuality, since they are able to experience more aspects of their own personalities along the different models of recognition. If these background convictions are now retrospectively made explicit, they yield two criteria that together can justify talk of progress in the relations of recognition. On the one hand, we see here a process of individualization, i.e., the increase of opportunities to legitimately articulate parts of one's personality; on the other hand, we see a process of social inclusion, i.e., the expanding inclusion of subjects into the circle of full members of society. It is easy to see how these two criteria are internally connected to the initial social-theoretical premises of a theory of recognition in the way that they outline two possibilities of an increase in social recognition. If social integration takes place by establishing relations of recognition through which subjects are confirmed in different aspects of their personalities and thus become members of society, then the moral quality of this social integration can improve through an increase in either the "recognized" parts of the personality or the inclusion of individuals – in short, through individualization or inclusion. From here it then seems justified to understand the breakthrough to the modern, liberal-capitalist social order as moral progress, since the differentiation of the three recognition spheres of love, legal equality, and the achievement principle went along with an increase in the social possibilities for individualization as well as a rise in social inclusion. Essential to this qualitative improvement is above all the fact that with the decoupling of legal recognition from social esteem, on the most basic level the idea came to the fore that, from now on, all subjects must have the same chance of individual self-realization through participation in relations of recognition.

Having thus briefly established why the moral infrastructure of modern, liberal-capitalist societies can be regarded as the legitimate starting point for a political ethic, the question then arises of how moral progress can be evaluated within such societies. It is clear that a solution to this problem can only be found within the framework of the tripolar model of justice that develops with the differentiation of three spheres of recognition as a normative reality. Because what is henceforth to be called "just" is to be measured, according to the sphere, by the idea of responsiveness to need, legal equality, or the merit principle, the parameters of moral progress within the new social order can also only be defined with reference to all three principles. What this could mean can be explained, in a first step, with the help of the idea of a "surplus of validity," which I already mentioned when introducing the three recognition spheres. Only then can I show, in a second step, that the critical task of a recognition-theoretical conception of justice need not be restricted to an advocatorial appeal to this sphere-specific surplus of validity, but can also include examination of the lines of demarcation between the spheres. In any event, here too I will have to be content with short explanations.

Progress in the conditions of social recognition takes place, as I said, along the two dimensions of individualization and social inclusion: either new parts of the personality are opened up to mutual recognition, so that the extent of socially confirmed individuality rises; or more persons are included into existing recognition relations, so that the circle of subjects who recognize one another grows. It is not clear, however, whether this (double) criterion of progress can find any application in the new, tripartite recognition order brought about by modern capitalist society. For each of the three recognition spheres is distinguished by normative principles which provide their own internal standards of what counts as "just" or "unjust." In my view, the only way forward here is the idea, outlined above, that each principle of recognition has a specific surplus of validity whose normative significance is expressed by the constant struggle over its appropriate application and interpretation. Within each sphere, it is always possible to set a moral dialectic of the general and the particular in motion: claims are made for a particular perspective (need, life-situation, contribution) that has not yet found appropriate consideration by appeal to a general recognition principle (love, law, achievement). In order to be up to the task of critique, the theory of justice outlined here can wield the recognition principles' surplus validity against the facticity of their social interpretation. As against the dominant interpretive praxis, it is shown that there are particular, hitherto neglected facts whose moral consideration would require an expansion of the spheres of recognition. To be sure, such critique can only attain a perspective that enables it to distinguish grounded from ungrounded claims by translating the previously outlined general criterion of progress into the semantic of each sphere of recognition. What can count as a rational or legitimate demand emerges from the possibility of understanding the consequences of implementing it as a gain in individuality or inclusion.

Even if this formulation might at first seem to recall the Hegelian philosophy of history, it is in fact meant only to name the theoretical conditions under which the recognition-theoretical conception of justice can now take on a critical role. We can only identify morally justified claims, which seems necessary for such a task, if we first name those principles of justice with reference to which legitimate demands can be made in the first place. In my model, this corresponds to the idea that we face three fundamental recognition principles in our societies, each with a specific normative surplus of validity that allows appeals to differences or states of affairs that have not yet been considered. But in order to now pick out morally justified particularities from the multitude of those typically asserted in social struggles for recognition, it is first necessary to apply a criterion of progress, however implicit. For only demands that potentially contribute to the expansion of social relations of recognition can be considered normatively grounded, since they point in the direction of a rise in the moral level of social integration. The two measures of individualization and inclusion, which I outlined above, represent the criteria by means of which this weighing can be accomplished.

Now, more would certainly need to be done to show how the criterion of progress could be applied within the three spheres of recognition. For what it means to speak of progress in the application of the equality principle only seems somewhat clear in the sphere of modern law,[90] while nothing comparable can be claimed for the spheres of love and achievement. As in many normative contexts, it may be helpful first to negatively reformulate the positive criteria, and thus to take the idea of eliminating obstacles as our starting point.[91] Moral progress in the sphere of love might then mean a step-by-step elimination of the role-clichés, stereotypes, and cultural ascriptions that structurally impede adaptation to others' needs; and in the recognition sphere of social esteem, it might mean radically scrutinizing the cultural constructions that, in the industrial-capitalist past, saw to it that only a small circle of activities were distinguished as "gainful employment."[92] However, such a sectorally differentiated model of progress faces a further difficulty which I would like to address in conclusion, since it clarifies the full complexity of our task.

In explaining the fact that, with the construction of the social-welfare state, the principle of equal legal treatment made its way into the sphere of achievement-based esteem, it already emerged how moral progress in the modern social order can also be achieved by drawing new borders between the individual spheres of recognition. For there can be no question that it was in the interest of the classes constantly threatened by poverty to decouple part of social status from the achievement principle and instead make it an imperative of legal recognition. We can thus speak of moral progress in such cases of boundary-shifting when a partial shift to a new principle lastingly improves the social conditions of personal identity-formation for members of particular groups or classes. And it seems above all to be processes of legalization – expanding the principle of equal legal treatment – that have the inherent potential to correctively intervene into other recognition spheres, ensuring the protection of the minimum preconditions of identity. This shows the moral logic that forms the basis of every boundary-shift from the sphere of law in the direction of the other two recognition spheres. Since the normative principle of modern law, understood as the principle of mutual respect among autonomous persons, has an inherently unconditional character, those affected can call on it the moment they see that the conditions for individual autonomy are no longer adequately protected in other spheres. Examples of such processes of legalization triggered "from below" include not only struggles for the realization of social rights, but also the complex debates taking place today over the legal guarantee of equal treatment within marriage and the family. Here, the central argument is that, in view of the structural domination of men in the private sphere, the preconditions for women's self-determination can only be secured when they take the form of contractually guaranteed rights, and hence are made an imperative of legal recognition.[93]

These considerations must lead to the conclusion that a recognition-theoretical conception of justice can take up the task of critique not only where what is at stake is a defense of moral progress within the respective spheres of recognition. Rather, we must always reflexively examine the boundaries that have been established between the domains of the different recognition principles, since we can never rule out the suspicion that the existing division of labor between the moral spheres impairs the opportunities for individual identity-formation. And not infrequently, such questioning will lead to the conclusion that an expansion of individual rights is required, since the conditions for respect and autonomy are not adequately guaranteed under the normative principle of "love" or "achievement." In any event, the critical spirit of such a conception of justice can conflict with its own preservative function, since there will also always be a need to maintain the separation of spheres, all the moral legitimation for boundary-shifting notwithstanding. For, as we have seen, in modern society the conditions for individual self-realization are only socially secured when subjects can experience intersubjective recognition not only of their personal autonomy, but of their specific needs and particular capacities as well.

Notes

* For advice, suggestions, and critical commentary, I would like to thank Alessandro Ferrara, Rainer Forst, Martin Frank, Christoph Menke, Beate Rössler, and Hartmut Rosa.

1 Cf. esp. Nancy Fraser, "What's Critical About Critical Theory? The Case of Habermas and Gender," "The Struggle Over Needs: Outline of a Socialist-Feminist Critical Theory of Late Capitalist Political Culture," and "Foucault on Modern Power: Empirical Insights and Normative Confusions," in *Unruly Practices: Power, Discourse, and Gender in Contemporary Social Theory* (Minneapolis & London 1989); Fraser, *Justice Interruptus: Critical Reflections on the "Postsocialist" Condition* (New York & London 1997).

2 Charles Taylor, "The Politics of Recognition," in Amy Gutmann, ed., *Multiculturalism and the Politics of Recognition* (Princeton 1994).

3 Axel Honneth, *The Struggle for Recognition: The Moral Grammar of Social Conflicts*, trans. Joel Anderson (Cambridge, MA 1995) and "Eine Gesellschaft ohne Demütigung? Zu Avishai Margalits Entwurf einer 'Politik der Würde'," in *Die zerrissene Welt des Sozialen*, expanded edition (Frankfurt/Main 1999).

4 Cf. the similar argument, if with fundamentally different goals, by Richard Rorty, *Achieving Our Country: Leftist Thought in Twentieth-Century America* (Cambridge, MA 1999), ch. 3.

5 See Karl-Werner Brand, *Aufbruch in eine andere Gesellschaft: neue soziale Bewegungen in der Bundesrepublik* (Frankfurt/Main 1986); Joachim Raschke, *Soziale Bewegungen: ein historischsystematischer Grundriß* (Frankfurt/Main 1988).

6 See, *inter alia*, Taylor, "The Politics of Recognition"; J. Goldsteun and J. Rayner, "The Politics of Identity in Late Modern Society," *Theory and Society* 23 (1994): 367–84; Jean Cohen, "Strategy or Identity: New Theoretical Paradigms and Contemporary Social Movements," *Social Research* 52 (1985): 663–716.

7 See Helmut Dubiel, *Theory and Politics: Studies in the Development of Critical Theory*, trans. Benjamin Gregg (Cambridge, MA 1985), pt. A.

8 Pierre Bourdieu et al., *The Weight of the World: Social Suffering in Contemporary Society*, trans. Priscilla Parkhurst Ferguson (Stanford 1999). Cf. *Daedalus*, issue on "Social Suffering," 125, no. 1 (1996).

9 Bourdieu, *The Weight of the World*, 627.

10 Albert Hirschman, "Social Conflicts as Pillars of Democratic Market Societies," in *A Propensity for Self-Subversion* (Cambridge, MA 1995).

11 Craig Calhoun, "The Politics of Identity and Recognition," in *Critical Social Theory* (Oxford & Cambridge, MA 1995), 215.

12 Taylor, "The Politics of Recognition."

13 Calhoun, "The Politics of Identity and Recognition," 216. Many texts by Isaiah Berlin offer further support for Calhoun's continuity argument; see, e.g., "Benjamin Disraeli, Karl Marx, and the Search for Identity," in *Against the Current: Essays in the History of Ideas* (New York 1980), 252–86; see also Dieter Senghaas's succinct essay, "Die Wirklichkeiten der Kulturkämpfe," *Leviathan* (1995): 197–212.

14 See, e.g., Edward P. Thompson, *Customs in Common: Studies in Traditional Popular Culture* (New York 1993); Barrington Moore, *Injustice: The Social Basis of Obedience and Revolt* (New York 1978).

15 Jean Cohen, *Class and Civil Society: The Limits of Marxian Critical Theory* (Amherst 1982), offers a convincing critique of the historical-philosophical implications of Marxist class theory.

16 Still first-rate in this respect is Jeffrey Alexander, *Theoretical Logic in Sociology: Durkheim* (London 1982), esp. chs. 2, 3, and 6; also excellent: David Lockwood, "The Weakest Link in the Chain? Some Comments on the Marxist Theory of Action," *Research in the Sociology of Work* 1 (1981): 435ff.

17 For a relatively early version of this thesis in Habermas, see the essays collected in the fourth section of *Zur Rekonstruktion des Historischen Materialismus* (Frankfurt/Main 1976); partial translation in *Communication and the Evolution of Society*, trans. Thomas McCarthy (Boston 1979). A revised version has since appeared in *Between Facts and Norms: Contributions to a Discourse Theory of Law and Democracy*, trans. William Rehg (Cambridge, MA 1996).

18 See Joshua Cohen, "The Arc of the Moral Universe," *Philosophy & Public Affairs* 26, no. 2 (1997): 91–134.

19 Formally, this is Barrington Moore's argument in *Injustice*.

20 Thompson, *Customs in Common*.

21 Richard Sennett and Jonathan Cobb's *The Hidden Injuries of Class* (Cambridge, MA 1972) was path-breaking here.

22 Tzvetan Todorov, *Life in Common: An Essay in General Anthropology*, trans. Katherine Golsan and Lucy Golsan (Lincoln, NE 2001); Michael Ignatieff, *The Needs of Strangers* (New York 1985); Avishai Margalit, *The Decent Society*, trans. Naomi Goldblum (Cambridge, MA 1996).

23 See on this the suggestive observations in Christopher F. Zurn, "The Normative Claims of Three Types of Feminist Struggles for Recognition," *Philosophy Today* 41, supplement (1997): 73–78; Lawrence Blum, "Recognition, Value, and Equality: A Critique of Charles Taylor's

and Nancy Fraser's Accounts of Multiculturalism," *Constellations* 5, no. 1 (1998): 51–68.

24 On the concept of "self-relation," cf. Ernst Tugendthat, *Self-Consciousness and Self-Determination*, trans. Paul Stern (Cambridge, MA 1986).

25 See Jonathan Lear, *Love and its Place in Nature* (New York 1990).

26 See Philip Ariès, *Centuries of Childhood: A Social History of Family Life*, trans. Robert Baldick (New York 1962).

27 Cf. the sociological analysis by Tilman Allert, *Die Familie. Fallstudien zur Unverwüstlichkeit einer Lebensform* (Berlin 1997), esp. pts. 4.1 and 4.2.

28 Cf. Axel Honneth, *The Struggle for Recognition*, p. 179 ff.

29 Cf. Heinz Kluth, *Sozialeprestige and sozialer Status* (Stuttgart 1957) and "Amtsgedanke und Pflichtethos in der Industriegesellschaft," *Hamburger Jahrbuch für Wirtschafts- und Gesellschaftspolitik* 10 (1965): 11–22; Claus Offe, *Industry and Inequality: The Achievement Principle in Work and Social Status*, trans. James Wickham (New York 1977), esp. ch. 2.

30 On the dissolution of the honor principle, see Peter Berger, Brigitte Berger, and Hansfried Kellner, *The Homeless Mind: Modernization and Consciousness* (New York 1973), 83–96; Hans Speier, "Honor and Social Structure," *Social Structure and the Risks of War* (New York 1952), 36ff.

31 See Frank Parkin, *Class Inequality and Political Order: Social Stratification in Capitalist and Communist Societies* (New York & Washington 1971), esp. chs. 1 and 3; Reinhard Kreckel, *Politische Soziologie der sozialen Ungleichheit* (Frankfurt/Main & New York 1992), esp. ch. 2.

32 Richard Münch, "Zahlung und Achtung. Die Interpenetration von Ökonomie und Moral," *Zeitschrift für Soziologie* 23, no. 5 (1994): 388–411.

33 See e.g., Georg Simmel, "The Metropolis and Modern Life," in Kurt S. Wolff, ed., *The Sociology of Georg Simmel* (New York 1950), and *Brücke and Tür*, ed. Margarete Susman and Michael Landmann (Stuttgart 1957), 227–42. For a recent general approach to the analysis of such anonymous patterns of interaction, see Uwe Sander, *Die Bindung der Unverbindlichkeit* (Frankfurt/Main 1998).

34 I have recently essayed a reactualization of the *Philosophy of Right* that centers on the grounding of the shift to the sphere of ethics in the theory of freedom. Axel Honneth, *Suffering from Indeterminacy: An Attempt at a Reactualization of Hegel's Philosophy of Right, Spinoza Lectures* (Assen 2000).

35 I here am correcting the thesis, still maintained in my *Struggle for Recognition*, that love "does not admit of the potential for normative

development" (p. 282). I am now convinced that love itself possesses a surplus of normative validity that emerges through (interpretive) conflicts.

36 Cf., e.g., Habermas, *Between Facts and Norms*, esp. ch. 9 and "Struggles for Recognition in the Democratic Constitutional State," *The Inclusion of the Other: Studies in Political Theory* (Cambridge, MA 1998).

37 Christoph Menke, *Tragödie im Sittlichen. Gerechtigkeit und Freiheit nach Hegel* (Frankfurt/Main 1996), offers a convincing interpretation of such a tension in Hegel.

38 See Honneth, *The Struggle for Recognition*, ch. 9 and *Suffering from Indeterminacy*.

39 See Axel Honneth, "Zwischen Gerechtigkeit und affektiver Bindung. Die Familie im Brennpunkt moralischer Kontroversen," in *Das Andere der Gerechtigkeit. Aufsätze zur praktischen Philosophie* (Frankfurt/Main 2000), 193–215.

40 On the social construction of "gainful work," see the short but very informative article by Jürgen Kocka, "Erwerbsarbeit ist nur ein kulturelles Konstrukt," *Frankfurter Rundschau*, May 9, 2000, 24.

41 For one of the most convincing analyses of this "naturalism" (as the "naturalization of social classifications") in German, see Regine Gildemeister and Angelika Wetterer, "Wie Geschlechter gemacht werden. Die sociale Konstruktion der Zweigeschlechtigkeit und ihre Reifizierung in der Frauenforschung," in *Traditionen Brüche. Entwicklungen feministischer Theorie* (Freiburg 1992), 201–54. Reflecting the ethnomethodology of authors such as Garfinkel and Goffman, the article is primarily indebted to Mary Douglas, *How Institutions Think* (Syracuse, NY 1986).

42 See Kreckel, *Politische Soziologie der sozialen Ungleichheit*, 92f.

43 See Münch, "Zahlung und Achtung." For a theory aligned with this process, now see Frank Nullmeier, *Politische Theorie des Sozialstaats* (Frankfurt/Main & New York 2000).

44 On the logic of this classical argument for the introduction of social rights, see Thomas H. Marshall, *Class, Citizenship, and Social Development* (Garden City, NY 1964).

45 For the methodological claim of such a "moral" historical explanation, see Cohen, "The Arc of the Moral Universe."

46 Karl Marx, "Critique of the Gotha Programme," in *Marx/Engels Collected Works, vol. 24, 1874–83* (Moscow 1975), esp. pt. IV.

47 Jürgen Habermas supplies the framework for such a critique of Marx in "Historical Materialism and the Development of Normative Structures," in *Communication and the Evolution of Society*.

48 For reservations in this regard similar to my own, see Iris Marion Young, "Unruly Categories: A Critique of Nancy Fraser's Dual Systems Theory," *New Left Review* 222 (March–April 1997): 147–60. Arguing

against the prevalent trend, Young attempts to locate the dimension of recognition in the so-called distribution struggles themselves.

49 The best material for reincorporating such a concept of social struggle into social theory is still offered by historical or ethnological studies. Along with the above-mentioned work by E.P. Thompson and Barrington Moore, two books by James C. Scott are here especially important: *Weapons of the Weak: Everyday Forms of Peasant Resistance* (New Haven 1985) and *Domination and the Art of Resistance: Hidden Transcripts* (New Haven & London 1990). In my *Struggle for Recognition*, ch. 8, I have already defined the outlines of a systematic theory of recognition as, *inter alia*, an effort to link such studies with moral theory: this through a focus on experiences of social disrespect as the actual motivation for resistance. The present text involves an effort to further clarify such a linkage by considering the moral justification of the experiences.

50 See the impressive collection of material in: Robert C. Solomon, *A Passion for Justice: Emotions and the Origins of the Social Contract* (Reading, MA 1990); cf. Karl Marx, "Proceeding of the Sixth Rhine Province Assembly. Third Article: Debates on the Law on Thefts of Wood," trans. Clement Dutt, in *Marx/Engels Collected Works, vol. 1, August 1835–March 1843* (Moscow 1975): 224–63.

51 Habermas, *Between Facts and Norms*, ch. 9.

52 This formulation is above all directed against objections to my approach to recognition, like that of Alexander García Düttmann, that argue that I ignore the constitutive role of the experience of "difference" in favor of a philosophy of reconciliation. See Düttmann, *Between Cultures: Tensions in the Struggle for Recognition*, trans. Kenneth B. Woodgate (New York & London 2000), 137–66.

53 One of the most convincing attempts in the German-speaking world to show the subjective tension between normative achievement principle and "unjust" evaluation comes from a research team led by Lothar Hack et al., *Leistung und Herrschaft. Soziale Strukturzusammenhänge subjektiver Relevanz bei jüngeren Industriearbeitern* (Frankfurt/Main & New York 1979), esp. ch. 8.

54 For an overview, see Gildemeister and Wetterer, "Wie Geschlechter gemacht werden"; Angelika Wetterer, ed., *Profession und Geschlecht. Über die Marginalität von Frauen in hochqualifizierten Berufen* (Frankfurt/Main & New York 1992); Wetterer, ed., *Die soziale Konstruktion von Geschlecht in Professionalisierungsprozessen* (Frankfurt/Main & New York 1995).

55 For numerous examples, see Anne Witz, *Professions and Patriarchy* (London & New York 1992).

56 For such a perspective in the case of ethic conflicts, influenced by

Pierre Bourdieu, see Klaus Eder and Oliver Schmidtke, "Ethnische Mobilisierung und die Logik von Identitätskämpfen. Eine situationstheoretische Perspektive jenseits von 'Rational Choice'," *Zeitschrift für Soziologie* 27, no. 6 (1998): 418–37.

57 Kreckel, *Politische Soziologie der sozialen Ungleichheit*, 100.

58 See e.g., Marshall Sahlins, *Culture and Practical Reason* (Chicago 1976), esp. chs. 4 and 5.

59 Cf. Jürgen Habermas, *"Technik" und "Wissenschaft" als Ideologie* (Frankfurt/Main 1968); partial translation in *Toward a Rational Society*, trans. Jeremy Shapiro (Boston 1970).

60 Honneth, *The Struggle for Recognition*, esp. ch. 8.

61 To this extent, I also consider Martin Fuchs' objection that I treat "confrontations over social value models" as if they played no role in social "struggles for recognition" unjustified (*Kampf um Differenz. Repräsentation, Subjektivität und soziale Bewegungen. Das Beispiel Indiens* (Frankfurt/Main 1999), 323). I do maintain, however, that such value conflicts are usually channeled through reference to specific principles of recognition held to be legitimate.

62 Fraser, "Struggle over Needs."

63 Will Kymlicka, *Finding Our Way: Rethinking Ethnocultural Relations in Canada* (Toronto 1998), esp. ch. 6. My thanks to Martin Frank for referring me to this book.

64 This should not, however, lead to the conclusion that distinctions between "desired, self-identified" and "non-intentional, subjectivized" collectives are no longer meaningful. The question is only whether such distinctions are now still significant from a normative point of view. On the problem in general and the corresponding terminology, see Carolin Emcke, *Kollektive Identitäten. Sozialphilosophische Grundlagen* (Frankfurt/Main 2000).

65 See Bernhard Peters, "Understanding Multiculturalism," *IIS-Arbeitspapier* 14, 1999, Bremen University.

66 On the connection between anti-discrimination policies and the equality principle, now see Rainer Nickel's meticulous dissertation, *Gleichheit und Differenz in der vielfältigen Republik* (Baden-Baden 1999), esp. ch. 2.

67 Peters, "Understanding Multiculturalism."

68 See Martin Frank's excellent dissertation, *Probleme einer interkulturellen Gerechtigkeitstheorie*, J.W. Goethe Universität, Frankfurt/Main, 1999.

69 Peters, "Understanding Multiculturalism."

70 Considerations of this kind are to be found in Avishai Margalit's *The Decent Society*, pt. 4.

71 See Nickel, *Gleichheit und Differenz*, esp. ch. 3.

72 Charles Taylor has called attention to this in "The Politics of Recognition," esp. 67ff; see also Peters, "Understanding Multiculturalism."

73 See Habermas, "Struggles for Recognition in the Democratic Constitutional State."

74 See e.g., Frank, *Probleme einer interkulturellen Gerechtigkeitstheorie.*

75 See Axel Honneth, "Reply to Andreas Kalyvas," *European Journal of Social Theory* 2, no. 2 (1999): 249–52.

76 Considerations of this kind, already present in my *Struggle for Recognition* (esp. chs. 4 and 5), have been further developed in Honneth, "Postmodern Identity and Object-Relations Theory: On the Supposed Obsolescence of Psychoanalysis," *Philosophical Explorations* 2, no. 3 (1997).

77 Interesting references to such a concept of social legitimation, which tie the moral acceptability of a society's legal order to the opportunities for experiencing social recognition, are found in Lawrence Thomas, "Characterizing the Evil of American Slavery and the Holocaust," in David Theo Goldberg and Michel Krausz, eds, *Jewish Identity* (Philadelphia 1993), 153–76. The notion of a "social contract," as developed by Barrington Moore in *Injustice*, should of course also be understood in precisely this sense.

78 I am here naturally playing on the corresponding concept in the early Habermas (*Knowledge and Human Interests*, trans. Jeremy Shapiro (Boston 1971)), which I believe retains its value in altered form. I find a similar orientation in Jonathan Lear's argument (*Love and its Place in Nature*, esp. ch. 7) that human love represents "a basic natural force."

79 Adam Smith, *An Inquiry into the Nature and Causes of the Wealth of Nations* (London 1910), 351f.

80 See John Rawls, *A Theory of Justice*, revised edition (Cambridge, MA 1999), ch. 2, § 15; Joseph Raz, *The Morality of Freedom* (Oxford 1986), ch. IV; G.W.F. Hegel, *Elements of the Philosophy of Right*, ed. Allen W. Wood, trans. H.B. Nisbet (Cambridge 1991).

81 See Habermas, *Between Facts and Norms*, ch. 3.

82 Rawls, *A Theory of Justice*, ch. 7, § 67.

83 With this historicist reformulation, I hope to at least in part respond to the objections of Christopher Zurn, "Anthropology and Normativity: A Critique of Axel Honneth's 'Formal Conception of Ethical Life'," *Philosophy & Social Criticism* 26, no. 1 (2000): 115–24.

84 David Miller, *Principles of Social Justice* (Cambridge, MA 1999).

85 For such a distinction between "first-order" and "second-order" justice that does allow appeals for an ethic of care in the name of universal justice (as impartiality) on the second level, see Brian Barry's impressive reflections in *Justice as Impartiality* (Oxford 1995), chs. 9 and 10.

86 Michael Walzer, "Liberalism and the Art of Separation," *Political Theory* 12 (1984).

87 This is of course the danger I see facing Nancy Fraser's normative-political proposals. To this extent, the one-sidedness of her social diagnosis (see section I above) would correspond to a one-sidedness on the level of the application of her normative conception of justice.

88 Maeve Cooke, "Between 'Objectivism' and 'Contextualism': The Normative Foundations of Social Philosophy," *Critical Horizons* 1, no. 2 (2000).

89 Indications of such a conception of moral progress, which takes account of an "expansion" of relations of recognition, are already to be found in my *Struggle for Recognition*, ch. 9.

90 See e.g., Habermas, *Between Facts and Norms*, ch. 9.

91 On such a negative procedure, see e.g., Margalit, *The Politics of Dignity*; Jonathan Allen, "Decency and the Struggle for Recognition," *Social Theory and Practice* 24, no. 3 (1998): 449–69.

92 See Kocka, "Erwerbsarbeit is nur ein kulturelles Konstrukt."

93 For arguments of this sort see in general: Susan Moller Okin, *Justice, Gender, and the Family* (New York 1989); Jeremy Waldron convincingly defends such a concept of rights in "When Justice Replaces Affection: The Need for Rights," in *Liberal Rights: Collected Papers 1981–1991* (Cambridge 1993), 370–91.

Translated by Joel Golb and James Ingram

3

Distorted Beyond All Recognition:
A Rejoinder to Axel Honneth

Nancy Fraser

Those who would renew the project of Critical Theory today face a daunting task.[1] Unlike earlier Frankfurt School thinkers, they cannot assume a political culture in which emancipatory hopes find focus in socialism, labor holds pride of place among social movements, and social egalitarianism enjoys broad support. Rather, they face an "exhaustion of [left-wing] utopian energies" and a decentered proliferation of social movements, many of which seek recognition of group difference, not economic equality.[2] Unlike their predecessors, too, today's exponents of Critical Theory cannot treat orthodox Marxism as an influential foil against which to assert the claims of culture and psychology. Rather, thanks to the confluence of neoliberalism and "the cultural turn," they must theorize the relation of culture and capitalism in a climate that conspires to repress the critique of political economy. Unlike earlier left-Hegelians, moreover, they cannot conceive society as a culturally homogeneous bounded whole, in which political claims can be adjudicated ethically, by appeal to a single shared value horizon. Rather, thanks to the complex processes that go under the shorthand term "globalization," they must address contexts in which value horizons are pluralized, fractured, and cross-cutting. Unlike their predecessors, finally, today's critical theorists cannot assume that all normatively justified claims will converge on a single program for institutional change. Rather, they must take on the hard cases – those, for example, in which claims for minority cultural recognition conflict with claims for gender equality – and tell us how to resolve them.

These conditions frame my debate with Axel Honneth. It is in response to their challenges that each of us has proposed to reconstruct the conceptual underpinnings of Critical Theory. And it is in the hope of satisfying their imperatives that each of us has devised a framework in which the category of recognition plays a major role. In both our theories, that category responds to several needs: on one level, it helps position critique in relation to contemporary social struggles; on another, it serves to theorize the place of culture in present-day capitalism; on yet a third, it promises to supply standards of justice that can adjudicate current claims. For both of us, therefore, recognition is central to the effort to reconstruct Critical Theory in a form adequate to present conditions.

Nevertheless, Honneth and I situate recognition very differently. He proposes a monistic framework in which that concept holds exclusive sway. In his view, a properly "differentiated" account of recognition is all that is required in a Critical Theory. There is no need for a second categorial axis oriented to distributive injustice and to the economic logic of globalizing capitalism. Recognition alone suffices to capture all the normative deficits of contemporary society, all the societal processes that generate them, and all the political challenges facing those seeking emancipatory change.

My own use of recognition is entirely different. Far from comprehending the totality of moral life, recognition for me is one crucial but limited dimension of social justice. And far from single-handedly orchestrating all social subordination, the "recognition order" of capitalist society is but one aspect of a larger complex that also includes market mechanisms. For me, accordingly, an approach centered exclusively on recognition cannot suffice. Rather, Critical Theory must situate recognition as one categorial axis in a framework that also encompasses distribution. Thus, I have proposed a "perspectival-dualist" framework of redistribution and recognition as an alternative to Honneth's monism.

Which of these approaches should critical theorists prefer? The choice depends on three issues that have become central to the present debate. The first concerns what we may call "the empirical reference point" of Critical Theory. At a time when Marxian metanarratives have lost all credibility, there can be no metaphysically designated agent of emancipation and no a prioristically identified addressee of critique. Absent such essentialist guarantees, the critic confronts decentered congeries of social movements, whose claims often concern issues of identity and are normatively ambiguous. In this context, there is no escaping the pressing question: How should Critical Theory position itself in relation to the current political conjuncture and especially to movements that seek recognition? How shall it establish both a foothold in the empirical world and a critical stance?

A second issue concerns the place of culture in the emerging new phase of capitalist society. Characterized alternatively as post-Fordism, globalization, and the information age, this phase is one in which culture has assumed a new salience – witness the growing weight of religion and ethnicity in the constitution of social identities, the heightened awareness of cultural differences, the expanding reach of global media, and the intensified cultural contestation that marks today's struggles for recognition. In this context, intellectual paradigms that posit the primacy of the economic appear deeply inadequate, while approaches that prioritize culture are attractive to many. The result is a new set of challenges for Critical Theory: How should it understand the emerging phase of capitalism, in which cultural contestation plays so prominent a role? And with what social-theoretical tools? How shall it position itself in relation to the cultural turn in social theory?

A third issue concerns the normative standards informing

critique. The background here, once again, is accelerated globalization, in which heightened economic interdependence coexists with increased transcultural interaction. In this context, there exists no shared, authoritative ideal of human flourishing. Rather, everyone lives cheek by jowl with "others," whose views of the good life diverge from their own. In this situation, Critical Theory cannot rely on any single, determinate set of ethical ideals. But neither can it embrace the cheerful anti-normativism – always in any case cryptonormative – recently fashionable in poststructuralist circles. Under these conditions, what sort of normative standards can Critical Theory lay claim to, and on the basis of what sort of justification?

In what follows, I shall examine my differences with Honneth on these three issues. In each case, I shall assess the relative merits of his recognition monism and my perspectival dualism of redistribution and recognition. In each case, too, I shall argue that Honneth's approach is inferior. I shall claim, first, that it fails to secure a credible empirical reference point for Critical Theory; second, that it fails to furnish a tenable account of the place of culture in contemporary capitalism; and third, that it fails to supply a set of normative standards that can adjudicate today's claims for recognition. I shall also argue that the root problem in each case is the same: Honneth overextends the category of recognition to the point that it loses its critical force. Inflating that concept beyond all recognition, he transforms a limited but precise instrument of social criticism into a bloated and blunted catchall that fails to rise to the challenges of our time.

I. On the Place of Experience in Critical Theory: Against the Reduction of Political Sociology to Moral Psychology

The question of an "empirical reference point" arises in this debate because both Honneth and I endorse a defining feature of Critical Theory: its distinctive dialectic of immanence and transcendence. Both of us reject the externalist stance of traditional theories that purport to judge social arrangements from on high, claiming a God's-eye-view wholly independent of the society in question. Rather, both of us assume that critique achieves traction only insofar as it discloses tensions and possibilities that are in some sense immanent to the configuration at hand. And we both seek to develop a language of criticism that can speak to the social subjects we aim to enlighten. At the same time, however, both Honneth and I reject the strong internalism of historicist hermeneutics. Not content merely to explicate the meanings sedimented in given traditions, both of us assume that critique can harbor a radical potential only if the gap between norm and the given is kept open. And we both assume that valid norms transcend the immediate context that generates them. Thus, far from restricting ourselves to criticism that is strictly internal, we both seek concepts with "surplus validity."

In general, then, both Honneth and I espouse Critical Theory's signature goal of accommodating immanence and transcendence simultaneously. Seeking a *via media* between positivist externalism and historicist internalism, both of us seek a foothold in the social world that simultaneously points beyond it.

Nevertheless, Honneth and I disagree as to how best to achieve this shared aim. His strategy for accommodating immanence and transcendence is to ground Critical Theory in a moral psychology of prepolitical suffering. Identifying immanence with subjective experience, he proposes to connect critique with its social context by deriving its normative concepts from the sufferings, motivations, and expectations of social subjects. This strategy is risky, however, as it threatens to collapse normativity into the given. To forestall this danger, Honneth resolves to take distance from the political disputes of the present. Thus, he determines to secure transcendence by locating an "independent" stratum of moral experience, unaffected by public-sphere claims-making. Fearing over-identifi-cation with contemporary social movements, yet still seeking an empirical reference point, he professes to find a body of pristine experience in inchoate everyday suffering that has not been politicized. Claiming to reconstruct that experience, he then purports to uncover the single basic moral expectation underlying all social discontent: that one's personal identity be adequately recognized. It follows, in his view, that the drive to secure recognition of identity represents the core of all moral experience and the deep grammar of all normativity. Critical Theory, therefore, should inscribe this imperative as the center-piece of its categorial framework.

In general, then, Honneth grounds his recognition monism in a moral psychology of prepolitical suffering. But far from establishing a genuine dialectic of immanence and transcen-dence, this strategy encounters difficulties at every point. For starters, Honneth's reading of prepolitical experience is dubi-ous. His appeals to social research notwithstanding, it is by no means clear that daily discontent is always a matter of denied recognition. In fact, the idea that one single motivation under-lies all such discontent is *prima facie* implausible. A less tenden-tious reading of a broader range of research sources would doubtless reveal a multiplicity of motives – including resent-ment of unearned privilege, abhorrence of cruelty, aversion to arbitrary power, revulsion against gross disparities of income and wealth, antipathy to exploitation, dislike of supervision, and indignation at being marginalized or excluded. (The list would be far longer, of course, if it also included all those less admirable motives, such as hatred of those who are different, that also suffuse daily discontent.) If these motivations *could* be subsumed under an overarching normative rubric, the latter could not be anything so determinate as the expectation that one's personal identity be recognized. Rather, it would have to be something more general, such as the expectation that one be treated fairly. That thesis could encompass experiences that Honneth's cannot, such as the felt unfairness of social arrangements that doom some people to stark deprivation, while others enjoy fabulous wealth – an experience documented, *inter alia*, in Michael Harrington's *The Other America*.[3] Certainly, such arrangements violate fundamental notions of the equal moral worth of human beings (an idea I shall examine in section III); and they clearly impede parity of participation in social life. But they are not best interpreted as violations of personal identity. To insist on construing them as such is to shift the focus away from society and onto the self, implanting an excessively personalized sense of injury.[4] Far from clarifying matters, the net effect is to stretch the concept of recognition to breaking point. Thus, instead of treating denied recognition as the normative kernel of all daily suffering, one would do better to construe it as one kind of felt unfairness among others.

The misreading of prepolitical suffering is hardly the only difficulty with Honneth's strategy, however. More troubling still is his designation of such suffering as Critical Theory's privileged reference point. That designation is questionable on several levels. Empirically, it is by no means clear that such suffering is really untainted by publicly circulated vocabularies of normative judgment. Certainly, in democratic societies, no firewall insulates daily life from political contestation in the public sphere. As a result, the quotidian experiences of injustice that Honneth casts as politically innocent are in fact mediated by idioms of public claims-making – witness Jane Mansbridge's ethnography of "everyday feminism," which reveals that US women's apparently nonpolitical experiences of daily suffering are suffused with interpretative schemata drawn from political feminism.[5] Conceptually, moreover, the appeal to a stratum of experience that is simultaneously empirical and primordial is incoherent. An instance of "the myth of the given," it fails to appreciate that we can never have access to moral experience unmediated by normative discourses, as the latter necessarily infiltrate not only the experiences of social actors but also the perspectives of those who study them.[6] Thus, to borrow an expression from Richard Rorty, there can be no "independent" moral psychology that captures "Morality's Own Language."[7] Normatively, finally, it is doubtful that prepolitical experience really constitutes a better reference point than the social-movement claims that Honneth dismisses. The latter, after all, have the advantage of being subject to critical scrutiny in open debate. Inarticulate suffering, in contrast, is by definition sheltered from public contestation. Thus, if Critical Theory's reference points should be normatively reliable – if, in other words, they should help us to conceptualize what really *merits* the title of injustice, as opposed to what is merely *experienced* as injustice – then social-movement claims are at least as plausible candidates as untested prepolitical discontent.[8]

Nevertheless, I do not intend to champion such claims as an alternative foundation for Critical Theory, Honneth's mischaracterization of my position notwithstanding. On the contrary, I object in principle to *any* proposal to ground a normative framework on one privileged set of experiences. That strategy is flawed in part because it puts all its eggs in one basket. Insisting on the necessity of one, and only one, privileged reference point, it invests the latter with too much authority, effectively treating it as an incorrigible foundation. In fact, however, no set of experiences, prepolitical or otherwise, should be insulated from critical scrutiny. The wiser course is to establish multiple points of entry into social reality, according absolute privilege to none of them, and submitting each to potential revision in light of the others. The need for such cross-checks is especially pressing in the case of subjective experiences, which Honneth, alas, takes at face value. Notoriously unreliable, such experiences need to be situated in relation to more objective, experience-distant touchstones, such as those afforded by structural analyses of social subordination and political sociologies of social movements. These latter reference points are empirical, to be sure, but they do not arise directly from subjective experience. On the contrary, they represent indispensable benchmarks for assessing the validity of experience's claims.

Honneth, however, is unwilling to put experience to the test. For him, rather, moral psychology settles everything in advance. In his framework, moral-psychological questions of subjective motivation assume priority over questions of social explanation and normative justification. Thus, the issue of what motivates the subjective experience of injustice sets the parameters for how he approaches other key critical tasks, such as identifying the hegemonic grammars of political claims-making, the social processes that institutionalize injustice, and the normative criteria for adjudicating claims. For Honneth, in other words, once moral psychology purports to establish that misrecognition is the sole bonafide experience of injustice, then everything else follows in train: all political demands must be translated into claims for recognition; all modes of subordination must be interpreted as denied recognition and traced to the recognition order of society; and all criteria of justice must be reduced to subvarieties of recognition. The result is a surprisingly traditional theoretical edifice: a foundationalist construction in which moral psychology grounds, and unduly constrains, political sociology, social theory, and moral philosophy, illegitimately truncating those inquiries and infringing their relative autonomy.

Taken together, these difficulties doom Honneth's attempt to establish a viable dialectic of immanence and transcendence. Far from constituting a genuinely immanent empirical reference point, his invocation of prepolitical suffering serves as a pretext for introducing a quasi-transcendental moral psychology, which purports to establish once and for all that recognition is always and everywhere the sole and sufficient category of morality. The effect is to entrench the primacy of recognition anthropologically, below the level of historical contingency, and thus to belie the pretension to immanence. To be sure, Honneth admits some scope for historical development, as he allows that recognition becomes "differentiated" as society progresses. But instead of leading to genuine historical thinking, this approach predetermines the course of history: historical developments can only ever differentiate recognition into various "spheres"; they can never generate new moral categories that are not variants of recognition. His historicizing gesture notwithstanding, then, Honneth ends up subordinating the moment of immanence to that of transcendence. And yet the transcendence, too, proves illusory in the end. Recognition monism does not, after all, provide a critical vantage point on contemporary political culture. On the contrary, it uncritically reflects today's one-sided fascination with the politics of recognition. As a result, it functions more to ratify the current fashion than to interrogate the latter's adequacy. And so the overall conclusion is clear: Honneth fails to establish a foothold in the existing social world that can also point beyond it.

What, then, is the alternative to his strategy? The approach I have proposed begins not with subjective experience, but with *decentered discourses of social criticism*. Thus, it does not seek to mirror the perspective of any social subject, whether individual or collective, prepolitical or political. Rather, I connect critique with its social context by focusing initially on the *folk paradigms of social justice* that constitute a society's hegemonic grammars of contestation and deliberation. Far from reflecting unmediated experience, these folk paradigms constitute depersonalized discursive formations that mediate moral disagreement and social protest. As such, they represent a nonsubjective reference point for Critical Theory. The effect is to detach the theory from the subject-centered philosophy assumed by Honneth and to resituate it within the linguistic turn.

Let me explain. Folk paradigms of justice do not express the perspective of any determinate set of social subjects. Nor do they belong exclusively to any one societal domain. Rather, they are transpersonal normative discourses that are widely diffused throughout democratic societies, permeating not only political public spheres, but also workplaces, households, and

civil-society associations. Thus, they constitute a moral grammar that social actors can (and do) draw on in *any* sphere to
evaluate social arrangements. As I explained in chapter one,
today's principal folk paradigms of justice are recognition and
redistribution. *Pace* Honneth, they are invoked not only by
organized movements, but also by unorganized individuals in
everyday contexts.[9]

In my approach, then, folk paradigms serve as an initial
empirical reference point. But they do not enjoy any absolute
privilege. Unlike Honneth's prepolitical suffering, they do not
constitute an incorrigible foundation from which to derive the
normative framework of Critical Theory. On the contrary, the
critical theorist must evaluate their adequacy – from at least
two independent perspectives. She or he must determine, first,
from the perspective of social theory, whether a society's
hegemonic grammars of contestation are adequate to its social
structure, and second, from the perspective of moral philosophy, whether the norms to which they appeal are morally
valid.

Evaluated in these ways, today's folk paradigms of justice get
mixed reviews. On the one hand, social-theoretic examination
discloses that both redistribution and recognition correspond to
modes of societal integration and social subordination that are
integral to contemporary society. Thus, it establishes their *prima
facie* plausibility as categories for critical reflection on present
conditions. On the other hand, social theory also discloses that
distribution and recognition are inextricably intertwined in
social reality. Thus, it reveals the inadequacy of a political
culture that decouples them from each other and casts them as
mutually incompatible. Similarly, moral-philosophical examination yields mixed results. On the one hand, it discloses that
both distribution and recognition are bonafide dimensions of
justice, thus establishing that both can generate principles with
normative validity. On the other hand, it also establishes their
mutual irreducibility and co-implication, thus revealing not
only the inadequacy of any monism, whether distributive or

recognition-based, but also the shortcomings of a political culture that fails to integrate both dimensions within a broader overarching moral framework. The upshot is that today's folk paradigms of justice are neither wholly misguided nor wholly satisfactory. At once plausible and in need of reconstruction, the current grammar of contestation represents an empirical reference point whose full and adequate development points beyond the present constellation.

In general, then, my approach, unlike Honneth's, is non-foundational. As a result, its internal structure diverges from his. In particular, the shift in focus from experience to discourse decenters moral psychology, thus opening space for the study of political culture, which now joins social theory, moral philosophy, and political theory as a constitutive element of Critical Theory. Yet none of these inquiries is the ground of the others in Honneth's sense. None is immune from revision. Rather, each is responsive to the others, which provide checks and correctives where necessary. And the results of the process cut both ways: on the one hand, today's emphasis on recognition spurs a critical look at social theories and moral philosophies that neglect culturally rooted injustices of status; on the other hand, as I just noted, that emphasis is itself subject to correction by the latter disciplines. The result is a hermeneutical circle in which a plurality of nonfoundational elements is brought into a decentered process of mutual correction aimed at achieving reflective equilibrium. Thus, in my approach Critical Theory simultaneously learns from contemporary political culture and preserves its critical independence.

It follows that my conception of Critical Theory differs from Honneth's. As we saw, he assumed a foundationalist edifice in which moral psychology grounded, and constrained, social theory and moral philosophy. For me, in contrast, Critical Theory is polycentric and multilateral. After all, once we reject the idea that experience can serve as the theory's foundation, then moral psychology loses its privileged place. Questions of subjective motivation lose their primacy over questions of social explanation and normative justification, ceasing to limit reflection on the causes of injustice and the criteria for justifying claims. Instead, both of those inquiries regain their relative autonomy. In social theory, we are freed to conceptualize types of injustice, their causes and their remedies, independently of how they are experienced. In moral theory, likewise, we may identify norms for adjudicating justice claims, unconstrained by the dictates of a flawed psychology. And in political sociology, we can analyze the hegemonic normative grammars that structure conflict and contestation. The effect is to free Critical Theory from the artificial restrictions of an *a priori* monism, which inflates the idea of recognition to the point of unrecognizability, thereby draining it of critical force.

At the same time, the polycentric alternative I have proposed provides a structure within which the demands of both immanence and transcendence can be met. Clearly, folk paradigms of justice occupy a position of immanence in the social world, as do the folk norms embedded within them. But they are not static repositories of fixed normativity. Far from being inevitably mired in the given, under modern conditions they are open to historical extension, radicalization, and transformation. Under pressure to confront new problems, and subject to creative reappropriation, the norms contained within folk grammars transcend the social world in which they originate. The idea of participatory parity is a case in point. As I shall explain in section III, this idea is a radicalization of widely held folk norms of equality, whose scope and substance have greatly expanded in the course of history. Thus, the principle of participatory parity has a foothold in the existing social world. At the same time, however, it points beyond that world, as its thoroughgoing implementation would require major social-structural change. Thus, participatory parity, like the folk norms from which it descends, represents an important reference point for Critical Theory – a nonsubjective reference point on which the demands of immanence and transcendence converge. And so the conclusion here, too, is clear: it is not the case, *contra*

Honneth, that, absent an "independent" foundation in moral psychology, my approach remains mired in the given. On the contrary, it allows for – indeed fosters – a radical critique of contemporary society.

Axel Honneth has suggested that the core difference between us is that his approach is oriented to deep philosophical issues, whereas mine is motivated by political opportunism. Thus, he disparages my approach as a form of "shortsighted presentism," which seeks only to mirror the claims of contemporary social movements. Nothing, it should now be clear, could be further from the truth. Far from insulating such claims from critical scrutiny, the entire thrust of my theory is to question their adequacy. Moreover, the irony of Honneth's charge is painfully clear. Failing to problematize current discourses, and so drawing unselfconsciously on hegemonic paradigms, his recognition monism is a far less critical mirror of the present *Zeitgeist* than my perspectival dualism of redistribution and recognition.

II. On the Cultural Turn in Social Theory: Against the Reduction of Capitalist Society to its Recognition Order

The second major focus of this debate is the place of culture in contemporary society. At issue here is the question of how critical theorists should understand the social structure of present-day capitalism. Within that structure, how far down does cultural ordering extend? What is its relation to market mechanisms, on the one hand, and to distributive outcomes, on the other? Is misrecognition the root cause of all subordination in capitalist society, and is recognition alone sufficient to redress it? Should Critical Theory unreservedly embrace "the cultural turn"? Should it replace an economistic paradigm that privileged production with one that privileges culture?

Such questions are by no means new. They have been

central to Critical Theory from its beginnings, when Frankfurt
School thinkers sought to complicate orthodox Marxism by
theorizing culture's relative autonomy. Today, however, they
assume a new guise. On the one hand, globalizing capitalism
has greatly heightened the salience of culture, speeding the
flow not only of capital, but also of images, signs, and people
across national borders. The effect is to intensify awareness of
"difference" and encourage its politicization. On the other
hand, Marxism is no longer a force to be reckoned with,
having been supplanted by culturalist paradigms, both in politics
and in the academy. In this situation, critical theorizing is less
likely to succumb to orthodox economism than to the neoliberal amnesia that represses the critique of political economy.
The result is a new set of challenges for Critical Theory: how
should it understand the salience of culture in globalizing
capitalist society? In particular, how should it assess the critical
potential of the cultural turn?

Both Axel Honneth and I seek to rise to these challenges.
Both of us believe that culture is no mere reflection of political
economy, but a vehicle of social ordering in its own right.
Both of us maintain, too, that culture often serves as a medium
of domination, hence that society harbors injustices whose
deepest roots lie not in political economy, but in institutionalized patterns of value. Finally, both Honneth and I theorize
these matters in terms of recognition. Both of us employ that
category to conceptualize the social weight and moral significance of culture in contemporary capitalism. Thus, each of us
proposes a framework for Critical Theory that aims to incorporate the best insights of the cultural turn.

Nevertheless, we proceed in different ways. Honneth con-
ceptualizes society as a network of recognition relations. Subordinating social theory to his moral psychology, he stipulates
that the former's task is to identify the concrete way in which
recognition expectations are institutionalized in a given society.
Then, having parsed the society's "recognition order," Critical
Theory should show how misrecognition arises within it and

grounds social conflict. Applying this method to capitalist society, Honneth discerns three institutionalized "recognition spheres," each governed by a different normative principle. In the sphere of "love," recognition should be governed by the principle of attentiveness to the specific needs of the unique individual. In that of law, by contrast, it should be governed by the principle of equal respect for the autonomy of persons. In the sphere of labor, finally, recognition should be regulated by the principle of achievement, which determines the level of one's wages according to the value of one's social contribution. From Honneth's perspective, therefore, struggles over distribution are really struggles over recognition, aimed at changing the cultural interpretation of achievement. For him, moreover, recognition goes all the way down. The primary medium of societal integration, recognition-interpretations govern social processes in every sphere, dictating not only the contours of intimacy and law, but even the distribution of income and wealth. It follows that there is nothing distinctive about market-mediated social interactions, which are regulated, like all interactions, by cultural schemas of evaluation. Thus, there is neither any point in, nor any possibility of, conceptualizing specifically economic mechanisms in capitalist society. Far from requiring a second, distribution-oriented level of analysis, capitalist society effectively *is* its recognition order.

In general, then, Honneth's social theory, like his moral psychology, is monistic. Viewing all social processes through the single lens of interpersonal psychology, it posits the "primacy of moral integration," in which social action is coordinated through shared understandings and interpretative schemas. The effect is to view capitalism exclusively from the perspective of recognition − hence to assume that all social processes in capitalist society are directly regulated by cultural schemas of evaluation; that all subordination derives from culturally rooted hierarchies of status; and that all can be remedied by cultural change. All of these assumptions, however, are problematic.

To begin with, it is doubtful that any society is simply a recognition order. Virtually all societies contain more than one kind of societal integration. Above and beyond the moral integration privileged by Honneth, virtually all include some form of system integration, in which interaction is coordinated by the functional interlacing of the unintended consequences of a myriad of individual strategies. To analyze any society exclusively as a recognition order is illegitimately to totalize one mode of integration, truncating the full range of social processes. The effect is to obscure a key question: in a given society, how precisely does the recognition order interact with other modes of social order to produce relations of subordination?

Moreover, what is true for any society holds especially for capitalist society. The latter's distinguishing feature, after all, is its creation of a quasi-objective, anonymous, impersonal market order that follows a logic of its own. This market order is culturally embedded, to be sure. But it is not directly governed by cultural schemas of evaluation. Rather, the economic logic of the market interacts in complex ways with the cultural logic of recognition, sometimes instrumentalizing existing status distinctions, sometimes dissolving or circumventing them, and sometimes creating new ones. As a result, market mechanisms give rise to economic class relations that are not mere reflections of status hierarchies. Neither those relations nor the mechanisms that generate them can be understood by recognition monism. An adequate approach must theorize both the distinctive dynamics of the capitalist economy and its interaction with the status order.

These considerations apply in spades to the labor markets of capitalist societies. In those arenas, work compensation is not determined by the principle of achievement. Granted, capitalist societies are permeated by ideologies about the extent to which various activities contribute to community well-being; about the supposed fit between various occupations, on one side, and various genders and "races," on the other; and even about what counts as work at all. And granted, too, these ideologies have real effects. But they are hardly the only factors that affect wage rates. Also important are political-economic factors such as the supply of and demand for different types of labor; the balance of power between labor and capital; the stringency of social regulations, including the minimum wage; the availability and cost of productivity enhancing technologies; the ease with which firms can shift their operations to locations where wage rates are lower; the cost of credit; the terms of trade; and international currency exchange rates. In the broad mix of relevant considerations, ideologies of achievement are by no means paramount. Rather, their effects are mediated by the operation of impersonal system mechanisms, which prioritize maximization of corporate profits. Recognition monism, however, is congenitally blind to such system mechanisms, which cannot be reduced to cultural schemas of evaluation. As a result, it is disabled from understanding the processes that generate distributive injustice in capitalist societies. Only an approach that theorizes the imbrication of recognition and distribution can adequately theorize those processes.

It follows that not all struggles over distribution are in fact struggles over recognition, aimed at enhancing esteem for the claimants' labor. To be sure, *some* movements for redistribution do contest reigning interpretations of achievement − witness the struggles for "comparable worth" I discussed in chapter one.[10] But, *pace* Honneth, not all distributive struggles are like comparable worth. Consider today's struggles against neoliberal globalization. Targeting transnational trade and investment regimes that serve the interests of large corporate shareholders and currency speculators, such struggles aim to end systemic maldistribution that is rooted not in ideologies about achievement, but in the system imperatives and governance structures of globalizing capitalism. *Contra* Honneth, this sort of maldistribution is no less paradigmatic of contemporary capitalism than the sort fueled by nonrecognition of women's carework − witness the fate of much of sub-Saharan Africa, eastern

Germany, and the south Bronx. The vast deprivation in question here stems not from undervaluation of labor contributions, but from economic-system mechanisms that exclude many from labor markets altogether. This exclusion is facilitated by racism, to be sure, as profit-maximizing imperatives interact with status distinctions and with the legacies of past depredations. But it cannot be remedied simply by changing Eurocentric standards of achievement. What is required, rather, is wholesale restructuring of global systems of finance, trade, and production. Such matters escape the conceptual grid of recognition monism, however. They can only be captured by a two-dimensional framework that encompasses both the system dynamics and status dynamics of globalizing capitalism.

In general, then, Honneth vastly exaggerates the role of recognition in capitalist society. Focused exclusively on value-regulated interaction, he takes valid insights about the ubiquity and irreducibility of culture and inflates them beyond all recognition. He goes from the true premise that markets are always culturally embedded to the false conclusion that their behavior is wholly governed by the dynamics of recognition. Likewise, he goes from the valid insight that the capitalist economy is not a purely technical, culture-free system to the untenable proposition that it has no economic dynamics worth analyzing in their own right. Finally, he goes from the valid insight that all social struggles have a cultural dimension to the insupportable conclusion that all are cultural *simpliciter*, and in exactly the same way. Thus, far from successfully incorporating the best insights of the cultural turn, Honneth capitulates to the latter's worst excesses. Instead of passing beyond economism to arrive at a richer theory that encompasses both distribution and recognition, he has traded one truncated paradigm for another, a truncated economism for a truncated culturalism.

What, then, represents a better approach? All the considerations marshaled here point in a single direction, to a *two-dimensional* framework that encompasses both recognition and distribution. Avoiding not only vulgar economism but also reductive culturalism, such a framework would not reduce capitalist society to a network of recognition relations. To understand that society, rather, it would analyze the interplay of two distinct ordering dimensions, mutually irreducible but practically intertwined: an economic dimension, associated with marketized interaction, and a cultural dimension, associated with value-regulated interaction. Such an approach offers several advantages. Instead of focusing exclusively on moral integration, it attends also to system integration and then studies the interaction of the two. Moreover, far from assuming that recognition imperatives alone directly govern all social action, it allows for marketized interactions in which cultural schemas of evaluation are refracted through an economic logic. Likewise, instead of reducing all social subordination to misrecognition, rooted in hierarchies of cultural value, this approach allows for distributive injustices that do not simply reflect status hierarchies, even as they interact causally with the latter. Far from assuming, finally, that all injustices in capitalist society can be remedied by cultural change, it requires that struggles for recognition be joined to struggles for egalitarian redistribution.

This is precisely the sort of approach I have proposed. By calling it *perspectival dualism*, I have signaled a special, counterintuitive way of understanding distribution and recognition. In lieu of spatial and substantial interpretations, which equate those categories with societal domains, I construe them perspectivally, as analytically distinct ordering dimensions which cut across institutional divisions. For me, accordingly, distribution and recognition do not occupy separate spheres. Rather, they interpenetrate, to produce complex patterns of subordination. Thus, institutionalized value patterns continue to permeate marketized interactions, even though they do not directly govern the latter; and instrumental considerations continue to suffuse value-regulated arenas, even though they do not enjoy a free hand. It follows that distribution and recognition can never be fully disentangled. All interactions partake simultaneously of both dimensions, albeit in different proportions.

Hence all must be analyzed bifocally and evaluated from both perspectives. *Pace* Honneth, therefore, perspectival dualism introduces no "unbridgeable chasm" between the material and the symbolic. Its guiding aim is, on the contrary, to investigate how precisely institutionalized patterns of cultural value interact with capitalist economic dynamics to generate maldistribution and misrecognition. Doing so, however, requires distinguishing distribution and recognition analytically and tracking their practical imbrication. It will not suffice to totalize culture, obliterate the economic, and negate the distinction by fiat.

The rationale for this approach lies in a two-dimensional conception of capitalist society. I assume that this society encompasses two analytically distinct orders of subordination: class stratification, rooted primarily in economic system mechanisms, and status hierarchy, based largely in institutionalized patterns of cultural value. These two orders do not map neatly onto one another, although they interact causally. Thus, in capitalist society there exist gaps between status and class. Moreover, each of these orders of subordination corresponds to an analytically distinct type of injustice. Whereas class stratification corresponds to maldistribution, status hierarchy corresponds to misrecognition. Morally speaking, however, the effect in both cases is the same: some members of society are prevented from participating on a par with others in social interaction. Thus, both orders of subordination violate a single overarching principle of justice, the principle of participatory parity. Yet each does so in a different way. Whereas class subordination denies some actors the resources needed to interact with others as peers, status subordination denies some the requisite standing. In both cases, therefore, redressing the injustice involves overcoming obstacles to participatory parity. Redressing maldistribution requires restructuring the economic system to eliminate resource disparities, while redressing misrecognition requires changing institutionalized patterns of cultural value. In both cases, too, the aim is to establish social arrangements that permit all to participate as peers.

Unlike Honneth's, therefore, my framework situates the recognition dimension of capitalist society in relation to the distributive dimension. In addition, it understands the recognition dimension in a different way. For me, that dimension concerns status equality, not intact identity; and its institutional expression is the *status order as a whole*. The status order is understood broadly, moreover, as spanning the full gamut of contemporary social institutions. A composite of the various value patterns that regulate interaction at different sites, it encompasses not only family and law, but also communications media and religion, to name just two more. Unlike Honneth, therefore, I do not divide the recognition dimension into three separate spheres, each associated with a different social institution, a different psychological injury, and a different normative principle. Rather, I assume that the status order of contemporary society is far too dynamic, pervasive, and plural to respect any such a priori division. At the same time, however, I also contend that beneath all the cultural complexity lies a single moral imperative: the principle of participatory parity.

To see why, consider the gender injustices associated with marriage. Included here are wives' vulnerability to marital rape and domestic violence; primary carework responsibilities that prevent them from participating in paid work and politics on the same terms as men; inferior social welfare entitlements; diminished rights of asylum and naturalization; and a host of other legal disabilities. *Contra* Honneth, these injustices are not best conceived psychologically, as violations of personal identity rooted in a lack of sensitivity to individual need in the sphere of intimacy, which is governed by the principle of care. Rather, they are better conceived socially, as forms of subordination rooted in an androcentric status order, which pervades society and is imbricated with its economic structure, systematically disadvantaging women in *every* sphere. *Contra* Honneth, moreover, marriage has never been regulated by the principle of care. For most of history, rather, it has been a legally regulated

220   REDISTRIBUTION OR RECOGNITION?

economic relation, concerned more with property accumulation, labor organization, and resource distribution than with care.[11] In fact, what Honneth calls affective care is actually women's labor, ideologically mystified and rendered invisible. It follows that the status subordination of wives in marriage cannot be remedied by further individualizing care. What is required, rather, is deinstitutionalizing androcentric value patterns throughout society in favor of alternatives that promote gender parity. Participatory parity, not care, is the key to reforming the institution of marriage.

Consider, too, the injustices that have occasioned today's struggles over cultural difference: for example, the display of the Christian cross in Bavarian schools, the US police practice of racial profiling, and a built environment that disadvantages people with disabilities.[12] *Contra* Honneth, such injustices are not best understood as belonging to "the sphere of law." They have no more intrinsic relation to law than does any other kind of status subordination, including the marital injustices just discussed.[13] Like the latter, these derive from a status order that cannot be localized in any one sphere – in this case an ethnocentric status order that institutionalizes majority cultural norms, denying participatory parity to minority-group members. Like marital injustices, too, these can only be redressed by deinstitutionalizing those value patterns throughout society, not only in and through law. As with marital injustices, finally, the guiding principle here is participatory parity, which gives concrete democratic substance to the ideal of equal autonomy, a point I shall elaborate in the final section.

The point about law is worth pursuing, given Honneth's claim that my approach overlooks struggles for legal equality. In fact, perspectival dualism *does* account for such struggles, albeit not by treating law as a sphere. Rather, it conceives law as pertaining to both dimensions of justice, distribution and recognition, where it is liable to serve at once as a vehicle of, and a remedy for, subordination. On the recognition side, some legal struggles aim to undo expressly juridified status subordination – witness campaigns to legalize gay marriage; others resort to law to redress *nonjuridified* status subordination – witness campaigns to outlaw racial profiling or to mandate handicapped access. Far from being localized in a special sphere, such struggles target parity-impeding norms wherever they appear, across the whole of the status order, from family to occupational practice to the built environment. On the distribution side, meanwhile, efforts to change class-biased tax and inheritance laws seek to mitigate legally sanctioned economic inequality, while struggles to enact new laws that would curtail corporate property rights, control international currency speculation, and establish a universal, unconditional Basic Income seek a more fundamental transformation. Aimed at restructuring the political economy, these struggles, too, confound efforts to compartmentalize law.

Law aside, the chief conclusion here is this: not only does perspectival dualism situate the recognition dimension of capitalist society vis-à-vis the distribution dimension; it also illuminates the recognition dimension better than Honneth does. Whereas he analyzes misrecognition psychologically, my approach foregrounds its *social* character as a matter of *status subordination*. Thus, instead of distinguishing kinds of misrecognition according to types of identity injury, I underscore the societal consequence common to them all: the constitution of some classes of persons as less than full members of society in a way that prevents them from participating as peers. The result is a critical sociology of recognition that is appropriate for contemporary globalizing capitalism: instead of dividing the cultural order into three recognition spheres, I theorize the cross-cutting *status orders* that run throughout every sphere. At the same time, perspectival dualism also affords a socially pertinent moral theory: instead of designating a different normative principle for each category of psychical damage, it establishes that all types that merit the title of injustice do so because they violate a *single* principle: the principle of *participatory parity*. Finally, this approach entails a politically responsible practical conclusion: instead of proposing to remedy each type of misrecognition by fine-tuning its designated principle, it discloses the social redress that is common to all: deinstitutionalizing patterns of cultural value that impede parity of participation and replacing them with patterns that foster it.

Axel Honneth has suggested that my categorial distinction between redistribution and recognition remains arbitrary and ungrounded for want of a theory of societal reproduction. This, it should now be clear, is not the case. Premised, rather, on a bilevel conception, perspectival dualism assumes that capitalist societies differentiate a systemically integrated market order from value-regulated social orders. As a result, both system integration and social integration are essential to those societies. Unlike Honneth's approach, accordingly, mine attends to both those dimensions and elucidates their mutual interaction.[14] In this way, perspectival dualism accords due significance to moral integration without construing the latter, implausibly, as "primary" and inflating it beyond all recognition. The result is a social-theoretical framework that appropriates the best insights of the cultural turn. Taking some distance from current culturalist fashions, this approach makes possible a *critical* theory of the place of culture, and of recognition, in contemporary capitalism.

III.   On Liberal Equality: Against the Reduction of Justice to an Ethics of Intact Identity

The third focus of this debate is the normative component of Critical Theory – its understanding of justice and its moral criteria for adjudicating claims. Although such matters have long constituted the core concerns of moral philosophy, they assume a new urgency today. Now, as globalization is accelerating flows of people and communication across borders, divergent value horizons are colliding with startling results. Everyone experiences a new proximity of "the other" and a new salience of identity and difference. The effect is to fracture all self-enclosed status orders and to unleash intensified struggles for recognition. Such struggles, to be sure, are not new. But they assume a new prominence in this context as they burst through the national frames that prioritized distributive politics in the preceding era of Keynesian Fordism. Today, accordingly, struggles for recognition are decreasingly bounded by country or region and increasingly decoupled from struggles for redistribution, despite worldwide exacerbation of economic inequality. The result is renewed pressure on our normative judgments. Buffeted by competing claims for recognition, from amid conflicting schemas of value, we are called on to decide: which claims are genuinely emancipatory and which are not? Which recognition struggles foster justice and which do not? Which merit our support and which do not?

The problem is to secure a standpoint for making such judgments. In the present context, it is hardly possible to regard society as a culturally homogeneous, bounded whole, in which recognition claims can be adjudicated ethically, by appeal to a single shared value horizon. Rather, we must evaluate claims across divergent value horizons, no single one of which can reasonably claim to trump all the others. The result is that Critical Theory needs a *nonsectarian* theory of justice. Far from simply assuming a particular scheme of ethical value, such a theory must be compatible with a diversity of reasonable visions of the good life. At the same time, however, it is equally implausible to assume that all *prima facie* meritorious claims will automatically converge. Rather, we must be prepared to encounter hard cases – as, for example, when claims for cultural recognition conflict with claims for gender equality. The upshot is that Critical Theory needs a *determinate* theory of justice. Far from simply counseling live-and-let-live, such a theory must provide criteria for adjudicating conflicts and resolving dilemmas.

In general, then, what is needed is clear. Critical Theory must incorporate a theory of justice that meets two conditions simultaneously. On the one hand, it must be sufficiently *general* to avoid sectarianism. On the other hand, it must be sufficiently *determinate* to adjudicate conflicts. Only a theory of justice that is simultaneously general and determinate can meet the challenges of globalization.

Both Axel Honneth and I have sought to develop such a theory. In so doing, both of us have returned to the core concepts of the liberal tradition, namely, the equal autonomy and moral worth of human beings. And both of us have sought to rearticulate those ideals in forms that are sufficiently general and determinate to meet current challenges. For both of us, finally, the category of recognition plays a major role in explicating both the meaning of equal moral worth and the requirements of justice.

Once again, however, we proceed in different ways. Honneth contends that it is impossible adequately to articulate liberal ideals in the absence of a theory of the good life. Thus, he grounds his theory of justice in a conception of human flourishing. The conception he advances is psychological, moreover, in keeping with his prioritization of moral psychology. For Honneth, accordingly, the chief ingredient of human flourishing is an "intact identity."[15] It follows in his reconstruction of liberalism that a society is just if and only if it permits its members to develop intact identities. This in turn requires three types of healthy self-relation, grounded in three different kinds recognition: self-confidence assured via loving care, self-respect based in legal rights, and self-esteem rooted in social appreciation of the value of one's labor. For Honneth, therefore, justice requires a recognition order that provides individuals with the care, respect, and esteem that a good life requires.[16] As we saw, moreover, he maintains that this tripartite understanding of recognition exhausts the entire meaning of justice. Thus every bonafide justice claim is a claim for recognition, aimed at consolidating an intact identity. And every recognition claim is justified teleologically, as a means to the good life as Honneth understands it.

This approach is faithful to Honneth's project in both its monism and its stress on psychology. But it is deficient as a theory of justice. In particular, it fails to satisfy the requirements of nonsectarianism and determinacy. Or rather, it can succeed in satisfying one of those requirements only by failing to meet the other.

Consider that to avoid sectarianism, Honneth must deny that his conception of human flourishing has any substantive content. For if he were to supply content to that notion, it would effectively become one concrete ethical ideal among others. In that case, his theory of justice would not be able to justify binding obligations on those who subscribe to alternative ethical ideals, as to do so would violate their autonomy. Analogous strictures against substance apply to all of Honneth's key normative categories, including recognition and identity-intactness, as well as care, respect, and esteem. Because all of these notions are construed as ingredients of human flourishing they, too, must be kept free of content. For, again, if any of them acquired concrete substance, the entire conceptual structure would devolve into one sectarian view of the good life among others. In that case, Honneth's theory of justice would be fatally compromised. It would not be able fairly to mediate conflicts across different value horizons.

To meet the requirement of nonsectarianism, therefore, Honneth must construe his normative categories as purely *formal*. He must maintain that care, respect, and esteem are formal requirements of *any* life that could reasonably be considered good from within *any* reasonable ethical horizon. But this creates difficulties of another sort. Once its recognition principles are emptied of content, Honneth's theory of justice lacks sufficient determinacy to adjudicate conflicting claims.

Take the principle of achievement. As we saw, Honneth invokes that principle to adjudicate claims for redistribution, which he construes as demands for a proper valuation of the claimant's labor. The principle of achievement cannot be construed concretely, however, as implying a substantive ethical horizon for assessing labor's social value. For if it were, it would not be able to fairly adjudicate distributive conflicts in contexts of ethical pluralism, where social actors do not subscribe to a single shared value horizon. So the principle of achievement must be understood formally. But in that case what does it require? Honneth tells us that justice enjoins a proper estimation of everyone's social contribution. But he does not tell us how, in the absence of any agreed upon substantive yardstick, we are to arrive at such an estimation. Nor does he tell us how we are to know when and whether any proposed estimation is just. Nor, finally, does he tell us how we should answer neoliberals, who insist that the correct estimations are precisely those assigned by unregulated markets. Frustratingly silent on these matters, Honneth's "achievement principle" provides no basis for distinguishing warranted from unwarranted claims. A normative standard in appearance only, it avoids sectarianism only by forfeiting determinacy.

Analogous problems plague Honneth's principle of care. Assigned to an "intimate sphere" whose constitution is as politically contested as it is culturally variable, that principle, too, must be construed formally in order to escape ethical sectarianism. In that case, however, it, too, lacks sufficient determinacy to adjudicate conflicting claims. How, after all, can a purely formal understanding of care tell us how to assess the relative merits of traditional full-time mothering, on the one hand, and feminist models of degendered parenting, on the other?

To be sure, achievement and care are especially vulnerable to the dilemma of sectarianism and indeterminacy. But even the venerable principle of equal respect runs into difficulties on Honneth's account. As we saw, he associates that principle with the "sphere of law" and invokes it to adjudicate struggles for legal equality. It is under this rubric, moreover, that he locates cultural and religious disputes, such as the controversy over the *foulard* discussed in chapter one. For Honneth, accordingly, such controversies should be resolved by appeal to the principle of equal respect for autonomous personhood. This approach promises to avoid sectarianism by eschewing ethical evaluation of the disputed practices. But its capacity to determine a clear resolution remains in doubt. Recall that for Honneth respect is justified as a vital ingredient of an intact identity. Thus, one might suppose that he means to interpret this principle psychologically, as requiring that the law license whatever practices are essential to claimants' subjective sense of their dignity. In that case, however, the principle would be unable to adjudicate conflicts in which one group's experienced dignity is tied to another's experienced humiliation. Let us assume, therefore, that equal respect, too, must be understood formally. But then what precisely does it require? Does equal respect require only that law manifest formal equality and facial neutrality, as conservatives insist? Or does it entail the more demanding principle of equality of opportunity, as liberals maintain? Or, finally, does it require a still more stringent, result-oriented standard, such as the principle of participatory parity, as I contend? Once again, Honneth is silent on the crucial issue.[17] As a result, his recognition principle of equal respect is insufficiently determinate to distinguish warranted from unwarranted claims. Unable to adjudicate conflicts that pit one group's recognition demands against another's, it too avoids sectarianism only to sacrifice determinacy.

In general, then, none of Honneth's three principles satisfies both those requirements simultaneously. When the three principles are considered together, moreover, additional difficulties arise. As we saw, Honneth assigns each recognition principle to its own social sphere, as if to ensure that the principles won't conflict. In fact, however, the recognition spheres do not, and cannot, remain separate, as the example of income distribution attests. I just noted that Honneth submits disputes in this area to the merit-based principle of achievement. Yet he also remarks, with apparent approval, that the democratic welfare state generated another standard, derived from the principle of equal respect. This second, "social-citizenship" standard precludes income disparities that endanger some people's standing as equal citizens.[18] Here, then, are two different norms of distributive justice, which are liable to conflict: whereas the achievement norm privileges individual desert, the respect norm prioritizes social solidarity.[19] Thus, a theory of distributive justice cannot encompass both unless it ranks the principles in order of priority. This, however, Honneth fails to do. Speaking, rather, of three "equally important" principles of recognition, he neglects to tells us what we should do in cases where esteeming the labor contributions of some entails denying equal citizenship to others. Absent a method for resolving such conflicts, his tripartite recognition monism falls prey to another dimension of indeterminacy.

The upshot is that Honneth fails to provide a practicable theory of justice. The root problem, I contend, is his teleological starting point. By grounding his account of justice in a theory of the good life, he is forced to take extraordinary steps to avoid capitulating to ethical sectarianism. Constrained to construe his normative principles formally, he must drain them of substantive content – hence, of normative force. In seeking to resist teleology's built-in temptation to sectarianism, he ends up succumbing to indeterminacy. Ironically, then, an ethical starting point designed to overcome empty formalism itself descends into moral vacuity.

What, then, represents a viable approach? What sort of theory of justice can satisfy the requirements of nonsectarianism and determinacy simultaneously? The approach I have proposed begins not with a theory of the good life, but with the central moral ideal of modern liberalism: the equal autonomy and moral worth of human beings. In my understanding, this ideal needs no grounding in an ethic of self-realization, as its basic point is to enable the subjects of morality to formulate such ethics for themselves. But its full meaning needs to be explicated and its normative implications spelled out. For me, the implications of equal autonomy can only be articulated deontologically, via a theory of justice that is compatible with a plurality of reasonable views of the good life. Nonsectarian from the outset, the normative principles comprising such a theory need not be emptied of content. On the contrary, as I shall show, they can be sufficiently rich in moral substance to adjudicate conflicting claims.

In my approach, the implications of equal autonomy are spelled out in a theory of justice whose core principle is *parity of participation*. Deontological and nonsectarian, this principle assumes both the reasonableness of ethical disagreement and the equal moral worth of human beings. It is compatible in principle with all those understandings of the good life that themselves respect equal autonomy – of both those who subscribe to a given understanding and those who do not. At the same time, however, the principle of participatory parity articulates a specific interpretation of what such respect requires. Rejecting formal notions of equality as insufficient, it maintains that to respect the equal autonomy and moral worth of others one must accord them the status of full partners in social interaction. That, moreover, means assuring that all have access to the institutional prerequisites of participatory parity – above all, to the economic resources and the social standing needed to participate on a par with others. On this view, anything short of participatory parity constitutes a failure of equal respect. And denial of access to parity's social prerequisites makes a mockery of a society's professed commitment to equal autonomy.

Participatory parity constitutes *a radical democratic interpretation* of equal autonomy. Far more demanding than standard liberal interpretations, this principle is not only deontological but also substantive. On the one hand, it enjoins removal of economic obstacles to full social participation, thus supplying a standard for adjudicating claims for redistribution: only claims that diminish economic disparities are warranted. On the other hand, it also enjoins dismantling of institutionalized cultural obstacles, thereby supplying as well a standard for adjudicating claims for recognition: only claims that promote status equality are justified. In both cases, to be sure, one must guard against perverse effects. Thus, one must apply the parity standard bifocally, ensuring that reforms aimed at reducing class disparities do not end up exacerbating status disparities – and vice-versa. Likewise, one must also apply the standard with an eye to cross-cutting axes of subordination, ensuring that reforms aimed at fostering, for example, gender parity do not worsen disparities along other axes, such as sexuality, religion, and "race." In the end, moreover, as such matters are highly contentious, the parity standard can only be properly applied dialogically, through democratic processes of public debate. But as I explained in chapter one, drawing on the arguments of Ian Shapiro, that condition holds for any account of *democratic justice*.[20] Construed as the principal idiom of public reason, the principle of participatory parity is sufficiently rich in moral substance to adjudicate conflicting claims – for both the recognition and distribution dimensions of justice.

Thus understood, the view of justice as participatory parity is simultaneously deontological and substantive. As a result, it bursts the bounds of Honneth's account of the possible options in moral philosophy. In his account, there are only two possibilities: the thick "teleological liberalism" favored by him and the thin "procedural liberalism" associated with Habermas and Rawls. Justice as parity of participation, however, fits neither of those two ideal types. It diverges from teleological liberalism in eschewing ethical foundations, while also parting company with liberal proceduralism in articulating substantive requirements of justice. Thus, this approach attests to a possibility overlooked by Honneth. Rejecting both teleological sectarianism and proceduralist formalism, justice as participatory parity exemplifies a third genre of moral philosophy, which could be called *thick deontological liberalism*.

The question remains, however: what justifies thick deontological liberalism? More specifically, what justifies the radical democratic view of justice as participatory parity? For Honneth, recall, such a view can only be arbitrary absent an ethical foundation in a theory of the good life. In fact, however, participatory parity finds the right sort of philosophical support in two complementary lines of argument, neither of which is ethical. The first line of argument is conceptual. The basic idea is that equal autonomy, properly understood, entails the real freedom to participate on a par with others in social life. Anything less fails to capture the full meaning of the equal moral worth of human beings. That idea is not adequately embodied, for example, in equal formal rights that lack "fair value" due to the absence of the necessary preconditions for their exercise. For such rights remain purely notional, despite their symbolic importance. Only when all the conditions are in place, ensuring that all can really interact as peers, is the equal moral worth of each individual respected. Thus, participatory parity simply *is* the meaning of equal respect for the equal autonomy of human beings *qua* social actors. Certainly, this conceptual argument assumes the normative validity of the core liberal norm of equal respect and will not persuade anyone who rejects that ideal. Nevertheless, it lends support to the radical-democratic interpretation of equal autonomy – in a manner befitting thick deontological liberalism.

The second argument for participatory parity is historical. It invokes historical considerations in support of a radical democratic interpretation of equal autonomy. From this perspective, participatory parity appears as the outcome of a broad, multifaceted historical process that has enriched the meaning of liberal equality over time. In this process, which is by no means confined to the West, the concept of equal moral worth has expanded in both scope and substance. In early modernity, the scope of liberal equality was restricted to religious freedom and equality before the law. Later, however, its reach was extended to more arenas of social interaction, including politics (thanks to suffrage struggles), labor (thanks to the trade unions and socialist parties), family and personal life (thanks to feminist and gay liberation movements), and civil society (thanks to struggles for multiculturalism). In substance, likewise, the

meaning of equality has also expanded. Earlier, formal rights
were deemed sufficient to meet the requirements of equal
moral worth. Today, however, one increasingly encounters the
expectation that equality be manifest substantively, in real social
interactions. Thus, the right to sue in a court of law now entails
the right to legal counsel. Similarly, "one person, one vote" is
now widely thought to entail public electoral campaign financ-
ing.[21] Likewise, the career open to talents, long linked to equal
public education, is increasingly viewed as entailing abolition
of the gender division of carework. Such examples suggest that
the norm of equality is becoming substantialized. No longer
restricted to formal rights but also encompassing the social
conditions for their exercise, equality is coming to mean
participatory parity. Participatory parity, then, is the emergent
historical "truth" of the liberal norm of the equal autonomy
and moral worth of human beings.

Together, these two arguments provide strong support for
the view of justice as participatory parity. But they do not
appeal to a theory of the good life. *Contra* Honneth, then, my
approach does not require an ethical account of the sorts of
participation that are required for human flourishing. It
assumes, rather, that the participants will decide that for themselves by their own lights. Far from pre-empting their choices,
justice as participatory parity seeks to ensure them the chance
to decide freely, unconstrained by relations of domination.
Thus, it seeks to remove obstacles to parity in all major social
arenas – including politics, labor markets, family, and civil
society. In this way, it aims to enable social actors to participate
as peers in any and every arena they choose to enter. Included
here are what we might call "deliberative meta-arenas": critical
discursive spaces where interlocutors debate the merits of
various types of social participation, mooting proposals to
reform or abolish existing arenas and to establish new ones.

In general, then, the approach I propose avoids appealing to
ethical arguments. Unburdened by teleology, it has no need to
drain its normative principles of determinate content. Thus,

this approach is free to articulate a substantive, radical democratic interpretation of liberal ideals. Construing equal autonomy as parity of participation, it expands that ideal's scope and substance, deepening its emancipatory force. The result is a thick deontological theory of justice that avoids both sectarianism and indeterminacy. Thus, this approach, unlike Honneth's, meets the requirements for a Critical Theory of justice in the era of globalization.

Let me conclude by recapping the key points. Those of us who hope to rejuvenate Critical Theory face difficult challenges in the period ahead. To ensure the continuing relevance of our tradition, we must adapt it to a world in which struggles over status are proliferating amidst widening economic inequality. With its capacity to analyze such struggles, the concept of recognition represents a promising vehicle for reconstructing Critical Theory in an era of accelerating globalization.

Nevertheless, recognition alone cannot bear the entire burden of critical theorizing. By itself, it is not sufficient to capture the normative deficits of contemporary society, the societal processes that generate them, and the political challenges facing those seeking emancipatory change. To ask that of recognition is to overextend the concept, distorting it beyond recognition and depriving it of critical force. Such an approach, I have argued here, can provide neither a suitable empirical reference point, nor a viable account of culture, nor a defensible theory of justice. What is needed, in contrast, is clear: *Critical Theory should situate recognition as one dimension of a perspectival-dualist framework that also encompasses distribution.*

Nothing I have written here detracts from the powerful moral and emotional force of Axel Honneth's emphasis on recognition. But there is a distance between the emotional appeal of a concept and its translation into a viable critical-theoretical framework. By integrating redistribution and recognition in a single framework, I hope that I have shortened that distance.

Notes

1 I am grateful to several colleagues for helpful comments on and discussions of this chapter. Thanks to Amy Allen, Seyla Benhabib, María Pía Lara, Martin Saar, and Eli Zaretsky.

2 Jürgen Habermas, "The New Obscurity: The Crisis of the Welfare State and the Exhaustion of Utopian Energies," in *The New Conservatism: Cultural Criticism and the Historians' Debate*, ed. Shierry W. Nicholson (Cambridge, MA 1990).

3 Michael Harrington, *The Other America: Poverty in the United States* (New York 1981).

4 This construal is also problematic for a second reason, which I shall elaborate in section III. To stress the victim's subjective feelings of injury is to endanger the possibility of a democratic adjudication of justice claims. The latter requires public deliberation aimed at determining the validity of the claims in question, a matter which in turn requires that claimants press their case via public reasons, not subjective feelings.

5 Jane Mansbridge, *Everyday Feminism* (Chicago, forthcoming).

6 Wilfred Sellars, "Empiricism and the Philosophy of Mind," in Herbert Feigl and Michael Sriven, eds, *Minnesota Studies in the Philosophy of Science*, vol. 1 (1956).

7 I borrow the expression "Morality's Own Language" from Richard Rorty, *Philosophy and the Mirror of Nature* (Princeton 1980). Interestingly, Honneth himself seems to concede this point when he acknowledges, later on in his essay, that moral experience is in fact "shaped" by socially and historically elaborated idioms of normative judgment. Yet he fails to acknowledge its full import and scope. Illegitimately restricting such "shaping" to his three subtypes of recognition discourse, he fails to allow for the historical elaboration and institutionalization of moral vocabularies that are not centered on recognition.

8 In fact, such claims are plausibly viewed as articulated reconstructions of previously inarticulate suffering. Moreover, as the self-organized expression of such suffering, social movements are at least as well positioned to articulate the experience of the subjects in question as the social scientists whose interpretations Honneth privileges.

9 Mansbridge, *Everyday Feminism*.

10 In that case, as I argued there, an androcentric pattern of cultural value is institutionalized in labor markets, channeling women into service-sector jobs that are coded "feminine" and assumed to require little skill. Since those jobs tend to be poorly paid, the result is to deny women

workers both the standing and the resources they need to interact on terms of parity with men. To redress the injustice requires, *inter alia*, that we deinstitutionalize the androcentric value patterns and replace them with patterns that promote parity. In this case, accordingly, Honneth's analysis overlaps partially with my own – although he assumes that cultural change by itself is sufficient and that its point is to valorize feminine identity, both propositions I consider erroneous.

11 Granted, bourgeois society purveyed ideals of companionate marriage as a "haven in the heartless world" of emergent capitalism. But far from eliminating the institution's economic functions, the effect was rather to mystify them, largely to the detriment of women – witness the increased invisibility of their household labor in industrial society.

12 Such injustices supply the chief inspiration for the current revival of recognition theory. Yet they were ignored entirely in Honneth's book *The Struggle for Recognition: The Moral Grammar of Social Conflicts*, trans. Joel Anderson (Cambridge 1995). In the present volume he considers them effectively as an afterthought, asking which recognition sphere they belong to and assigning them to the sphere of law, hence to the principle of equal autonomy.

13 Honneth's difficulties in handling these injustices are compounded by his cultural monism – his quasi-Durkheimian assumption that society is (or should be) ethically integrated via a single, overarching horizon for assigning esteem, which is centered in the system of labor. Treating labor as the sole source of differentiation in social identity, this model obliterates differences, such as those based in language, ethnicity, or religion, which do not correspond to occupational divisions. The effect is to render invisible claims for recognition of cultural difference. Thus, the most salient struggles of our age elude Honneth's framework.

14 In this respect, my approach resembles that of Jürgen Habermas. Unlike him, however, I do not substantialize the distinction between system and lifeworld. By treating it perspectivally, rather, I enable a more complex account of their mutual imbrication than his one-directional conception of the "colonization of the lifeworld." For Habermas's approach see *The Theory of Communicative Action*. For a critique, see Nancy Fraser, "What's Critical About Critical Theory? The Case of Habermas and Gender," *Unruly Practices: Power, Discourse and Gender in Contemporary Social Theory* (Minneapolis & London 1989).

15 Actually, there is an ambiguity here. In some passages, Honneth treats the consolidation of an intact identity as the *chief ingredient* of human flourishing, effectively equating the good life with one enjoying adequate recognition. In other passages, in contrast, he treats the consolidation of an intact identity as the *chief prerequisite* for human flourishing, effectively

instrumentalizing recognition as a means to the good life. In both cases, however, psychological intactness is treated as the only relevant factor in human flourishing. Thus, whether construed as ingredient or prerequisite, identitarian integrity is assumed by Honneth to be both necessary and sufficient for self-realization.

16 There is also an ambiguity here. In some passages, Honneth contends that justice requires recognition relations that *really supply* the requisite forms of recognition to all individuals. In other passages, in contrast, he contends that justice requires only that recognition relations provide individuals with *equal chances* to gain the requisite forms of recognition. Neither approach is wholly satisfactory, however. The first one works well for rights-based respect, which a just society ought to really guarantee, but poorly for achievement-grounded esteem, which it cannot. Conversely, the second approach works well for self-esteem, where equal opportunity is the appropriate standard, but poorly for self-respect, where real equality is called for.

17 To be sure, he speaks suggestively of a "moral dialectic of universality and particularity," which *might* mean something akin to participatory parity. But absent further clarification, no practicable standard emerges here.

18 In fact, the social citizenship principle could be interpreted along the lines of my notion of participatory parity. In that case, it would guarantee all social actors the resources they need to interact with others as peers, regardless of their social contributions.

19 One could also invoke Honneth's notion of care to derive yet a third distributive principle. Such a care-based principle could be understood either in terms of need (e.g., as requiring satisfaction of some specified level of "basic need") or in terms of welfare (as requiring some specified level of individual welfare). Either way, the effect would be to introduce a further prospect of conflict among principles, hence a further dimension of indeterminacy.

20 For a recent elaboration and defense of this sort of democratic approach to justice, see Ian Shapiro, *Democratic Justice* (New Haven 1999).

21 It should go without saying that "one person, one vote" also entails a uniform system for casting and counting votes. But, as we learned in December 2000, that condition is scandalously lacking in the United States.

4

The Point of Recognition: A Rejoinder to the Rejoinder*

Axel Honneth

Nancy Fraser has devoted a thorough critique to my attempt to develop a recognition-based framework for Critical Theory in reponse to her objections. The reformulation of her premises and the transparency of her counterarguments make it easier to continue our conversation. Yet the multitude of issues she touches on, and the sheer number of her objections, render this task harder and would, if I wanted to respond defensively, require complicated corrections, clarifications, and explanations – which would be tiresome for most readers. For long stretches it is easy to follow Fraser's reflections and see the core of our disagreement. In certain especially heavy-going places, however, I had to rub my eyes to be quite sure that I was meant to be the author of such absurd-sounding conclusions. Under these circumstances, it seems to me to make the most sense to respond not defensively but offensively to her rejoinders by working out once again in sharpened form the point that I see connecting the three clearly outlined levels of a recognition-theoretical "monism." My impression is that, despite her clear and nuanced analysis, at central points Fraser has incorrectly or inadequately construed the real field of our debate. The attempt to more precisely outline these problem zones in the reactualization of Critical Theory will therefore be more useful, pro-

ductive, and helpful than the cramped enterprise of going step
by step through her objections.

As a first approach, the three points of divergence distinguished by Fraser following my proposal seem suitable for
designating the essential difficulties confronting an attempt to
continue Critical Theory today. Each of the questions she
identifies outlines a field in which intervening historical and
theoretical transformations have led to controversy about how
the old, complex demands of the Frankfurt School can be
revived. A first point concerns the problem of how to conceive
of a theoretical approach to social reality that allows for an
immanent justification of moral claims. Here Fraser rightly uses
the formula of "a dialectic of immanence and transcendence" –
without, to be sure, in my view doing justice to what "transcendence" could mean in this context (I). The second and
certainly most complex point of divergence concerns the social-
critical question of how the social order of the new capitalism
should be conceptualized from the standpoint of a theory of
justice. This problem seems to be connected in a not entirely
clear way to considerations about the relationship between
"social integration" and "systemic integration," even if Fraser's
use of the two concepts in her "perspectival dualism" still seems
quite unclear to me (II). The final point, which opens up
almost unbridgeable divergences between us, once again
touches on the question of the normative foundations of a
critical theory of society. Here I still do not see how a purely
deontological approach is to accomplish all the tasks Nancy
Fraser has in view, particularly if she takes into account
historical processes of normative progress (III).

I. Critical Social Theory and
Immanent Transcendence

The idea that a critical analysis of society needs to be tied to an
innerworldly instance of transcendence represents the legacy of

THE POINT OF RECOGNITION

Critical Theory's left-Hegelian tradition.[1] Only for a very few of the approaches today making a claim to critique does this challenge still even represent a meaningful enterprise, but for those who feel bound to it, it involves a number of difficult problems. For the earlier representatives of the Frankfurt School, the necessity of having a standpoint of critique within society was so closely connected to identifying a revolutionary subject that they scarcely thought the problem of its methodological structure had to be dealt with independently. As long as the proletariat could be pretheoretically regarded as a social class with an inherent interest in overthrowing capitalist relations, no further explanation seemed to be required of which experiences or practices could guarantee that the given social order could be transcended. And as soon as doubts grew for empirical reasons about the readiness of the industrial working class for revolution, the instance of transcendence was in general simply moved one level deeper: no longer the working subjects themselves, but the structure of social labor was declared the guarantor of a permanent overcoming of capitalism. But this solution, too – which in historical-philosophical form constituted the core of Western Marxism – did not last for long. Already in *The Dialectic of Enlightenment*, published two years after the demise of National Socialism, another change emerged insofar as the social labor process itself was now seen as a cause of advancing reification and domination, so that it could no longer be considered a social guarantor of the possibility of transcendence.[2] The situation that thus emerged was worked through on the highest level by Cornelius Castoriadis in France in the 1950s[3] and Jürgen Habermas in West Germany in the 1960s,[4] in their contributions to the critique of Marxism. Since then, the question of what other instances, experiences, and practices could pretheoretically secure the possibility of overcoming the given order has become the main source of new models in critical social theory.

The particular difficulties that go along with this problem, to be sure, only become clear if a central premise that was always tacitly assumed in the inheritance of left-Hegelianism up to Adorno and Horkheimer is made explicit. For Marx, there was no doubt that the practices on which he believed he could base his theory – labor oriented toward use-value and revolutionary activity – already contained precisely the normative structures that would shape the new social order to be established by overthrowing the old one. To this extent, the instance or practice that could socially guarantee the possibility of transcendence had to be of the same normativity or "reasonableness" that would later become socially manifest in the theoretically anticipated upheaval.[5] These conceptual constraints arise not only in Marx's case, however, but are common to all his successors' attempts to understand the project of a critical social theory as a continuation of the social detranscendentalization of reason: within the given relations, an element of practice or experience must always be identifiable that can be regarded as a moment of socially embodied reason insofar as it possesses a surplus of rational norms or organizational principles that press for their own realization. The concept of "emancipatory interest," coined by Habermas in his earlier work, may come closest to this left-Hegelian idea. It was connected to the certainly over-ambitious idea that the human race could have a deep-seated interest in responding to the experience of self-generated but thus far non-transparent domination and objectification with self-reflective efforts to establish domination-free relations.[6]

Our discussion might then benefit from a short, necessarily schematic overview of the alternative strategies with which critical theorists responded to the disintegration of the labor or production paradigm. After it was realized that the practice of social labor could not automatically produce an emancipatory interest, three or four distinct approaches emerged which tried to localize a different source of inner-social transcendence. A certain oversimplification is unavoidable in the following enumeration:

a) Cornelius Castoriadis responded to the obsolescence of the production paradigm by trying to relocate the permanent re-emergence of revolutionary tendencies on an ontologically deeper level, conceptualizing it as an expression of an impulse of presocial reality represented in the individual psyche. In this idea of a "magma," psychoanalytical approaches play an essential role insofar as human subjects are said to be dominated by a "desire for total unity" sustained by the drives, which is reflected at a higher level by the constant organic flow of new creations.[7] The work of Hans Joas can today be taken as an attempt to use the action-theoretical elements of Castoriadis – maintaining his desire-theoretical considerations and using the notion of "practice" – to develop a concept of creative action in the tradition of American pragmatism and in continuous dialogue with the Habermasian theory of action and discourse. Here, extraordinary situations, in which the individual opens up new values by overthrowing old boundaries, are understood as the source of structures of meaning that always point beyond the given social order and values.[8]

b) Not unlike Castoriadis, Herbert Marcuse also responded to the disintegration of the production paradigm in *Eros and Civilization* by shifting the necessity of transcending the social order to human drives. Marcuse, however, did not see the source of all later "revolutionary" ideational and affective achievements in the "break" with early childhood fantasies of omnipotence, but rather in the natural endowment of a pleasure principle that constantly drives individuals to transgress the institutionally embodied reality principle.[9] A further difference consists in the fact that with Marcuse it is not easy to see how an internal connection can be made between his drive theory and normative questions concerning the social order. While with Castoriadis such a mediation is achieved through the concept of autonomy, which distinguishes a form of society that does not suppress new creations but reflexively processes them, a comparable bridging concept is completely lacking with Marcuse. One attempt to preserve the critical heritage of Freudian drive theory through Marcuse and Castoriadis can be found today in the work of Joel Whitebook. Distancing his work from intersubjectivism and cautiously working through new insights from developmental psychology, Whitebook tries to find a social guarantor for the overcoming of the given social order in the sublimation of libidinally-driven fantasies of omnipotence.[10]

c) The intersubjectivism of Jürgen Habermas can of course be understood as a third approach to finding another guarantor of the possibility of social transcendence. His writings of the 1960s are explicitly guided by the aim of opening up a social sphere for Critical Theory with linguistically mediated interaction, whose normative surplus of validity is to ensure a lasting renewal of system-exploding energies and motivations.[11] This interaction-oriented proposal not only seems to me superior to the last two approaches in its sociological explanatory power. In my view, the greatest advantages of Habermas's theory concern the question of how a specific privileged instance can have normative force: the moral potential of communication is the engine of social progress and at the same time also indicates its direction. Today the circle of those who seek to push the communication-theoretical turn in Critical Theory forward by determining more concretely the normative content of social interaction – whether through a diagnosis of the times or on a more fundamental conceptual level – extends from Seyla Benhabib to Thomas McCarthy to Maeve Cooke.[12] My own efforts to make the Hegelian motif of a "struggle for recognition" fruitful for social theory can be understood as an attempt to set Habermas's ingenious conception "back on its feet." I will return to this point after discussing the fourth approach that can with some justification be understood as a way out of the disintegrating production paradigm.

d) It probably also makes sense to understand Michel Foucault's late writings as a whole as an answer to the question of what other form of practice can take over the transcending role of labor within a critical analysis of society. For the idea put forth in his essays on Kant that the performance of a subversive, decoding operation represents the necessary condition for the realization of critique can be understood as indicating the kind of experience that can subvert the existing rules of order in any society.[13] This "transcendental" reading is today supported above all by the writings of Judith Butler, in which Foucault's scattered remarks are developed in a direction that shows the outlines of a social-ontological theory of the connection between power and subversive practice. According to this approach, the establishment of a social recognition order brings about, with a certain necessity, behaviors that lead to the explosion of available forms of social existence, which are too narrow – too constraining – for unruly human subjectivity.[14] These considerations also show, however, that such an approach cannot be sustained without borrowing psychoanalytical hypotheses like those that played a role for our first two figures. For only if the idea of a human psyche structurally directed against the unreasonable demands of society is added to the above-mentioned connection between social order and subversion can one speak of the necessity of a practice of transgression.

In the context of our discussion, the enumeration of these four approaches is meant only to highlight the difficulties facing those who take up the inheritance of Critical Theory's left-Hegelian tradition. Here it cannot be sufficient merely to discover an empirical reference point in social reality on which to base the theory's immanent justification. If the task were limited to that, it would indeed be sufficient to refer to unmet claims in the present and use them as social evidence for the necessity of critique. But the real challenge of our common tradition is being able to show that such a reference point – such demands – are not the result of contingent conflict situations, but rather express the unmet demands of humanity at large. Talk of "transcendence within social immanence" – which is of religious origin – means more than that unfulfilled, and to that extent transcending, social ideals and goals are still to be found within social reality at a particular time. Rather, it designates a normative potential that reemerges in every new social reality because it is so tightly fused to the structure of human interests. This line of thinking can be also be formulated such that this "transcendence" must be attached to a form of practice or experience which is on the one hand indispensable for social reproduction, and on the other hand – owing to its normative surplus – points beyond all given forms of social organization. The connection established in these ways of speaking between "transcendence" and "immanence" is hence stronger than Fraser seems to see: "transcendence" should be a property of "immanence" itself, so that the facticity of social relations always contains a dimension of transcending claims.

Now, I realize that the idea of such a connection must seem rather high-flown under present conditions. This is why I pointed out right at the outset that today only a very few approaches in critical social theory still really follow this left-Hegelian program. On the other hand, the enumeration of the positions connected to the names Castoriadis, Marcuse, Habermas, and Foucault should make it clear that a number of not insignificant approaches continue to try to fill the gap left by the disintegration of the production paradigm. And this list could even be extended by, for example, following Hinrich Fink-Eitel's suggestion that the work of Ernst Bloch involves a social phenomenology of utopian sentiments.[15]

But what is decisive for our discussion at this point is that our respective efforts to establish an "empirical reference point" for critique are guided by two completely different sets of ideas: while Fraser's proposal to start with folk paradigms of justice only pursues the aim of anchoring theory in present-day society, my moral-psychological reflections in fact seek a quasi-transcendental justification of critique in the structure of social reality. As this short overview hopefully made clear, taking up such a program means once again finding an instance in the facticity of social processes that time and again presses beyond the given social order. Consequently, my proposal that this place be filled by feelings of humiliation and disrespect must be judged according to its social-ontological and social-anthropological persuasiveness. Essentially, my idea amounts to the hypothesis that all social integration depends on reliable forms of mutual recognition, whose insufficiencies and deficits are always tied to feelings of misrecognition – which, in turn, can be regarded as the engine of social change. This formulation also shows very clearly how the left-Hegelian tradition is at the same time connected to explanatory intentions that go far beyond what Fraser has in mind: the same instance that is in principle to guarantee the possibility of transcending the given order must also be able to explain historically how normative changes and improvements in the forms of social organization have come about. I will try to counter the objections Fraser has made against my moral-psychological reflections through two further clarifications.

a) I really thought I was far enough from the tendency of treating feelings of misrecognition as something given to us in an unmediated way, without being shaped by history. It was only due to the logic of my presentation that I first outlined the importance of such feelings for the normative legitimacy of social orders before explaining in the second section how they are semantically shaped by established principles of recognition; and I only dealt with the question of the moral justifiability of social claims arising from historically mediated feelings of mis-recognition in a third step. But Fraser's reproach that I fall into "myth of the given" – which can all too easily become a blunt, all-purpose weapon – seems to involve two different lines of

attack: on the one hand, it is meant to make the objection that
I treat moral feelings of humiliation as something ahistorically
given; on the other hand, I am criticized for even speaking of
an elementary structure of human feelings of justice in the first
place.

Indeed, unlike Fraser (and Rorty), I am convinced that we
can try to identify the experience upon which all perceptions
of social injustice rest, provided we keep in mind that it will be
the risky and self-evidently falsifiable result of generalizations
from our own horizon of experiences. The proposal that we
locate the core of such feelings of injustice in the feeling of
violation of what are taken to be legitimate expectations of
recognition implies a web of other social-theoretical assumptions, which together represent nothing other than an empirically-based generalization of especially striking contemporary
experiences. But to this extent, objections to my project must
also take the form of empirically-based counterarguments like
those Fraser herself seems to announce when she brings in
other kinds of feelings of social injustice (abhorrence of cruelty,
resentment of unearned (!) privilege, dislike of supervision,
etc.). Our discussion of this point would then turn on the
question of how we can discover a unitary structure of feelings
of illegitimately withheld recognition in this multitude of
expressions of dissatisfaction.

b) It will perhaps also help clarify our positions if I briefly try
to outline how my own proposal can be seen as a further
development of the Habermasian theoretical project. In my
brief overview, I have already made it clear that Habermas has
given the tradition of critical social theory a decisive turn
insofar as he has transferred the emancipatory, transcending
potential from the practice of labor to the action model of
linguistically mediated interaction. Of the four authors I named,
he is thus the only one who did not finally seek a way out of
the breakdown of the production paradigm by normatively
charging the human psyche or drives, but rather rehabilitated

another form of action. In my view, however, a certain ambivalence is still inherent in his efforts, since it is not entirely clear whether the transcending potential is to reside in the normative presuppositions of human language or in social interaction. Even if this distinction appears artificial – since all complex actions among people are linguistically mediated – in the end it makes a considerable difference whether social interactions themselves bear normative expectations or whether it is only through language that a normative element comes into communication.[16] I see the same ambiguity at work when Habermas uses the concept of "recognition" both for granting social status and for supporting language-based validity claims – without ever sufficiently distinguishing between the two.

However that may be, I understood my own proposal as an attempt to dissolve such distinctions in favor of the former interpretation by proceeding "social-anthropologically" from a core of expectations of recognition that all subjects bring to social interaction. Not everything that normatively underlies human communication in this way can take linguistic form, since recognition is often tied first of all to physical gestures or mimetic forms of expression.[17] To be sure, the real point of such a recognition-theoretical "monism" consists in the assertion that socially constitutive expectations of recognition vary historically with the principles that govern in which respects members can count on mutual approval in different societies. With this historicizing move I sought to counter the suspicion that the concept of recognition is merely a kind of anthropologized morality that proceeds from a constant set of "recognition needs." My impression is, however, that Fraser has not really taken note of this bridge between normative theory and social theory – which, in turn, does not make our discussion of the second point of divergence any easier.

II.   Capitalism and Culture: Social Integration, System Integration, and Perspectival Dualism

When I step back and consider the many problems that have to be reckoned with in our discussion of the second point of divergence, I feel completely overwhelmed. The questions that go along with the task of sociologically explaining the current developmental process of capitalism are so complex that the two of us cannot possibly clear them up in a few pages. Nothing less seems to be required than determining the relation between social integration and system integration – and, at the same time, the roles of the economy, law, and culture – in current structural transformations. In addition to the practical problems with this, from my perspective there are difficulties of mutual comprehension that make it even harder to enter a fruitful discussion. These emerge when Fraser wants to understand our disagreement mainly as a debate about the consequences of the "cultural turn"; continue when she accuses me of analyzing market processes in terms of "cultural" recognition alone; and culminate in the assertion that I want to explain the development of contemporary capitalism without any consideration of utility imperatives and the profit motive.

As my text could have shown, all this is fundamentally wrong. I do not see myself as a representative of the cultural turn in the social sciences; nor do I want to pronounce upon the determinants of the market process; and it certainly does not seem to me that an analysis of global capitalism that neglects the perspectives of firms' profitability and return on investment could be adequate. In general, the image of a totally naïve fellow, completely ignorant of economic imperatives, runs through Fraser's rejoinder – a picture in which I would not dream of recognizing myself. But it is precisely this gross exaggeration that gives me the impression that at this point our discussion does not suffer from particular, easily remedied comprehension problems, but rather from a fundamental misunderstanding: Fraser and I seem to have very different views of the task involved in developing social theoretical reflections in the present context. Thus, I want to first try again to explain the point of a recognition-theoretical conception of society before then turning briefly to particular aspects of our discussion.

My attempt to reconstruct the recognition order of modern capitalist societies was not connected to any explanatory aims; it was not a matter of establishing a basic categorial framework for adequately explaining development processes in such societies. My goal was much more modest: for the time being, I sought only to reveal the moral "constraints" underlying social interaction on different levels in this form of society. Here I have let myself be guided by the general idea that the inclusion of members of society always takes place through the mechanism of mutual recognition – that this is how individuals learn to intersubjectively affirm one another in particular respects or facets of their personalities. This – what we call, following David Lockwood, "social integration" as opposed to "system integration"[18] – should in my view be understood as a result of processes of recognition through which subjects are normatively incorporated into society by learning to see themselves as recognized with respect to certain characteristics. Elsewhere I have tried to show that this process of inclusion can also be understood as a mechanism mediated by language, gestures, or media through which individuals achieve public "visibility."[19] If we allow ourselves to be guided by these considerations, it becomes clear that social integration is always based on certain normative "constraints," which are mirrored in a society's recognition order. The institutionalized principles which together determine the respects in which individuals can count on achieving social recognition or "social existence" (Judith Butler) represent moral value perspectives or ideals to which social interactions among members of this society are subject. To this extent, my attempt to reconstruct the recognition order of modern capitalist societies aims only to uncover the normative principles that to a large extent structure communication processes from within.

But Fraser seems not to have seen the real point I was after with this at all. Like her, I am convinced that feelings of social injustice are always shaped by public discourses, and hence do not appear uninfluenced by the semantic space provided by a society. In contrast to her, however, my idea is that these discourses do not simply appear and disappear arbitrarily, but are connected to a repertoire of deeper normative principles that determine the linguistic horizon of socio-moral thoughts and feelings in a particular society. My concept of a "recognition order," which forms the basis for my remarks on social integration in modern capitalism, aims at this stratum – the epoch-specific grammar of social justice and injustice. Just as the space available for social-moral ideas is limited in all societies by the principles governing the legitimacy of claims for social recognition, so it is with this ordering structure. Such a conception is, of course, not sufficient to explain the dynamics of developmental processes in contemporary capitalism. But it is only meant to make clear the normative constraints embedded in such processes because subjects face them with certain expectations of recognition. The feelings of injustice that might be provoked by the most recent structural changes in the organization of work are "semantically" shaped by recognition principles in the form of historically achieved meanings and interpretations that govern the social division of labor.

Of course, with these reflections I have – to remain within Lockwood's framework – conceded a certain primacy to social integration as against system integration. I continue to assume that even structural transformations in the economic sphere are not independent of the normative expectations of those affected, but depend at least on their tacit consent. Like the integration of all other spheres, the development of the capitalist market can only occur in the form of a process of symbolically mediated negotiation directed toward the interpretation of underlying normative principles. It is precisely at this point, however, that another of Fraser's serious misunderstandings comes in, which seems to impute that I see the capitalist labor market as restrained by the merit principle alone. Here I thought that my excursion into the development of welfare-state regulations made it sufficiently clear that, from the partici-pants' perspective, the legitimacy of market processes must be measured at least as much by their conformity to certain historically achieved legal norms as by the fulfillment of specific achievement principles. Especially the current structural transformation of work – its increasing flexibilization and deregulation – shows unmistakably clear how much legal arrangements have contributed not to the system integration but to the social integration of the sphere of work. From the perspective of those affected, the social–legal constraints of the employment contract represent not merely a functional safe-guard of their capacity to work, but a moral guarantee of the social recognition of their dignity and status.[20] To be sure, such normative elements of the economic sphere can only be perceived if we are clear that the state's granting of subjective rights constitutes an independent source of social recognition, and Fraser and I seem to be talking past one another on this point.

In the revised version of her approach Fraser presents in this second round of our debate, law at least surfaces as a category of analysis. While it did not appear at all in her first essay, even now it merely takes the form of a secondary guarantor of claims achieved elsewhere. Fraser still does not want to grant subjec-tive rights – which make up the core of modern egalitarian legal systems – any independent significance in her theoretical program. Instead, state-sanctioned rights are to have only the purely instrumental function of equipping already achieved entitlements to cultural recognition or economic redistribution with certain enforcement powers after the fact. This instrumen-talism does not seem at all convincing to me, however, because it forgets that rights govern relations among actors in fundamental ways, and their significance to social interaction is thus not only functional. Rather, the subjective rights we grant one another by virtue of the legitimation of the constitutional state reflect which claims we together hold to require state guarantees in order to protect the autonomy of every individual. This interactive character of rights also allows us to explain why they should be understood as independent, originary sources of social recognition in modern societies: if subjective rights express the ways in which we regard one another as members of a democratic legal community entitled to autonomy, then their concession or denial must play a decisive role in subjective feelings about one's status in society. Only a social theory that, following Hegel, pursues this connection between equal rights and social recognition can in my view do justice to the normative peculiarity of modern societies. But such questions about the architectonic of the theory of recognition – the problem of which forms of social recognition should be distinguished in a particular social order – seem not to concern Fraser at all. She operates from start to finish with the preconceived dualism of cultural recognition and economic distribution without categorially testing whether there could be other types of recognition specific to particular societies. For this reason she is not in a position to see the tension between the principle of legal equality and factual inequalities as a source of social conflicts that have the independent character of a struggle for legal recognition.

This digression on the recognition content of modern law was above all necessary to make it clear that, in the contemporary expansion of capitalism, even economic processes are not simply normatively unmediated. Even on the problematic assumption that economic imperatives possess a pure, culturally unmediated form, we must still admit the influence of normative constraints that stem from achieved legal guarantees: the expectations individuals can articulate are continually undermined by supposedly anonymous, norm-free market processes because their claims to social recognition are already somehow institutionalized in legal regulations or payment schemes. Analyzing the development of the labor market without taking such recognition expectations based on law or achievement into account seems to me a typical product of the economists' fiction of the *homo oeconomicus*.[21]

At this point a dilemma arises for Fraser that deserves closer consideration because of its importance for the problems of constructing a critical social theory. Contrary to her assurances that she is restricting herself to a "perspectival dualism," at times Fraser succumbs to the temptation of talking about "social integration" and "system integration" in an essentialist sense. For example, she mentions that in social reality "impersonal system mechanisms" somehow combine with "cultural schemas of evaluation" (215f) – although this would have to mean that one and the same process is in a certain sense describable from both analytical perspectives. This revision of her original intention probably occurred because she wanted to insist against me on the empirical weight of economic mechanisms, which she accuses my approach of neglecting. Seduced by this critical aim, she sketches a picture of two different ways of coordinating social action – system integration and integration through values – which can certainly influence one another, but nevertheless represent separate domains of reality. This model, however, contradicts her point of departure, according to which the two (merely) analytically distinct spheres are to mirror the two normative principles of economic and cultural justice. For this postulate would require analyzing even processes of "system integration" as social processes that already reflect or can reflect certain normative principles: i.e., those of distributive justice. In order to sustain her normative dualism right down to her basic social-theoretical categories, Fraser should not have made use of the system-theoretical idea of norm-free integration processes, since this prevents economic processes from being described as open to normative transformations. Accordingly, she seems to be caught in a dilemma: due to her Marxist heritage, she wants to speak in social-theoretical terms

about anonymous economic processes, while she simultaneously has to conceive of the very same processes as strongly
dependent on value-mediated communication so that she can
accommodate immanent moral demands for redistribution
within them.

In my view, a conclusion must be drawn from this dilemma
concerning the categorial construction of a social theory that
can fulfill the strong normative objectives Fraser and I demand.
The "basic structure of society," to use John Rawls's
expression,[22] must if possible be analyzed in a social-theoretical
framework that allows the anticipation of points of departure
for normative improvements. For this purpose we cannot avoid
highlighting the stratum within the institutional spheres that
can be understood as an expression of the results of communication mediated by norms. If we accept this basic idea, it
quickly becomes clear that Fraser derives no great benefit from
the idea of system-integrative processes. For it precludes the
possibility she has in mind of understanding the economic
sphere as an institutionalization of particular interpretations of
distributive justice, just as she tries to trace the status order back
to a specific form of cultural recognition. Simply the fact that
those affected in western societies usually experience the deregulation of labor as a loss of rights and thus press for internal
corrections makes quite clear the extent to which even seemingly "anonymous" economic processes are determined by
normative rules. Indeed, the term "deregulation" itself is a
direct indication of the fact that the labor market is organized
by legal norms that express the moral interests of those
involved.[23] It is for such reasons that I spoke of the necessity of
being guided not by a "cultural" but by a "moral" monism. As
long as we hold onto the idea of a normatively substantial social
theory, we must always try to discover principles of normative
integration in the institutionalized spheres of society that open
up the prospect of desirable improvements.

Now, it is true that these theoretical-strategic considerations do not provide a sufficient basis for the further proposal that these principles of normative integration be traced back to moral norms of mutual recognition. This is where the arguments about the internal relationship between social integration and recognition come in. Moreover, we also need to avoid Fraser's repeated misunderstanding that I would claim that the institutionalized spheres always fall under just one principle of recognition. Just as today public schooling is normatively integrated by two competing principles of social recognition,[24] the family has for good reasons long been governed not only by the normative principle of love, but also increasingly by legal forms of recognition.[25] These remarks, however, do not yet show how I mean to use the idea of a primacy of normative integration for explanatory purposes – for example, in order to explain the current processes of accelerating marketization in capitalist societies. For reasons elaborated above, I think that Fraser's strategy of seeing only the "impersonal system mechanisms" of capitalist realization at work, unilaterally forcing a restructuring of the social, is wrong. On the other hand, here I cannot really satisfactorily outline how I would conceive an alternative explanatory model that would adequately take into account the requirements of normative integration. I will therefore make do with a few sentences.

It is probably most important to make clear that the whole opposition of social integration and system integration is problematic. It is true that some socially generalized media, like money or political power, can in fact coordinate social interaction relatively automatically, but even they depend on some belief in their legitimacy that can weaken or disappear altogether at any moment. Accordingly, the principle of profit maximization, which first of all determines only the conditions for the existence of capitalist firms, cannot be understood simply as a functional requirement that gives rise to a whole social sphere. It only becomes such a "subsystem" of social action after it has found sufficient normative agreement to constitute – with the help of legal norms – an institution in which a complex network of individual actions is coordinated seemingly automatically by the interplay of utility considerations. But economic processes are then not only normatively but also factually "embedded" in the normatively structured social order, even when the corporate perspective of profit maximization seems to dominate all other interests and intentions. For without being tied to general norms, habitual action patterns, and social networks, it would be impossible to secure the degree of cooperation, security, and innovation an effective allocation of economic resources requires.[26] Such social limits on markets must necessarily play the role of independent variables when trying to explain processes of economic development. There is thus little sense in merely appealing to the importance of capitalist imperatives without considering how changes in normative expectations and action routines have paved the way for social negotiations about the scope of these imperatives. It would be presumptuous even to sketch the contours of such an explanation of current transformations here. But it should have become clear that such an attempt could only be successful if the social recognition order played a decisive role among the different factors under consideration.

III. History and Normativity:
On the Limits of Deontology

Many problems Nancy Fraser and I confront in our attempts to devise basic social-theoretical concepts result from the fact that we both aim at a normatively substantial social theory. I understand this to imply more than is usually meant today when normative criteria for judging social conditions are demanded. We do not simply seek to apply what we take to be well-grounded normative principles to a given social order in order to arrive at judgments about morally justified corrections or improvements. Rather, social reality must be described in a way that shows how norms and principles considered justified could already have become socially valid. If "normatively substantial" is understood in this strong sense, methodological constraints arise regarding both basic social-theoretical concepts and the underlying principles used as criteria. Descriptions of social reality must always include a categorial dimension that can be understood as the embodiment of moral experiences and reflections – just as, conversely, we can only invoke norms and principles that are already in some way reflected in the institutional order of society. Although these meta-theoretical considerations have already played a central role in the first two sections of this chapter, I underline them again here because of their decisive importance for the third point of our debate. The lengths I went to in constructing the concept of a "social recognition order" in chapter two reflect my search for a categorial bridge between social theory and a conception of justice. I want to first once again make clear the particular point of my proposal before turning to the differences that continue to lie between Fraser and myself concerning theories of justice.

Of course, today a broad and impressive array of normative theories are available in which individual equal treatment, the determining principle of our societies, is further differentiated. Whether social equality should be defined with a view to resources available to individuals or with a view to the corresponding options, whether the merit principle should be restricted or the equality principle applied irrespective of achievement – all these questions have been discussed among these approaches with impressive acuity. What prevents me from simply joining these debates is first and foremost the fact that I want to take the moral infrastructure of modern society as my point of departure. The normative principles that give a theory its critical impulse should if possible be understandable as moral claims that are already valid within our social order. However, such an imbrication of social and normative validity can only avoid being orientated to the status quo if it can be shown with good reasons that the already valid principles possess a constitutive "surplus" of normative significance: moral claims concerning the just organization of social relations are broader or more demanding than what has already been realized in social reality. These meta-theoretical considerations strongly suggest taking the initially only descriptive reconstruction of the recognition order of modern society as the starting point for a normative conception of justice. In a certain agreement with David Miller's theory, it then appears that the modern idea of justice as equal treatment has in fact been "institutionalized" in three different ways, which require the consideration of individual needs, individual autonomy, and individual achievements. To this extent, the conception of justice on which I seek to base critical social theory assumes a pluralistic form. Instead of only one, here there are three principles that can inform analyses of social struggles and processes of transformation about which moral claims can be regarded as justified. Before going further into the implications of this pluralistic conception, I first of all want to contrast it to Fraser's approach.

In my view Fraser overdramatizes both the importance of moral psychology to my proposal and the significance of its ethical point of departure. It should have become clear that moral-psychological considerations about the function of recognition play a role in the conception of justice only insofar as they are to support the social-theoretical thesis that social integration works through forms of mutual recognition. Since subjects depend on stable patterns of recognition for the development of their personal identity, it is not implausible to suspect that, for them, the normative legitimacy and quality of the society depends upon the social guarantee of such relations. Now, for me this social-theoretical thesis – and not moral psychology as such – represents the key to determining the purpose of social justice. I take it that the reason we should be interested in establishing a just social order is that it is only under these conditions that subjects can attain the most undamaged possible self-relation, and thus individual autonomy. In terms of the distinctions on which John Rawls based his theory, here we have a weak idea of the good, without which a conception of justice would have no aim.[27] But the ethical idea I have just sketched already involves intersubjective determinations insofar as subjects are also presumed to have an interest in the freedom of the others from whom they expect social recognition. In contrast to Rawls, the idea of the good on which a recognition-theoretical conception of justice is based is tailored from the start to the intersubjective character of human relations. For it assumes that the subjects for whose sake just social relations are to be established are aware that their autonomy depends on the autonomy of their partners in interaction.[28]

It is this intersubjective orientation that I thought at least represented a point of convergence between Fraser and myself. But I still fail to see how Fraser means to introduce the idea of participatory parity without understanding it as a particular idea of the good – and at some places in her reflections I even find formations that could create the impression that it is a very substantial idea of the good indeed, since it sees participation in democratic politics as "the most important good in political life."[29] But, such internal ambiguities notwithstanding, we nevertheless agree that the goal of social justice must be understood as the creation of social relations in which subjects are included as full members in the sense that they can publicly uphold and practice their lifestyles without shame or humiliation. Here the point of recognition is the same as that of participatory parity: the development and realization of individual autonomy is in a certain sense only possible when all subjects have the social preconditions for realizing their life goals without unjustifiable disadvantages and with the greatest possible freedom.

However, the equality principle, which plays a decisive role in the last sentence, for me only comes into play as the result of historical development. While Fraser evidently believes she can derive the principle of "participatory parity" deontologically from the concept of the person, I am content to observe that in modernity the social recognition order has shifted from hierarchy to equality, from exclusion to inclusion. All members of society are from now on to be equally included in the network of recognition relations by which society as a whole is integrated. But since this mere finding is not sufficient to make a social fact into a morally justified starting point, a further justificatory step is needed: from the fact of the equality principle, we must be able to show that, judged by the standards that determine the quality of social integration, it represents a morally superior recognition order. For this purpose I have undertaken the – perhaps odd-seeming – attempt to develop criteria of moral progress, which are in a certain sense to emerge internally from the structure of social integration that arises through mutual recognition. And, in agreement with a number of other social theories, I reached the conclusion that such criteria are to be found in the extent of both social inclusion and individualization made possible by a social recognition order. Measured by these standards, the modern form of social integration, shaped by the equality principle, turns out to be a morally superior recognition order, so that in my view it can be treated as a legitimate starting point for constructing a conception of justice. Accordingly, I take the idea of the equal normative priority of the principles of love, legal equality, and merit to be the most suitable way to establish an internal connection between a conception of justice and the social theory on which it is based.

In contrast, the difficulties Fraser runs into when she tries to justify her idea of participatory parity deontologically emerge when she too implicitly tries to introduce a criterion of moral progress. I have to admit that I initially had trouble grasping her strategy for normatively justifying her theory of justice. On the one hand, Fraser wants to understand her approach according to the model of deontological proceduralism, whereby the duties of social justice are to be derived from the results of public deliberations in which all members of society, by reason of their equal autonomy, must be able to participate. Such a justificatory program fails to consider why the exercise of individual autonomy should be tied to participation in public discourses, but it is possible that here Fraser implicitly relies on Habermas's treatment of the issue.[30] The real problem of this understanding of her procedure, however, is that Fraser again and again seems to anticipate the results of these procedurally conceived debates by herself explaining the material content of social justice. Such anticipations, however, are incompatible with proceduralism in the strict sense, since determining content is precisely what should be left to the carrying out of the procedure. A way out could have been offered by understanding the material principles of justice as implications of the social preconditions for the free participation of all members in public procedures of deliberation.[31] But Fraser does not seem to have such a solution in mind, since she wants to relate the notion of participatory parity to participation not only in democratic deliberations, but in "social life" or "social reality" as a whole. If I thus already have problems understanding Fraser's approach to the theory of justice, I also do not see how her basic idea of "participatory parity" could avoid including a teleological perspective; and these difficulties are compounded when she suddenly and without further explanation includes historical transformations into her strategy of justification (231). Quite apart from the fact that such historical considerations are hard to combine with her deontological premises, it is above all unclear to me how Fraser could justify her recourse to the historical "expansion" of the idea of liberal equality on the basis of her own theoretical premises.

Certainly, it seems to make perfect sense to understand the development of the concept of equality over the last two hundred years as a learning process through which, under the pressure of social struggles, it gradually acquired new, hard to reject contents. Thus, today we seem to stand at a threshold

where the question of whether membership in cultural minorities needs to be protected and supported in the name of social
justice imposes itself for the first time.[32] But if we accept the
result of this historical process as the presupposition of our
conception of justice, not only does this historical fact unexpectedly and contrary to deontological premises become a norm;
Fraser is above all left without arguments that could justify
speaking of the actual development of the concept of equality
as moral progress. Such ambiguities are for me a clear sign that
Fraser does not quite know which of two strategies of justification to choose: on the one hand, she is inclined toward
discourse-ethical proceduralism, but without wanting to pay
the price of renouncing substantial statements about justice; on
the other hand, she is therefore always drawn back toward a
teleological ethics for the substantial remainder, but she does
not want to take on its justificatory burden because of her
reservations about ideas of the good. In my opinion, one
cannot have it both ways – a substantial idea of social participation and the thinnest possible procedural program of justification – within a single theory.

For this reason, I decided at the start to tie the conception
of justice to a weak idea of the good, which moreover fits
together with the structural conditions of social integration.
From this intention arose the proposal to treat the fact of
integration through forms of mutual recognition as a goal, for
whose sake we should want to establish social justice. For the
more such social integration does justice to the normative
expectations of the members of society – the "better" it takes
place – the more it includes all individuals into the relations of
recognition and helps them articulate their personalities. On
these premises it now seems justified to accept the historically
developed recognition order of modern society as the normative presupposition of an egalitarian concept of justice in order
to arrive at criteria for evaluating current processes of transformation. But here it turns out that we must proceed from not
one but three distinct principles of justice, since in our societies

the social recognition of subjects can refer to three different
characteristics (need, autonomy, achievement).

Fraser is of course right that at this point the normative
problems are not solved but in a sense only begin. For now it
must be shown how such a pluralistic conception of justice can
arrive at standards by means of which we can at least tentatively
and provisionally judge the social struggles of the present. For
me, the key to solving this problem is, as I already said, the
idea of the "surplus validity" of moral norms and principles.
Although Fraser does not explicitly take up this concept in her
response, it cannot be entirely unfamiliar to her, since she
herself makes use of it in her notion of a successive "expansion"
of the equality principle. For this can only mean that the idea
of social equality in a certain way possesses a semantic surplus,
which is gradually revealed by innovative interpretations without ever being completely or clearly determinable. I make this
time-tested model my own and apply it to the other two
recognition principles of "love" and "achievement." Accordingly, we should assume that modern societies underwent
normative processes of development in the course of which the
meaning not only of the equality principle, but also of the idea
of interpersonal love and the principle of individual achievement were successively enriched under the pressure of experi-
ence-based arguments. In the last few pages I have tried to
indicate what follows from this for a prospective application of
my conception of justice: these semantic extensions – which
can now be regarded, according to the criteria of the respective
spheres, as normatively expanding the three principles of recognition – can be interpreted as indicators of moral progress in
the sense that they can inform us about the desirability of
processes of social change.

It may be hardest to bring this idea to bear on the recognition principle I called "achievement" – the extent of one's
individual contribution to social reproduction. It did not take
Fraser's admonition for me to realize that the normative principle of individual achievement cannot be conceived apart from

the values that determine what is to count as how much of a contribution to social reproduction. Basically, insofar as my first response deals with the achievement principle, I am concerned with little else than the problems resulting from this imbrication with ethical objectives. The question is whether we can speak of a progressively redeemed surplus of validity when the core normative principle (achievement) can only be applied in social reality via value-based interpretations. To me, this seems conceivable if, instead of a positive learning process ("expansion"), we assume a negative process of overcoming the constraints of narrow horizons of interpretation. What we can then expect is fragmentary moral progress that consists in the serious interrogation of those ethical values that allow for a highly particularist recognition of actual contributions to reproduction. Of course, as Angelika Krebs' work shows in an exemplary manner,[33] such critique requires investment in a categorial imagination by means of which it can be shown why certain, hitherto ignored activities should be valued as "work," and accordingly given social recognition. But it would be wrong to take such conceptual innovation as only the business of philosophy and not to see the extent to which the affected themselves have always made use of the tool of conceptual critique. Thus, we can speak of a morally motivated struggle, rooted in experiences of social misrecognition and proceeding by argumentatively mediated claims to "difference," with reference to the achievement principle as well. To the extent that a critical social theory can advocatorially articulate this experience, it unfolds its normative power in the present.

This in a certain sense closes the circle that Nancy Fraser and I have worked through point by point in this second round of our debate. With the thesis that a critical social theory needs a conception of justice that can be seen as an articulation of the justifiable objectives of its addressees, I have essentially returned to my starting point. For normatively determining what should count as an indicator of emancipatory progress at a particular time is not independent of prior considerations about the

sources of transformative practice in the process of social reproduction. For the tradition Fraser and I both embrace, there is
a much closer connection between conceptions of justice and
social theory than is envisaged today within the spectrum of
liberal theories: it is not a matter of an external relation – of
applying normative criteria to a theory-independent reality –
but rather of revealing this reality guided by normative criteria,
which for their part must already have "sociological" or "social-
theoretical" content. The three-fold "point" of the category of
recognition, as I have tried to show once again, should consist
precisely in establishing such an internal connection: social
reality is revealed (social theory) by means of the same conception that, owing to its normative content, can be used to
evaluate social change (a conception of justice) in a way that
allows the perspectives of those affected to be articulated
(moral psychology). The question of whether it still makes
sense at least to attempt such a project probably depends on
the answer to a question Fraser and I have only indirectly
touched on: how the relation between theory and practice –
which our theoretical ancestors from Marx to Lukács to
Habermas endlessly disputed – can once again be reconceived
under transformed conditions.

Notes

* I am grateful to Rainer Forst and Rahel Jaeggi for advice and
suggestions.

1 Heinrich Fink-Eitel, "Innerweltliche Transzendenz. Zum gegen-
waertigen Stand kritischer Gesellschaftstheorie," *Merkur* 47, no. 3 (1993):
237–45; Axel Honneth, "The Social Dynamics of Disrespect: On the
Location of Critical Theory Today," *Constellations* 1, no. 2 (October
1994).

2 Max Horkheimer and Theodor Adorno, *The Dialectic of Enlighten-
ment: Philosophical Fragments*, trans. Edmund Jephcott (Stanford 2002); see
Axel Honneth, *The Critique of Power: Reflective Stages in a Critical Social
Theory*, trans. Kenneth Baynes (Cambridge, MA 1991), ch. 2.

3 Cornelius Castoriadis, *Political and Social Writings*, vols. 1–3, trans. David Ames Curtis (Minneapolis 1988, 1993).

4 Jürgen Habermas, *Theory and Practice*, trans. John Viertel (Boston 1973).

5 David Brudney, *Marx's Attempt to Leave Philosophy* (Cambridge, MA 1998).

6 Jürgen Habermas, *Knowledge and Human Interests*, trans. Jeremy Shapiro (Boston 1971).

7 Cornelius Castoriadis, *The Imaginary Institution of Society* (Cambridge, MA 1987). See also my interpretation, which is not uncontested: Honneth, "Rescuing the Revolution with an Ontology: On Cornelius Castoriadis' Theory of Society," in *The Fragmented World of the Social: Essays in Social and Political Philosophy*, trans. Kenneth Baynes (Albany 1995).

8 Hans Joas, *The Genesis of Values*, trans. Gregory Moore (Chicago 2001). See also Joas, "On Articulation," *Constellations* 9, no. 3 (2002).

9 Herbert Marcuse, *Eros and Civilization: A Philosophical Investigation into Freud* (Boston 1955).

10 Joel Whitebook, *Perversion and Utopia: A Study in Psychoanalysis and Critical Theory* (Cambridge, MA 1995). Also see our debate: Joel Whitebook, "Wechselseitige Anerkennung und die Arbeit des Negativen," and Axel Honneth, "Facetten eines vorsozialen Selbst. Eine Erwiderung auf Joel Whitebook," *Psyche* 55, no. 8 (2001): 755–89 and 790–802.

11 Habermas, *Theory and Practice*.

12 Seyla Benhabib, *Situating the Self: Gender, Community, and Postmodernism in Contemporary Ethics* (New York 1992); Thomas McCarthy, *Ideals and Illusions: On Reconstruction and Deconstruction in Contemporary Critical Theory* (Cambridge, MA 1991); Maeve Cooke, "Between 'Objectivism' and 'Contextualism': The Normative Foundations of Social Philosophy," *Critical Horizons* 1, no. 2 (2000).

13 Michel Foucault, *The Politics of Truth*, trans. Sylvère Lotringer (New York 1998).

14 See Judith Butler, *The Psychic Life of Power: Theories in Subjection* (Stanford 1997).

15 Hinrich Fink-Eitel, "Das rote Zimmer. Fragen nach dem Prinzip der Philosophie von Ernst Bloch," *Philosophisches Jahrbuch* 95, no. 2 (1988): 320–37.

16 Axel Honneth, "Anerkennungsbeziehungen und Moral. Eine Diskussionsbemerkung zur anthropologischen Erweiterung der Diskursethik," in Reinhard Brunner and Peter Kelbel, eds, *Anthropologie, Ethik und Gesellschaft. Für Helmut Fehrenbach* (Frankfurt/Main 2000), 101–11.

17 Axel Honneth, "Invisibility: On the Epistemology of 'Recognition'," *The Aristotelian Society*, supplementary vol. LXXV (2001): 111–26.

18 David Lockwood, "Social Integration and System Integration," in *Explorations in Social Change*, Georg Zollschan and W. Hirst, eds, (London 1964).

19 Honneth, "Invisibility." Similar thoughts appear in Hannah Arendt, *The Human Condition* (Chicago 1998), §§ 7, 24, 25.

20 Robert Castel, *Les métamorphoses de le question sociale: une chronique du salariat* (Paris 1995).

21 Robert Lane, *The Market Experience* (Cambridge 1991); Friedrich Kambartel, *Philosophie und Politische Ökonomie*, Essener Kulturwissenschaftliche Vorträge 1 (Göttingen 1998).

22 John Rawls, *Political Liberalism* (New York 1996), ch. 2.

23 Castel, *Les métamorphoses de le question sociale*.

24 François Dubet, "L'égalité et le mérite dans l'école démocratique de masse," *L'Année Sociologique* 50, no. 2 (2000): 383–408.

25 Axel Honneth, "Zwischen Gerechtigkeit und affektiver Bindung. Die Familie im Brennpunkt moralischer Kontroversen," in *Das Andere der Gerechtigkeit. Aufsätze zur praktischen Philosophie* (Frankfurt/Main 2000), 193–215. The excursus on Hegel's *Philosophy of Right* in my first rejoinder was meant to foreclose precisely this sort of misunderstanding.

26 Jens Beckert, *Grenzen des Marktes. Die sozialen Grundlagen wirtschaftlicher Effizienz* (Frankfurt/Main 1997), 403ff.

27 John Rawls, "The Priority of the Right and the Idea of the Good," in *Political Liberalism*.

28 Axel Honneth, *Suffering from Indeterminacy: An Attempt at a Reactualization of Hegel's Philosophy of Right* (Assen 2001).

29 Rawls, *Political Liberalism*, 206.

30 Jürgen Habermas, *Between Facts and Norms: Contributions to a Discourse Theory of Law and Democracy*, trans. William Rehg (Cambridge, MA 1996), e.g., ch. 2 and 3.

31 See my original proposal: "Diskursethik und implizites Gerechtigkeitskonzept," in E. Angehm and G. Lohmann, eds, *Marx und Ethik* (Frankfurt/Main 1986), 268–74.

32 Will Kymlicka, *Multicultural Citizenship* (Oxford 1995).

33 Angelika Krebs, *Arbeit und Liebe. Die Philosophischen Grundlagen sozialer Gerechtigkeit* (Frankfurt/Main 2002), esp. ch. 7.

Translated by Christiane Wilke and James Ingram

Index

achievement 258, 263–4
Adorno, Theodor
    The Dialectic of Enlightenment
        (with Horkheimer) 239,
        240
Aristotle 70–1
autonomy 258–9
    state guarantees 252
    transcendence 241–2

Barry, Brian 15
Benhabib, Seyla 242
Bloch, Ernst 244
Bourdieu, Pierre
    The Weight of the World
        118–20
Butler, Judith 60, 243, 249

Calhoun, Craig 121, 123
capitalist societies 3
    and achievement 155–7
    Hegel on 145–7
    and history 67, 122–4

instrumental-rational interests
    127
moral direction 184–90
new underclass 112
normative structure of 253–6
place of culture in 200,
    211–22
property forms 68–9
and sexuality 98–9n
social and system integration
    248–56
and social conflict 120
as social system 4–5, 105n
spheres of recognition 137,
    138–50
Castoriadis, Cornelius 239, 241,
    244
change
    paradigms for 13–14
class
    concept of 48–50
    exploitation and oppression
        16–17, 68

class (cont.)
    inequalities 3
    Marxist concept of 96n
    perceptions of injustice
        131–2
    and redistribution 11, 16–17
    and status 50–4, 218
    two-dimensional 23–4, 26
    under- 112
Cohen, Joshua 129
colonized people 132
communism 90
communitarianism 10
    majority participation 40
    repressive 76–7
communities
    constructing identity 162–5
Cooke, Maeve 183–4, 242
critical social theory
    different approaches 60–3
    empirical reference point
        200, 201–11
    and immanent transcendence
        238–47
    normative goals and 126–34
    perceptual underpinnings
        198–201
    pragmatism 45
    renewing Critical Theory
        111–13
    and status 59
    substantive dualism 61–2
    see also perspectival dualism
culture
    boundedness 103–4n
    of capitalist societies 248
    differences 220
    distribution 157–8
    domination by 212

in kin-governed societies
    54–6
patterns of value 57–8
and recognition 159, 160–70
status and class 50–4
structures of 13

deconstruction 106n
    and identity politics 12
    strategies for justice 75–6
democracy
    and justice 70–1
    participatory parity 43–5,
        47
Derrida, Jacques 106n
The Dialectic of Enlightenment
    (Adorno and Horkheimer)
    239, 240
difference 264
    and global non-sectarianism
        222–33
    question of existence 15
disability 162
Durkheim, Emile 184
Dworkin, Ronald 99n
    distributive justice 10

economics
    Basic Income 78–9, 221
    and class 16–17, 50–4
    and culture 19–22, 157–8
    and gender 19—2
    injustice 13
    restructuring 12–13
    and status 50–4, 57–8
Engels, Friedrich 58
environmental movements 115
equality 2
    and class 3

legal 152, 159, 169–70, 182, 226–7
  meaning of 263
  and moral progress 261–2
  principle of 259–60
  struggles for 220–1
Eros and Civilization (Marcuse) 241–2
ethnicity and race 11–12
  deconstructive strategies 76
  economic structures and 14
  nationalism 121
  and neoliberal globalization 215–16
  slave market 58
  two-dimensional 22–3, 26
existentialism 10
experience
  empirisim and critical theory 200, 201–11

families
  Hegel on 145–7
  and recognition 138–9
Farrakhan, Louis 121
female circumcision 42
feminism 8
  deconstructive strategies 76
  "everyday" 204
  and femininity 80–1
  women's distinction 46
Fink-Eitel, Hinrich 244
Forst, Rainer 99n
Foucault, Michel 243, 244
France
  headscarves in school 41–2, 81–2, 226
Frankfurt School 113–14, 134, 212, 237, 239

Institute for Social Research 110, 116
Fraser, Nancy
  Honneth outlines argument 110–14
  perspectival dualism 3
free will 178

Gadamer, Hans-Georg 169
gender 11–12
  achievement recognition 148, 153–4
  cross-redressing 83–4
  effect of Basic Income 79
  feminization of poverty 118–19
  history of women's movement 123
  injustice and 15
  and marriage 219–20
  perspectival dualism 66
  protests 132
  and religion 40–2
  status and 21
  two-dimensional 19–22
Gitlin, Todd 15
globalization
  current struggles 89–92
  and distribution 215–16
  ethical sectarianism 201, 222–33
  justice 88
Gramsci, Antonio 128

Habermas, Jürgen 128, 156, 230, 235n, 244
  action and discourse 241
  communication 242
  distribution 142

Habermas, Jürgen (cont.)
  popular sovereignty 178–9
  recognition 246–7
  transcendence 239, 240
Harrington, Michael
  The Other America 204
Hegel, Georg W. F. 184, 239
  and critical social theory
    243–4, 245
  Philosophy of Right 143–7,
    178
  recognition 1, 10, 132
  Sittlichkeit 28, 33
Hirschman, Albert 120
history
  feelings of misrecognition
    245–6
  historicism 202
  and participatory parity
    231–2
  and progress 207
  social conflicts 136–7
  and status 67
Horkheimer, Max
  The Dialectic of Enlightenment
    (with Adorno) 239, 240
human rights 92, 236n

identity formation 189
  changing everyone's 75–6
  and social structure 173,
    176–80
  three forms of recognition
    180
identity politics 111
  constructing communities
    162–5
  and deconstruction 12

demystifying struggles
    117–25
  exclusive 120–2
  historical sequence 122–4
  and multiculturalism 115
  redistribution and 8
Ignatieff, Michael 132
immanent transcendence 207,
    238–47
individuals
  autonomy of 178–80, 229
  see also participation, parity
    of
Islam
  headscarves in school 41–2,
    81–2, 226

Joas, Hans 241
Judaism 40–1
justice 101–2n
  affirming or transforming
    72–8
  claims for recognition 37–42
  cultural injustice 13–14
  democratic 70–2, 230
  distributive 1–2
  economic 13
  folk paradigms of 207–10,
    244–5
  and gender 19–22
  goals of recognition 126–34
  and the "good life" 172,
    173–80
  group-specific values 165–6
  institutions of 70–2, 86–8,
    103n
  international 88
  modern moral progress
    184–90

nonreformist reform 78–82
normative recognition 170–3
phenomenology of injustice
    114–17
self-realization and
    recognition 27–30
social experiences in 114
and status model of
    recognition 33
three principles of 180–2,
    227–8, 258, 263
two-dimensional 19–25,
    34–7
two types of claims 7–9
victims of injustice 14–15

Kant, Immanuel 243
    Moralität 28, 33
Krebs, Angelika 264
Kreckel, Reinhard 154
Kymlicka, Will 100*n*, 103–4*n*,
    162

labor
    Basic Income grants 78–9
    gendered division of 20
    recognition for 213
    respecting achievement
        141–3, 147–8
    of women 147–8, 153–4
language 135
law
    and equality 169–70, 182,
        226–7
    guarantees of autonomy 252
    and heterosexuality 18
    property rights 220–1
    same-sex marriage 39–40
liberalism, egalitarian 1

Lockwood, David 156, 249,
    250
Luhmann,, Niklas 142
Lukács, Georg 127

McCarthy, Thomas 242
Mansbridge, Jane 204
Marcuse, Herbert 244
    Eros and Civilization 241–2
Margalit, Avishai 132
marriage
    and gender injustices 219–20
    and sexuality 39–40, 220–1
Marx, Karl 184
    distribution conflicts 150–1
    historical-philosophical
        premises 124, 126
    melting status 58
    transcendence 240
Marxism
    class oppression 14, 68, 96*n*
    transcendence 239
    utilitarian anthropology 128
materialism
    distributive politics 8
Miller, David 181–2, 258
Moore, Barrington 131, 133
morality
    direction of capitalist societies
        184–90
    discontent of social
        movements 116–17
    evaluation of conflict 183
    the "good life" 172, 173–80,
        232
    and legal equality 152–3
    monism *versus* normative
        dualism 4

morality (*cont.*)
   motivating social conflict
      136–7
   normative recognition 170–3
   progress of 260–2
   psychology of 204–6
   sectarianism and globalization
      201, 222–33
   and social reality 256–8
   structure of norms 253–6
   surplus validity 263–4
multiculturalism 75, 106*n*
   and politics of identity 115
   postsocialist 94
Münch, Richard 141

nationality *see* ethnicity and race
needs 236*n*, 258
neoliberalism 2
   and economic transformation
      75
   free-market ideology 8
   and globalization 215–16

The Other America (Harrington)
   204

participation, parity of 36–7,
      101*n*, 210, 236*n*
   and autonomy 259
   conditions of 70
   cultural value 57–8
   and democracy 47
   deontological and
      nonsectarian 229–31
   and the "good life" 177–80
   and history 231–2
   and marriage 220
   and moral progress 260–2

normative recognition 171–2
   obstacles to 68, 73–4, 179
   political agenda 93–4
   status and class 218
   two-dimensional approach
      42–5
perspectival dualism 3, 93, 156,
      217–18, 222
   boundary awareness 86–7
   cross-redressing 83–5
   effects of political strategies
      64–7
   normative social structure
      253–6
   struggles for equality and
      220–1
Peters, Bernhard 163–6
phenomenology
   of social injustice 114–17
Philosophy of Right (Hegel)
      143–7, 178
Plato 70–1
politics
   current global struggles
      89–92
   dissociations 69
   distribution struggles 151
   social welfare 105*n*, 149
   unintended effects 64–7
poststructuralism
   anti-dualism 60, 63
poverty
   feminization of 118–19
   underclass 112
pragmatism 45–8
property rights 220–1

race *see* ethnicity and race
Rawls, John 99*n*, 230

basic goods 177–8
distributive justice 10
human relations 259
Political Liberalism 105*n*
self-respect 179
structure of society 254
Theory of Justice 179
Raz, Joseph 178
recognition
  for achievement 141–3,
    147–8, 188
  claims for 37–42
  concept of 1, 9–10, 96*n*,
    125–6, 133
  and cultural identity 159,
    160–70
  current global struggles
    89–92
  of distinctiveness 45–8
  false antithesis 11–16
  and Hegel 10, 143–7
  history and misrecognition
    245–6
  and justice 7–9, 14–15,
    34–7, 181–2
  for labor 213
  legal 139–40, 151–2, 159
  misrecognition 34–5
  mutual 262
  normative goals 126–34
  order of 250
  politics of 207
  reciprocal 146, 157
  and redistribution 2–3, 26–7,
    150–9
  and respect 135–6, 138–9
  and self-realization 27–30
  social relations 142–3, 146
  and status 17–19, 29–33

structure of culture 13
surplus of validity 186–7
three spheres of 137–44
see also justice; participation,
    parity of
redistribution
  and class 16–17
  concept of 1–2, 9–10, 95–6*n*
  conflicts of 150–9
  culture and economics 157–8
  current global struggles
    89–92
  economic structures 12–13
  false antithesis 11–16
  and neoliberal globalization
    215–16
  normative recognition 171–2
  and recognition 2–3, 26–7
  and social justice 7–9
  social welfare 64–7, 149
  status and class 218–19
  three principles of justice 182
religion 40–2, 81–2
resistance *see* social conflict
respect 160, 236*n*
Rorty, Richard 15, 205, 246

sectarianism 201, 222–33
Sen, Amartya 100*n*
sexuality 11–12
  affirming/transforming
    strategies 75
  and capitalism 98–9*n*
  constructing communities
    162
  cross-redressing 84–5
  and culture 97*n*
  injustice and 14–15
  and marriage 39–40, 220–1

sexuality (*cont.*)
  perspectival dualism 63
  status 17–18
  two-dimensional 24–5
Shapiro, Ian 230
social movements and conflict
  in capitalist societies 120
  geographical differences 118
  moral discontent of 116–17
  moral evaluation of 183
  morally motivated 136–7
  resistance and protest 131–2
  see also identity, politics of
socialism
  transformative strategies
    74–5, 78
society
  civil institutions 58–9
  and the "good life" 172,
    173–80
  reality and norms 256–8
status 3
  and class 50–4, 218
  concept of 48–50
  and gender 21
  historical developments 67
  in kin-governed societies
    52–6

  marketization 57–8
  and recognition 17–19,
    29–33, 93, 135–6, 138–9
  social subordination 221–2
  systems 248–56

Taylor, Charles 10, 103–4n,
  111, 152
  historical thesis 122–4
  misrecognition 32
  self-realization 28
terrorism
  and 9/11 2
Theory of Justice (Rawls) 179
Thompson, E. P. 98n, 131
Todorov, Tzvetan 132

Walzer, Michael 183
Weber, Max 17, 96n
The Weight of the World
  (Bourdieu) 118–20
welfare state 227
Whitebook, Joel 242
women *see* gender; sexuality
Wright, Eric Olin 102n, 107n

Young, Iris Marion 15, 60

39252143R00172

Made in the USA
Middletown, DE
09 January 2017